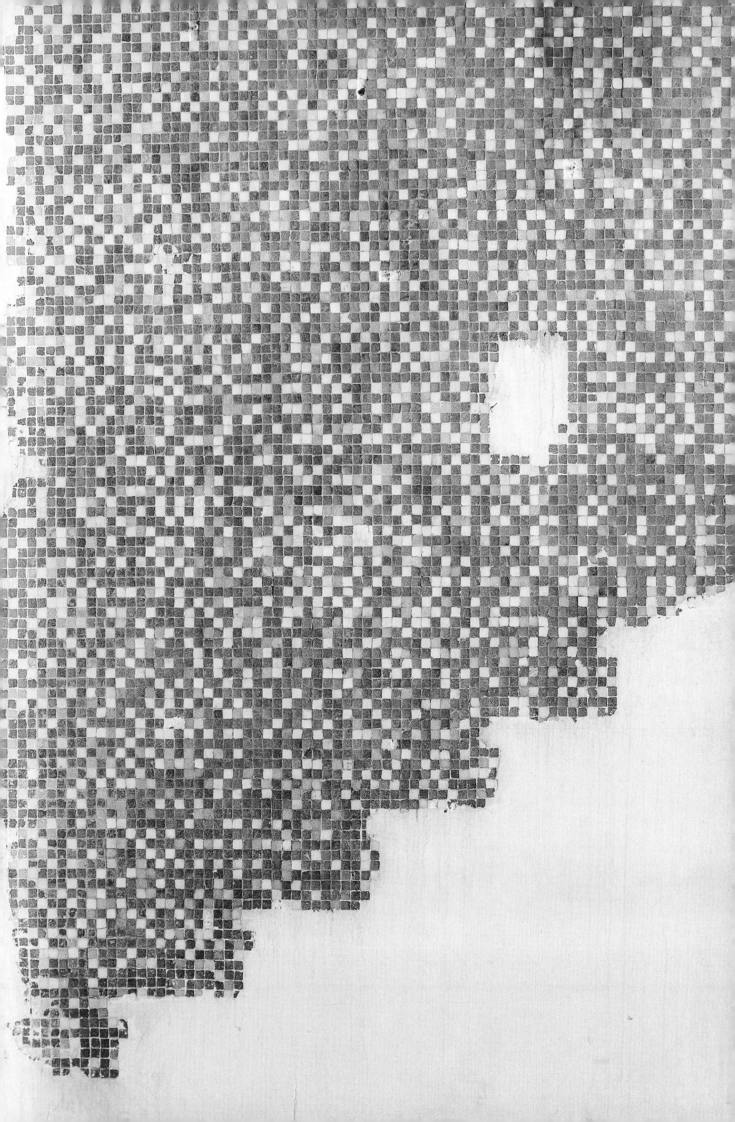

Rehabilitation of the former
Cooperative *Pau i Justícia*
Poblenou, Barcelona

Sala Beckett
International Drama Center
Flores & Prats

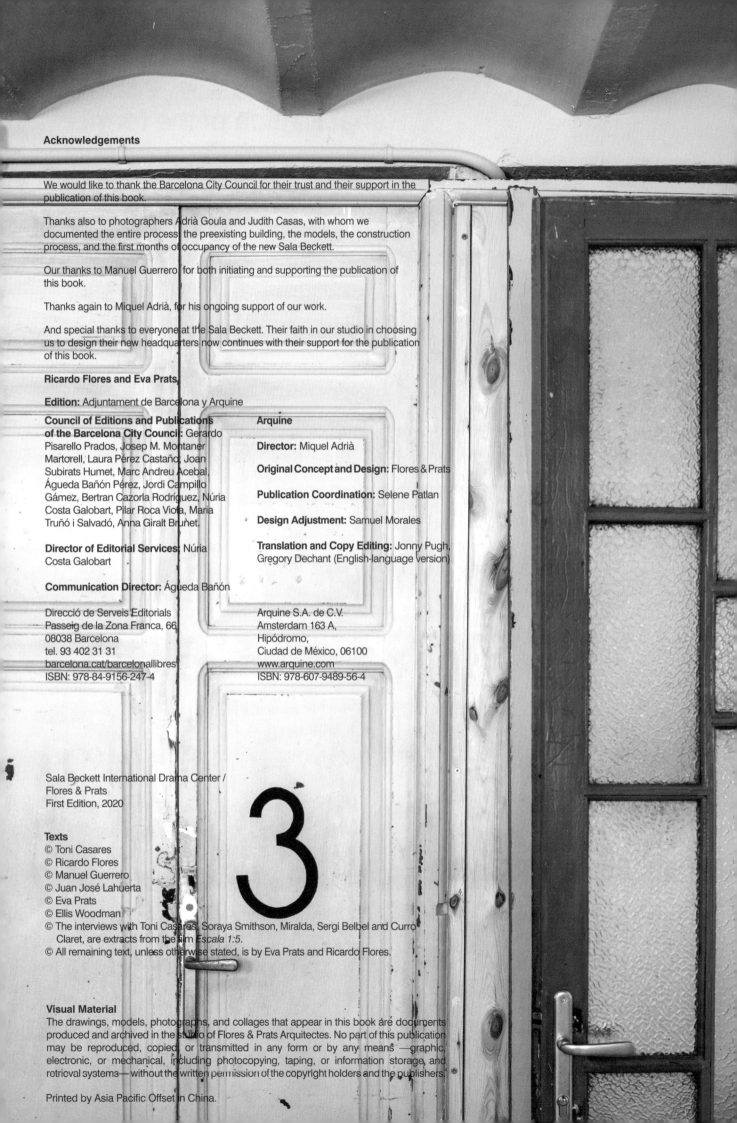

Acknowledgements

We would like to thank the Barcelona City Council for their trust and their support in the publication of this book.

Thanks also to photographers Adrià Goula and Judith Casas, with whom we documented the entire process: the preexisting building, the models, the construction process, and the first months of occupancy of the new Sala Beckett.

Our thanks to Manuel Guerrero, for both initiating and supporting the publication of this book.

Thanks again to Miquel Adrià, for his ongoing support of our work.

And special thanks to everyone at the Sala Beckett. Their faith in our studio in choosing us to design their new headquarters now continues with their support for the publication of this book.

Ricardo Flores and Eva Prats.

Edition: Adjuntament de Barcelona y Arquine

Council of Editions and Publications of the Barcelona City Council: Gerardo Pisarello Prados, Josep M. Montaner Martorell, Laura Pérez Castaño, Joan Subirats Humet, Marc Andreu Acebal, Águeda Bañón Pérez, Jordi Campillo Gámez, Bertran Cazorla Rodríguez, Núria Costa Galobart, Pilar Roca Viola, Maria Truñó i Salvadó, Anna Giralt Brunet.

Director of Editorial Services: Núria Costa Galobart

Communication Director: Águeda Bañón

Direcció de Serveis Editorials
Passeig de la Zona Franca, 66
08038 Barcelona
tel. 93 402 31 31
barcelona.cat/barcelonallibres
ISBN: 978-84-9156-247-4

Arquine

Director: Miquel Adrià

Original Concept and Design: Flores & Prats

Publication Coordination: Selene Patlan

Design Adjustment: Samuel Morales

Translation and Copy Editing: Jonny Pugh, Gregory Dechant (English-language version)

Arquine S.A. de C.V.
Amsterdam 163 A,
Hipódromo,
Ciudad de México, 06100
www.arquine.com
ISBN: 978-607-9489-56-4

Sala Beckett International Drama Center /
Flores & Prats
First Edition, 2020

Texts
© Toni Casares
© Ricardo Flores
© Manuel Guerrero
© Juan José Lahuerta
© Eva Prats
© Ellis Woodman
© The interviews with Toni Casares, Soraya Smithson, Miralda, Sergi Belbel and Curro Claret, are extracts from the film *Escala 1:5*.
© All remaining text, unless otherwise stated, is by Eva Prats and Ricardo Flores.

CONTENTS

How should the new Sala Beckett be?
An important decision

Toni Casares

That night I couldn't sleep…

We had to make the decision the following morning, at a meeting with the technical people and the representatives of the public authorities involved in one way or another in the project. Approval was required of the need for it, as well as its viability and, above all, financing. It was to be a consensus decision, but I knew that our opinion —the viewpoint of the people of the Sala Beckett and the theater people— would of course be taken into account and highly valued.

The choice had to be made, from among the five finalists, of which architecture firm was to handle the renovation of the former workers' cooperative *Pau i Justícia* in Poblenou, now owned by the municipality, undertaken thanks to pressure from neighborhood residents, who wished to salvage the ruin and transform it into a theater space: the new Sala Beckett.

The Sala Beckett had existed for twenty years, developing a character of its own and an acknowledged cultural influence. Originally a small alternative theater, located in an industrial building in the Gràcia neighborhood, it had grown gradually from almost marginal status to become a reference in the cultural ecosystem of the city. Now, as a change of venue was forced upon it by the vicissitudes of the real estate market, a conceptual redefinition was also required, of which the new building would inevitably constitute a standard and a display window, at once cause and consequence. The architects, therefore, and the architectural design needed to be chosen with solid judgement and a sense of responsibility. The *whos*, *whats*, and *hows* of the building and its circumstances would condition and represent our way of understanding theater and its relationship to the city and to culture in general.

So we were in the final phase of a selection process that had been long, complex, and very peculiar, owing in part to a certain naiveté in our approach to the rules of the game —perhaps a more conscious naiveté than might appear at first glance. We are theater people, and for theater people, in general, good interpersonal communication, a sense of participation and collaboration in a common project, a feeling for procedure, respect for *tempi* and for both the private and collective rhythms of creation, a persistent tendency to doubt and to question oneself, mutual trust, a balance between conceptual planning and intuitive action, between play and responsibility, etc., all these attitudes and approaches are necessary and even indispensable when facing any important work or process.

A parenthesis:

There were two decisions that definitively marked, from my point of view, the course and positive results of the entire process of the renovation and architectural transformation of the former *Pau i Justícia* as the site of the new Sala Beckett.

First, there was the acceptance by the city council of Barcelona, which owned the building, to cede the general formulation of the rules of the game prior to the competition —invitation, concept, conditions, competition bases, etc.— to those who were afterwards going to occupy and use the building, and to involve them in choosing (obviously by responsible consensus) the winner. In this way, their viewpoints and concerns were trustingly prioritized, for although they might not have all the technical know-how, they knew exactly what they wanted and what they needed.

The other important decision, assumed by the three governmental bodies involved —City council, Regional government, and State ministry—, was also to cede to the future user of the equipment (the Fundació Sala Beckett) the conceptual and technical direction of the project, and consequently the control and management of the budget, the quality of the work, and the execution schedule, all previously agreed upon.

In my view, both of these were courageous decisions and an example of what the role of government with regard to cultural policy should be: that of promoting, facilitating, and guaranteeing ambitious initiatives of cultural and social interest, while at the same time surrendering with confidence the conceptualization, execution, and management of the projects to others, but watching over the sense of responsibility, transparency, and common interest with which they are carried out. Things are not always done in this way.

Close parenthesis. To continue:

SAMUEL BECKETT

Paris
23.3.87

[handwritten letter in French]

Paris
23.3.87

Dear Señor Sinisterra

Thank you for your letter of the 19th and for remembering that distant Good Friday (!).

I would like to be with you next month, but it's out of the question, I'm afraid: no more travelling for me.

My best wishes for your Oh les B. J.

I accept with pleasure that your Sala bear my name. And that your Gestos para Nada be dedicated to me.

I am truly honored.

Affectionately to you all,

  Samuel Beckett

That morning, therefore, technicians, politicians, but also a group of "theater people" had the five finalist designs in front of us on the table. We had all had a chance to look them over and over again for several days, but how little a single plan drawn in ink on a single piece of cardboard explains, and how difficult it is to understand if you are not accustomed! Now they were to be defended by their respective authors for just a few brief moments: ten or fifteen minutes to explain an entire building designed to house a whole cultural project! Thereafter, in closed session, we would make the final decision about the winner.

"How ineffective, unfriendly, and disrespectful of the enormous task we have set all these professionals," I thought, "and how ill adjusted to the importance of the decision we are about to make!" I would have liked to postpone the decision until I had talked to each one of them for a few more days, a few more weeks or months, or who knows how long…

But the process could not be extended, and we had already made them think too hard, the poor architects, because of the conditions and procedures of a competition in which the criteria of esthetic and philosophic value implicit in the project seemed to be of almost greater importance than the technical and professional aspects customary in a competition of this kind.

This was not entirely so, but the truth is that there were some farfetched conditions we had come up with in order to come to a decision. Such as the collective meeting of all the candidates, joined around the same table, where for an entire afternoon they had to listen to explanations about the philosophy of the Sala Beckett and give their own opinions (!) about the importance of contemporary dramaturgy and its social significance in Catalonia. Or the obligatory visit, again with all of them together, to the building object of the competition. Or finally —yet another obligatory condition— the requirement to receive the director of the Sala Beckett in their own offices one afternoon, in order to explain to him viva voce, in "simple, understandable language", the way they worked and the general outline of the proposal they were going to present. Conditions set by "theater people" for building a theater. It seems obvious, but it's not at all common.

What was there behind this rather false naiveté, behind these seemingly uncommon conditions in a competition for an architectural renovation, and also —let's not forget— behind this daring yet trusting commitment by the government? There was an awareness, as I have pointed out above, that the architectural form of a new Sala Beckett would mark, at least in Barcelona, a particular way of conceiving contemporary theater and its relation to society for decades to come. And it was our responsibility, clearly, that this form should not be arbitrary or individual or whimsical, but rather the consequence of a shared artistic and social philosophy that would, among other things, connect with the work of previous decades —El Teatro Fronterizo and José Sanchis Sinisterra were the inspiration for it—, linking up a variety of people of different generations and leading with respect and emotion toward imaginaries we are still unaware of. That is no small thing.

And there was also a sense of political responsibility: the Sala Beckett, which, in order to carry out its development plan, was converted into a foundation that would guarantee the public interest of its objectives and the complete transparency of its management, also needed to ensure that it would maintain the direction and coherence of its esthetic and sociocultural goals, which have justified, among other things, the government financial aid it has received since its creation. Moreover, in spite of the change of dimensions to which it aspired through this competition, the Beckett was unwilling to lose its special character in the theater world and within the cultural panorama of the country as a whole. And neither is that a small thing.

What kind of theater do we want? In what kind of theater do we believe? How do we want it to relate to society, to the neighborhood it is in, to the country as a whole? Who creates it? For whom? Who will come to see it? And why? How is theater done nowadays? Is there only one way of doing it? How many other theaters are there in the city? Where are they? What do they do? What do we mean by contemporary theater? What languages, what disciplines, what codes, what verisimilitudes, what creative tools are we talking about? What is dramaturgy? Who makes use of it? What will the theater be like in a few years?...

Each one of these questions and so many others were behind the decision we made that day. Indeed, the same questions had been there when we chose the building of the former Pau i Justícia as the perfect site for the new Beckett, and they would continue to be there in future decisions, when we began to work with the architects selected.

Poblenou? The neighborhood of Poblenou, with its working class roots and its tradition of worker cooperatives, with its remarkable vitality of cultural association and activism, resistant to speculative and depersonalizing real estate operations, threatened by the assault of tourism and by gentrification, a process to which we ourselves —there is no getting around it— ran the risk of being accomplices: we had also wondered about Poblenou, of course, from the stupid vantage point of our centralist vision. We agonized: wouldn't Poblenou be just too far away? We wondered who would come.

A former cooperative? What exactly are we getting into? The only thing still to be glimpsed of what Pau i Justícia had been was summed up in a triangle that, for us, would be fundamental to our own redefinition: a bar, a theater, a school. The building, it alone, showed the way.

From this point on, it is impossible to say what there is of the original building in the theoretical and strategic design of the new Sala Beckett and what there is of the former Sala Beckett in Gràcia in the new building: it is impossible to say how much architecture there is in each one of the premieres and regular activities we are performing in the theater, or how much theater substance there is in every wall, every paving stone, every window… But it is clear there is an understanding, a dialogue, a preoccupation, a shared concern, a **time** conceived and experienced with shared intensity in every decision made.

This time, respected and shared, struggled for by so many people, is what can be seen spattered on the old and new walls of the present Sala Beckett: it is what makes it —everybody says— so powerfully appealing. The time of the former cooperative workers who constructed the building and filled it with meaning, that of the playwrights and actresses and actors and stage designers of the last twenty years of the Sala Beckett in Gràcia; the time of the carpenters and masons of the renovation, that of the builders and engineers, that of the members of the board of trustees of the Foundation, that of the theater technicians, the managers, the directors, and the politicians who intervened directly in the process of conceiving and designing the project and the building; and the time of the new playwrights, the new actors and actresses, and the spectators and students and neighborhood residents and people from farther away, and all those still to come, and that of the entire team of people working at the Beckett.

I would say that the word *time* has taken on a special meaning, radiating in multiple directions within the former *Pau i Justícia*, since we decided that **Eva Prats and Ricardo Flores** would help us to transform it into the new Sala Beckett.

A certain way of relating to time: this is noticed and understood by anyone who visits the studio of Flores & Prats on the Carrer Trafalgar. A way that has much more to do with the time of an artisan and that has a curious connection with the world of the theater. I will try not to give way to second-rate poetry… First of all, there is time stored up, with love and respect, in their studio. The memory of their past and of that of others. Old models and plans stored with the greatest care in wooden boxes, and meticulously explained in endless series of notebooks. There is the time of doubt and of error, in the form of boxes full of pencils and erasers on every worktable. Very visibly, there is the time of their direct, bodily relationship to the work in progress, because there are pieces of cardboard and glue and photographs tacked on the walls and rulers and compasses and plans and young architects deep in concentration; there is time for the coffee they never fail to offer you when you drop by, so that you can talk calmly, with no hurry, about this and that, from the smallest and most concrete detail of the project to the most general and abstract aspect. And there is also —and this is definitive— time for play: whole collections of models of all sizes! Models everywhere, designed for every decision to be taken. Models and people making more models for tentative answers. In the face of any doubt: a model!

A model is not just an object that appeals by its craftsmanship, though there is that too; it is not just an excellent way of understanding the volume and proportions of a space, though there is that too; a model is also, in addition to all that, a little theater. It is the perfect toy for helping to imagine the inhabitants of a particular space and the stories they will be part of. A model will keep a "theater person" occupied for a whole afternoon. Time stands still for the imagination.

And there was something else that appealed to me in the work of Flores & Prats, long before I was able to visit their studio. Among the photographs in their professional dossier —before I had even met them— there were some of the renovation, still unfinished at that time, of the Casal Balaguer in Palma de Mallorca. One of these photographs was the detail of a section of a curved concrete stairway, standing alone between old walls, with a wooden banister and a ray of light entering in through the skylight above, also of wood. The contrast between the coolness and warmth of the materials; the friendliness of that curving line, bathed in light; and the magical uncertainty of the moment captured in the photograph. I felt that sensation of balance, hospitality, and strangeness as a gentle esthetic jolt that invited me to imagine a possible change in the esthetic and relational forms of a space such as the Beckett: moving from the darkness of the underground hideout to the naturalness and audacity of generously shared light, from rectilinear and minimalist harshness to the friendliness and hospitality of curves, from an obsession with novelty to a respect and appreciation for the memory of walls with stories to tell. Along with a willingness, without losing even a hint of ambition for complexity in the gaze, to maintain a taste for the uncertainty of open, indefinite spaces. As if we had to "conquer" a right, to claim a more open, natural, daring, and nonchalant mood for contemporary theater and for culture in general in the society of our time.

In more prosaic terms, other things were also necessary, such as being able to maintain the theatrical character of the small or medium format and understanding that the growth of the Beckett had more to do with dignifying theatrical creation and experimentation than simply with the size of the productions we could offer or the spaciousness of the exhibition halls. It was a matter of increasing to a maximum to the number of work and encounter spaces available to professionals, and of improving the technical conditions of those spaces: rehearsal rooms, classrooms, laboratory spaces, etc. A revealing anecdote: one day an important figure from the most commercial theater in the city came to see the renovation work, and after observing the reduced dimensions of the Theater Downstairs, he said to me affectionately: *"Casares, you are going back to money-losing theater…"* But he immediately added: *"…money-losing, but very necessary."*

It was also natural to assume that the change in dimensions of the Beckett —from 900 m² to 3,000 m²— would lead us to open up and connect with more people, and doubtless in a different way. I'm not saying we would have to change the way we already had of connecting with the public through our performances, but that intuition of wagering on the light and spatial friendliness I have spoken of may have a little to do with the need to abandon certain slightly elitist attitudes, or in any case a certain tendency to overvalue artistic "encryption": attitudes that theater was often accused of in the 1990s, and particularly the kind of theater performed in the Sala Beckett.

In any case, in order to avoid another one of the esthetic risks typical of the cultural spaces and equipment that preceded us in the city, at the opposite extreme of what I have been talking about, one of the first conditions that we imposed on ourselves, architects and "theater people" alike, may also be significant: "Let's avoid solemnity at all costs!" The new Beckett was not to be a temple or a palace or a place of magnificence. A space for contemporary culture and creation is not a lofty, sacred site to which an obedient and respectful public ascends in order to be enlightened by the truth of the creator… definitely not. A place of culture and art and shared thought —however ritualized the ceremony of theater may be— is a domestic, democratic, comfortable place, where we all feel at home as citizens, the protagonists of our own stories, and where we dare to look each other in the face, in order to laugh and cry and rebel against the world and against ourselves. Culture is not something we access: we carry it within us. It defines us, as part of our own condition. It is our exceptional capacity to be seen from without and to share this discovery in community, without shame or prejudice or hierarchy. We need these spaces and mechanisms in order to develop this capacity together, with freedom and dignity and without complexes. That is what a theater offers today, among so many other things.

And if the truth be told, a respect for and trust in artists has been one of the keys of the Sala Beckett's philosophy of work from the very beginning. If Sanchis Siniterra is an excellent teacher, a genuine reference in the field of dramatic pedagogy, that is in large part because he knows how to give his students confidence. He is able to give them the tools to overcome the terror of the blank page: to avoid the dangers of demanding too much of themselves, of exaggerated importance, when they begin to write and produce.

The new Beckett also had to respond to this trust, in architectural terms. The artists and performers, the playwrights above all, but also the actors and actresses, the creative public and other users, had to feel comfortable and open to exchange, creativity, imagination… The building's circulations, its work and meeting spaces, the views from every corner of it, its colors and materials: they are all conceived to facilitate this trust.

There was also the decision —a brilliant one!— to bring the bar down from the upper floor, where it used to be, in the days of the Cooperative, to the ground floor, where it occupies an entire corner of the building: spacious, welcoming, warm, light, simple, and above all open to the neighborhood and to anyone who wants to come in. It is a space of encounter and conversation, designed to foster contact and mixing among people of different kinds and interests: established artists and artists just starting out, journalists and professors and professionals of all kinds, stage technicians and economists and theater-lovers and bird-watchers! People who want their time to themselves or who want to share it with others. People from the neighborhood and people from farther afield.

People from the neighborhood… People who are fully mindful of a building that has been salvaged thanks to them and that appreciate its past. Many of them have met each other in it: learned in it, gathered in it, had fun, argued, or thrilled in it, gone to buy something in it, or heard their parents or grandparents or aunts and uncles talk so much about it… We couldn't fail these people, letting so many emotions and so much life be lost. As theater people and people who make emotion a motor of communication and intelligence, we just couldn't fail them.

The competition and the decision about how to renovate this building had to take all this into account. Esthetic sensibility but also social sensibility. Thought about the place of theater in contemporary society. Ideas and solutions conceived with deliberation and collectively. Before definitively setting to work, we lived for a year on the upper floor of the building. We got to know, we explored and listened to it… Through activities with and without a public. And we made decisions in collaboration with technical people, playwrights, managers, politicians, office staff, neighborhood representatives, actors and actresses. With a due sense of responsibility and perfectionist ambition. Not just anyhow.

In the entire course of the process that this book describes, we had to modify the project on several occasions, moving from ideals to realities, giving up many things, pausing, arguing, doubting, making mistakes.

A lot of people used to say: "It's not the time, it's not the way, something like this is no longer possible. Where are you going to end up! How naive!"

"Slowly but surely," we said to ourselves.

Yes: Flores & Prats, Eva and Ricardo had —have— a certain naiveté in their gaze and expression. They also have intelligence, good hands, sensibility, and words and tools constantly open and attentive to every possibility. They are willing to pull up their sleeves and get their hands dirty. They doubt and make mistakes. They listen, ask, propose, erase, correct. And they're always there: always! They have time stored up in their studio, as I have said. They know how to play. With their models they play at imagining a world.

They were prepared for a professional and personal commitment of this magnitude. With an expression of anticipation in their eyes that made them look like children.

Children about to make a theater.

Backstage of the *Liquid Light* installation at the Biennale di Venezia 2018.
Fragment of the presentation of the Sala Beckett and the competition for its new headquarters in Poblenou.

La desaparició de Wendy
de Josep M. Benet i Jornet

Direcció: Oriol Broggi

Al Poblenou!
Pere IV,
228-232

Un tret al cap
de Pau Miró

Da 30/03 al 30/04/1

ROOF TESTS FOR THE COMPETITION ENTRY SCALE 1/200.

SAMUEL BECKETT ACCEPTS
TO GIVE HIS NAME TO THE SALA.

PERVERTIMENTO

SALA BECKETT ORIGINS IN 1977

EL TEATRO
FRONTERIZO
propone

PRIMER AMOR
de Samuel Beckett

MERCIER
T CAMIER
de SAMUEL BECKETT

La nuova Sala Beckett

Sala Beckett è un gruppo teatrale attivo a Barcellona da più di 20 anni.
La loro attività principale è la promozione di nuove scritture teatrali e la loro
messa in scena per la prima volta. Attento alla drammaturgia del suo tempo,
il gruppo produce spettacoli di autori con emporanei che mostrano interesse
nella sperimentazione e in nuove pratiche di scrittura drammatica.

The new Sala Beckett

Sala Beckett is a theatre group that has been working in Ba
for more than 20 years. Their main activity is to promote ne
drama stones, and to put them on stage for the first time.
on contemporary dramaturgy, they produce shows by
contemporary authors with an interest in experimentatio
forms of dramatic writing.

ATION MODEL SCALE 1/100.
11.

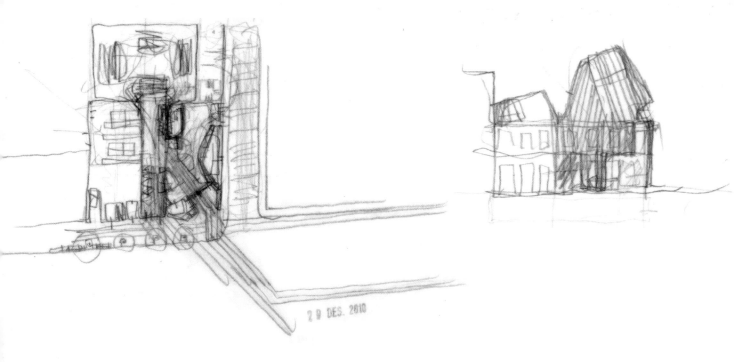

29 DES. 2010

The Competition Project Dec 2010 – Jan 2011

The New Sala Beckett
Flores & Prats

To accept the discipline of the existing —a ghost present throughout the life of a building— as the physical quality conferred on things by time.

The Pau i Justícia building has a spatial structure that will easily house the program proposed for the new Sala Beckett. What interests us for its future occupation is to acknowledge this structure and to organize the new design on the basis of it.

We understand that the recycling of the building must begin with its spatial structure. From there we can go on to restore the warmth offered by the various elements we salvage. Thus, façade and interior correspond: when you enter a building with an old appearance, you find an interior with traces of the different programs that have occupied it.

The aim is to achieve a building where everything works together, where old and new are indistinguishable, where there are signs of previous occupations, but where EVERYTHING is updated for new use, with structure and ornamentation working together.

The idea is to carry out the expansion required so that the original building may house the entire program in a unified way. Thus, just as on the inside the building is organized around the entrance passageway, its outside appearance is intended to show two things to the city around it: that it has been expanded with respect for the preexisting elements and that the expansion has been done in a unified way.

The result, therefore, is not simply a program piled onto a preexisting structure, but rather something more, something manifest on the inside in the large public lobby and on the outside in the large roof structure that transforms the former cooperative into a big house: **the playwrights' house.** *

* Excerpts from the competition project (January 2011).

2 5 DES. 2010

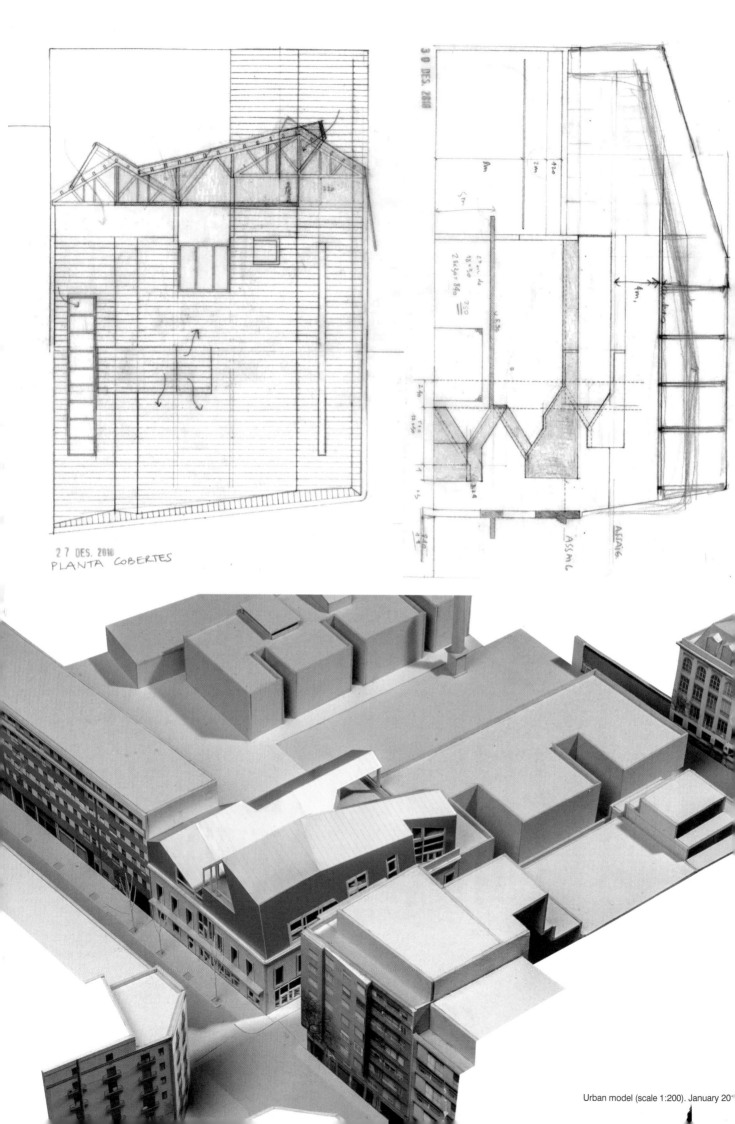

2 7 DES. 2010
PLANTA COBERTES

3 0 DES. 2010

Urban model (scale 1:200). January 20

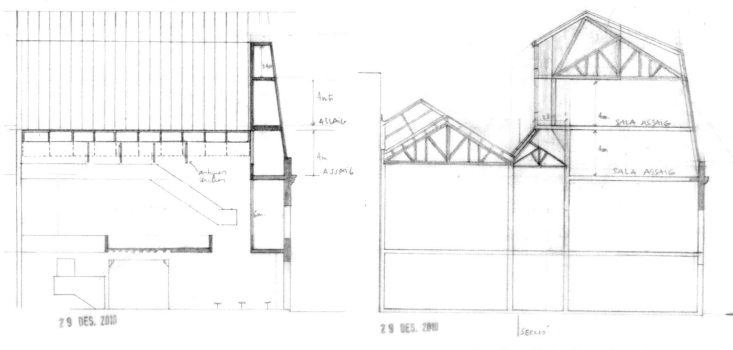

Study of the modification of the preexisting roofs.
Plan and sections (scale 1:200). EP, December 2010.

The World of the Roofs: A Corner Location

Currently resting atop the upper floor are the two large volumes occupied by the pitched roofs, four meters high, along with the former residence of the chairman of the cooperative.
*This current world is what must be transformed and expanded in order to make room for the rest of the program. One of the bays, that of the Theater Upstairs, will preserve its original silhouette. The other roof, the corner one, will grow two stories in order to house the two rehearsal halls, rising on top of the dramaturgy classrooms. The constructed volume is weighted toward the corner of the lot, freeing the upper part of the patio and then covering it again by reusing the wooden roof trusses. The two rehearsal halls are located above, where they receive plenty of natural light and ventilation, ready for long working days. ** *

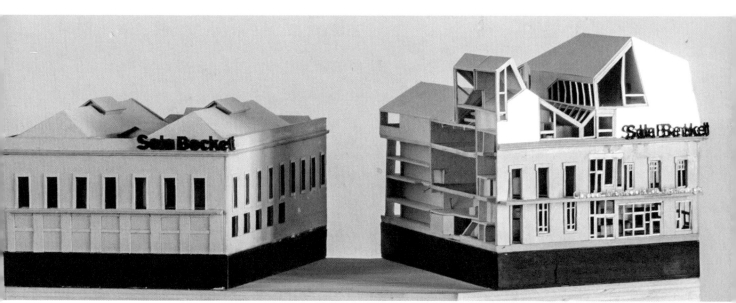

Models (scale 1:200) of the former *Pau i Justícia* cooperative building and of the new Sala Beckett. January 2011.

The move from the middle of a block in the Gràcia neighborhood to a corner building in Poblenou confers a new value on the new Sala Beckett, transforming it into a more public theater center, connected with the surrounding neighborhood. Nearby, less than a hundred meters away, is Can Felipa, a civic center where theater is also sometimes performed. It is an industrial building with an enormous Parisian-style mansard roof. We expected the Sala Beckett, with its new roofs, to be a worthy companion to it.

The program drawn up by the Sala Beckett for the competition amounted to 4,435 m². It included two rehearsal halls, two main theater halls, classrooms for both theory and acting classes, workshops for technicians, storage rooms, and lodgings for guest performers. Since the former cooperative building had around 3,000 m² of constructed area, the building needed to be expanded. In our design, the building expanded both below, with a basement level for storage areas, workshops, and machine rooms, and above, with two rehearsal halls and lodgings for guest performers.

17

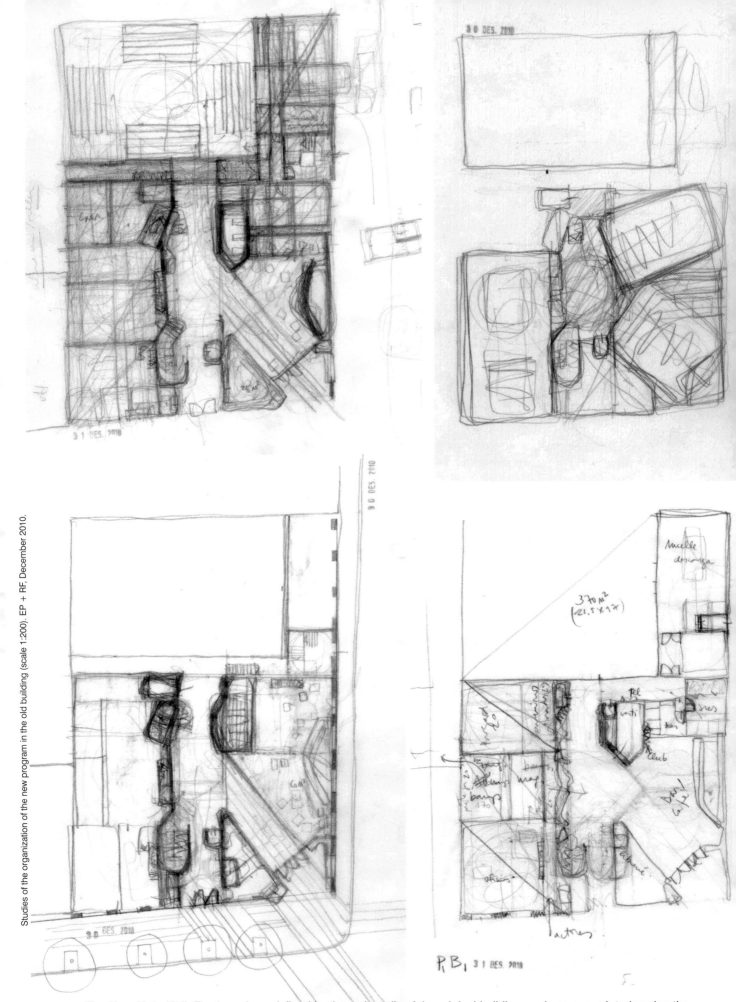

Studies of the organization of the new program in the old building (scale 1:200). EP + RF, December 2010.

The New Main Hall. *The large bays defined by the main walls of the original building are large enough to imagine the new program fitting within them. But one of the principal elements of the program, the Theater Downstairs, is the only one that cannot be inserted directly into the preexisting structure. And we have learned that, if this hall is to be sufficiently polyvalent, adapting to changes in the relationship between stage and audience in accord with successive productions, it needs to be at least fifteen meters wide: 4 meters of seating + 7 meters of stage + 4 meters of seating. The bays of the former cooperative, however, are just eleven meters wide…*

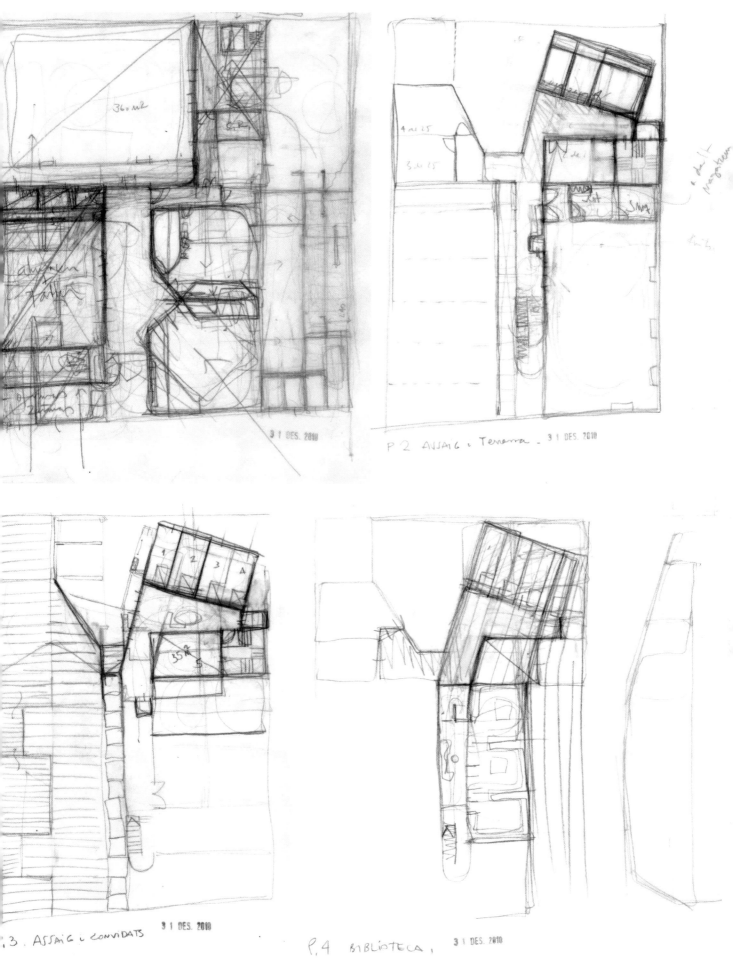

P 2 AVSAIG i Terrassa — 3 1 DES. 2010

.3. ASSAIG i CONVIDATS   3 1 DES. 2010

P.4 BIBLIOTECA,   3 1 DES. 2010

*That is why we have placed the large hall where the building will most easily accommodate it: where the two main bays end, at the back of the lot, occupying a space that was the final expansion of the former building. This space, fundamental to the new Sala Beckett, is located on the ground floor, at street level, where there is easy access for both people and goods. The location of this space within the building has been our first design decision and has determined the distribution of the program directly connected with it: the lobby bar through which it can be entered from the street, the loading dock area, the technical area, the stage equipment storerooms, the dressing rooms… *

A Very Public Ground Floor. *It is on the ground floor that the public program is concentrated, the public spaces of the project: bar, lobby, meeting/waiting area, entrance to the theater… The corner bar serves to connect the rest of the building with the surrounding neighborhood. It leads into the lobby, which also constitutes the foyer of the Sala Beckett. The three spaces —bar, lobby, theater— function as continuous spaces, equipped to absorb the large numbers of people who will occupy the ground floor on performance nights.*

The Different Entrances to the Building. *People will be coming to the building for different reasons, so we have divided the entrances as follows:*
- *General public and workshop participants: near the corner, by way of the large doors that open from Calle Pere IV onto the interior passageway, the bar, and the large central lobby.*
- *Sala Beckett staff and actors enter from Calle Pere IV, but separately from the general public.*
- *Guest performers go to their apartments by means of a separate doorway, which opens onto the stairway along Calle Batista.*
- *The loading and unloading of material takes place at the end of Calle Batista, out of the way of public circulation.* *

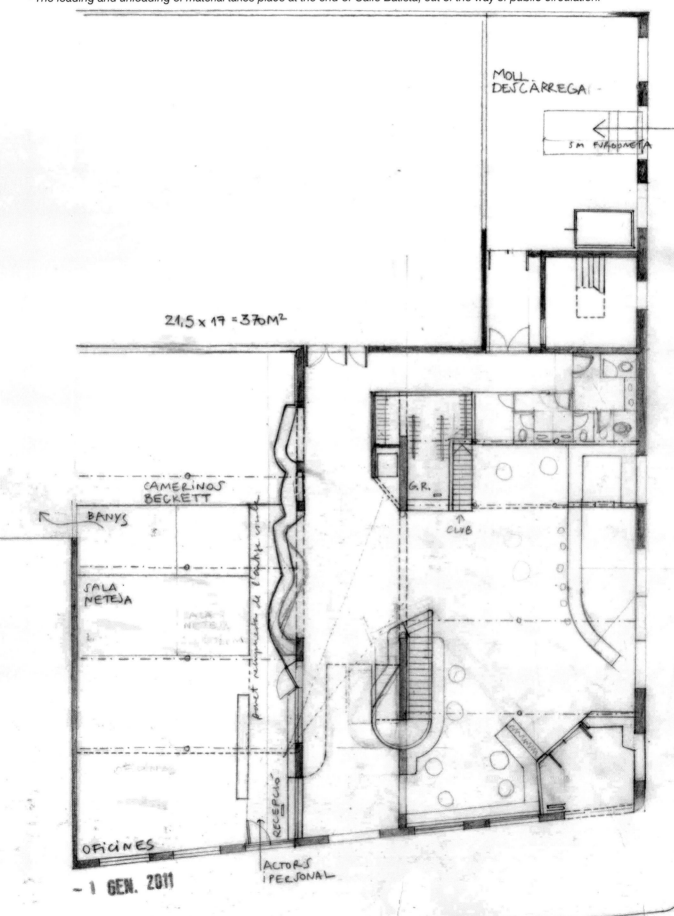

Plans in scale 1:200 from the first version of the competition project. EP, January 2011.

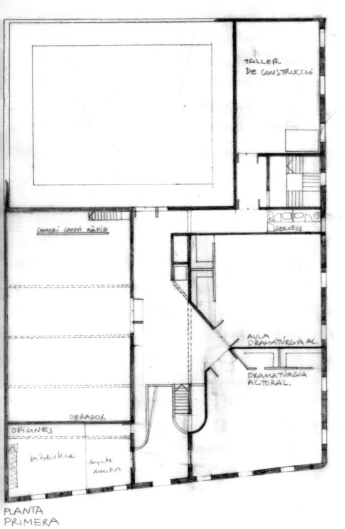

TALLER
DE CONSTRUCCIÓ

CAMERÍ CANVI RÀPID

SERVEIS

AULA
DRAMATÚRGIA AC.

DRAMATÚRGIA
ACTORAL.

OBRADOR

OFICINES

biblioteca   departament
                    direcció

PLANTA
PRIMERA
E. 1/200.
- 1 GEN. 2011

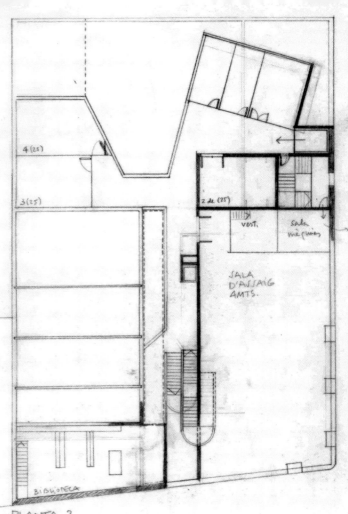

4 (25)

3 (25)

2 de (25)

VEST.

sala
mà(quines)

SALA
D'ASSAIG
AMTS.

BIBLIOTECA

PLANTA 2.
ASSAIG - AULES - TERRAVSA
E. 1/200.
- 1 GEN. 2010

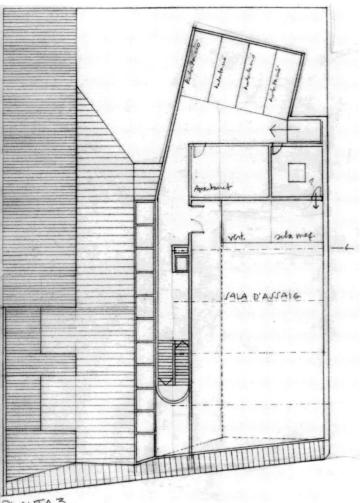

Apartament

vest.   sala maq.

SALA D'ASSAIG

PLANTA 3.
ASSAIG - CONVIDATS
E. 1/200.

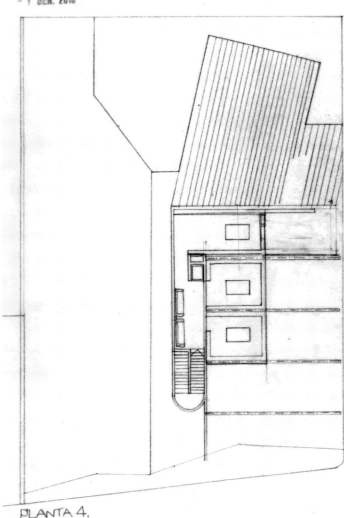

PLANTA 4.
BIBLIOTECA
E. 1/200. - 1 GEN. 2011

Definitive Version 5-8 January 2011.

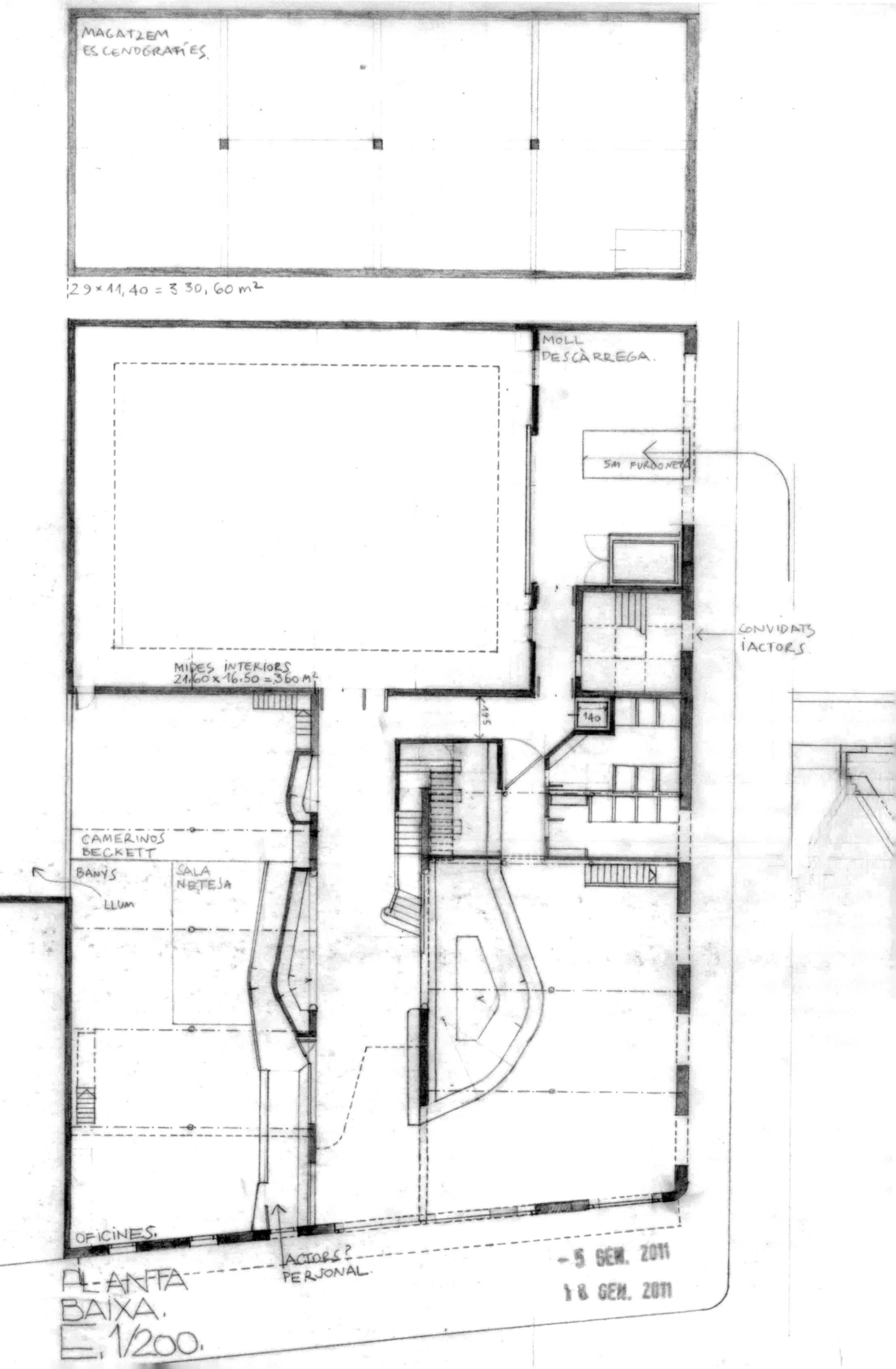

MAGATZEM
ESCENOGRAFÍES.
29 × 11,40 = 330,60 m²
MOLL
DESCÀRREGA.
5m FURGONETA
CONVIDATS
i ACTORS.
MIDES INTERIORS
21,60 × 16,50 = 360 M²
195
140
CAMERINOS
BECKETT
BANYS
LLUM
SALA
NETEJA
OFICINES.
ACTORS?
PERSONAL.
-5 GEN. 2011
18 GEN. 2011
PLANTA
BAIXA.
E. 1/200.

Plans of ground floor and mezzanine level in scale 1:200 from the definitive version of the competition project. EP, January 2011.

The Pocket Spaces. *Once the large volumes of the program have occupied their places within the structure —the Theater Downstairs, the Theater Upstairs, the dramaturgy classrooms and rehearsal halls, the bar…— the rest of the program is inserted into the interstices between these spaces. People will find themselves closer to one another in these smaller spaces —the library, the authors' club, the offices, the dressing rooms…— and there will be a noticeable spatial contrast between the large diaphanous halls and these more compact work and meeting spaces. The distribution of these "pocket" spaces is as follows:*

- *Dressing rooms, laundry room, and sewing room: between the two large halls, thereby guaranteeing accessibility for the performers from their dressing rooms and so ensuring, in the different configurations, that they will not run into the public or other users of the Theater Downstairs.*
- *Offices: between the Theater Upstairs and the main façade, so that there are as many windows as possible.*
- *Technical spaces: workshop, lighting storeroom, stage equipment storeroom, loading dock… around the Theater Downstairs.*
- *In a mezzanine above the bar, the authors' club, overlooking the intersection of Pere IV and Batista. ***

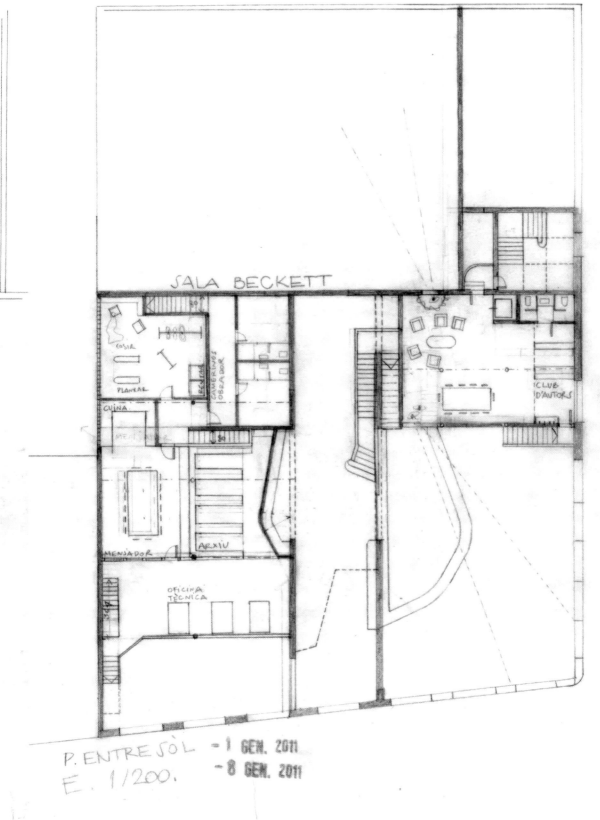

Natural Light and Circulation. *An intuitive circulation in the direction of natural light has guided the organization of the building. The former lobby of the* Pau i Justícia *cooperative comes to play a central role again. We have made use of the two preexisting walls —also a help in terms of budgeting— for the new 15-meter-high lobby. This constitutes the main entrance, with the full height of the original building and a depth of 25 meters, leading directly to the Theater Downstairs. The ceiling of the lobby is a skylight, transforming it into an interior landscape that traverses the building, leaving the various rooms and other parts of the program on either side and leading to a large exterior terrace where open-air activities are organized.*

This landscape —just another landscape of the neighborhood of Poblenou— makes it possible to understand the new Sala Beckett in a unified way. It is the place from which all of the doors open onto the various halls and classrooms. It is where chance encounters between different participants will take place: actors, playwrights, students, staff…

Vertical circulation is by way of a stairway resting against one of the two high walls: as it goes up, the light comes down alongside it, like a shower of rain… combining light and circulation. By means of this void at the center of the new building, we have ensured that natural light will reach the ground-floor lobby and all the rooms of the building. *

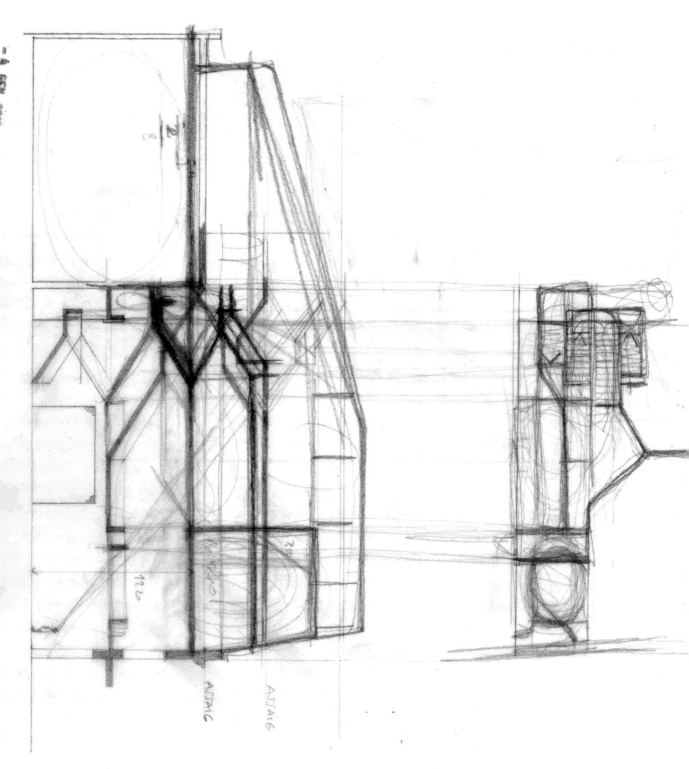

Studies of longitudinal section and second floor plan in scale 1:200 from the definitive version of the competition project. EP, January 2011.

Longitudinal section through the lobby, with the stairway located as close as possible to the center of the floor, connecting the programs on the Pere IV with those of the interior patio. Looking upward, as one enters the building, through the apertures on the second floor, on can see the sky through the skylight.

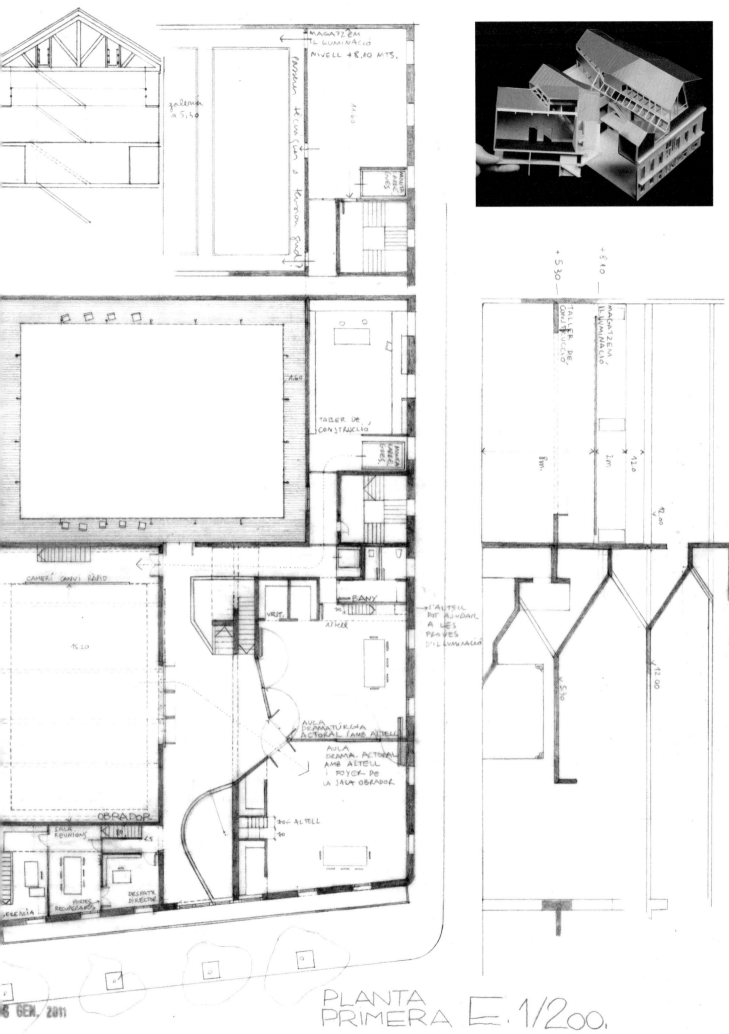

MAGATZEM
IL·LUMINACIÓ
NIVELL +8.10 MTS.

galería a 5.30

1.60

TALLER DE
CONSTRUCCIÓ

+ 5.30
+ 8.10

MAGATZEM
IL·LUMINACIÓ

TALLER DE
CONSTRUCCIÓ

8 m.

1 m.

+ 12.0

+ 12.00

CAMERÍ CANVI RÀPID

BANY

VRST.

l'ALTELL
POT AJUDAR
A LES
PROVES
D'IL·LUMINACIÓ

+ 5.30

+ 12.00

16.20

AULA
DRAMATÚRGIA
ACTORAL (AMB ALTELL

AULA
DRAMA. ACTORAL
AMB ALTELL
I FOYER DE
LA SALA OBRADOR

OBRADOR

SALA
REUNIONS

80

65

POC ALTELL
70

GERENCIA

PORTES
RECUPERADES

DESPATX
DIRECTOR

6 GEN. 2011

PLANTA
PRIMERA E. 1/200.

The Charm of the Second Floor. *On this second floor, the ambience of the original building can still be savored.
There are elements of the decoration —above all the woodwork with the colored glass— that it will be interesting to preserve
for the future Sala Beckett. These elements can be removed, restored, and then put back in the building. The former theater
hall will become the Theater Upstairs, with the same dimensions and the original wooden trusses.* *

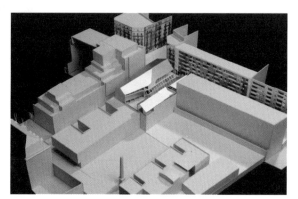
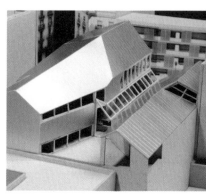

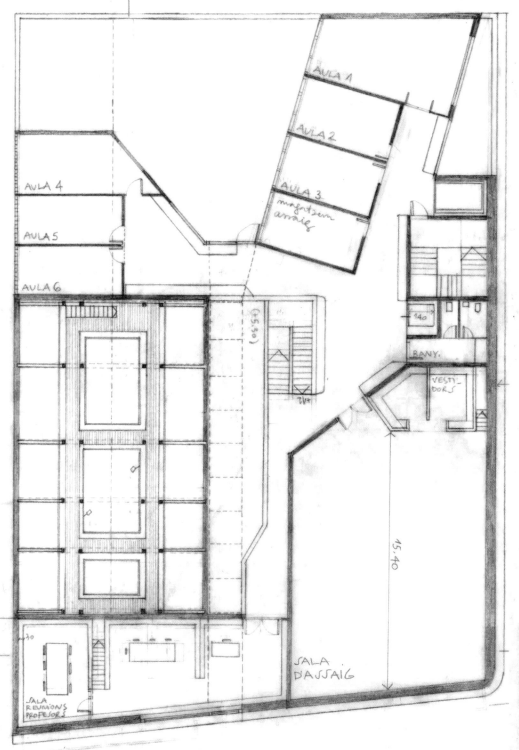

AULA A

AULA 2

AULA 3
magatzem
assaig

AULA 4

AULA 5

AULA 6

(+5,30)

140

BANY.

VESTI-
DORS

15,40

SALA
D'ASSAIG

SALA
REUNIONS
PROFESORS

ASSAIG - AULES - BIBLIOTECA.
E. 1/200. PLANTA 2.
- 6 GEN. 2011   2 0 GEN. 2011

PLANTA 3.
ASSAIG i CONVIDATS

2 0 GEN. 2011
- 6 GEN. 2011

The Interior Patio. *The building shares its block in the Poblenou neighborhood with schools and housing. There is a large interior patio occupied by sporting and recreational equipment, an interesting space in which the new Sala Beckett can venture to participate. The new building extends a large open terrace in the direction of this patio, onto which all of the theory classrooms look. These classrooms will therefore have plenty of natural light and ventilation. The terrace is a place for mixing and interaction between the lobby-landscape and the interior patio. ***

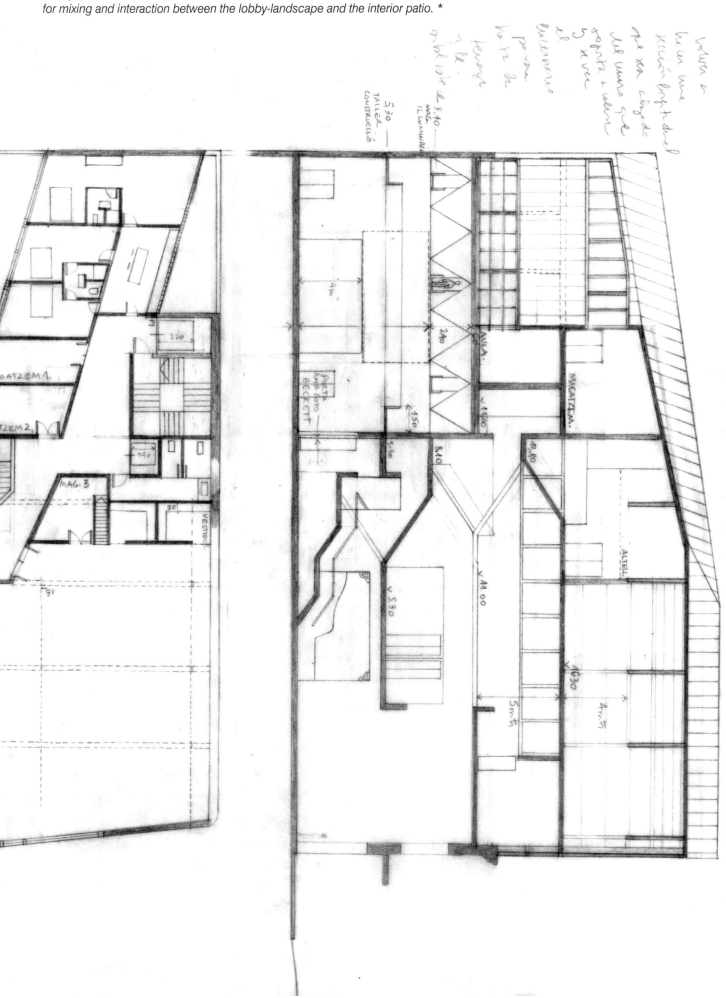

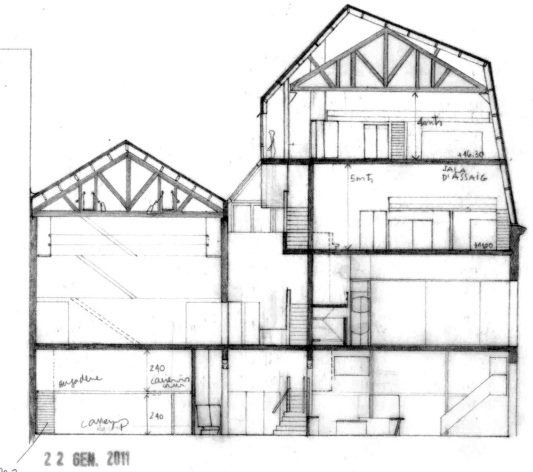

2 2 GEN. 2011

The loadbearing wall on the right is extended by means of a corbel on the second floor to support the metallic frames of the roof structure. This wall constitutes the main element of the expansion of the building. While the bay adjoining the party wall remains intact, the pair formed by the lobby and the right bay appears as a unit within the building, which continues to grow with the new program, pushing the roofs a few meters higher. The original wooden trusses have been salvaged and placed on the top floor.

ALZADO PEREN.
2 0 GEN. 2011

SITUATION
1/200

THE NEW SALA BECKETT IS LOCATED ON A CORNER OF AN OLD ROAD OF BARCELONA, NOW PERE IV STREET. THIS CORNER HOSTS THE MOST PUBLIC PART OF THE PROGRAM, WHILE THE ACADEMIC AREA IS ORIENTED TOWARDS THE INNER PART OF THE PLOT FACING THE SPORTS FIELDS OF TWO SCHOOLS OF THIS CITY BLOCK.

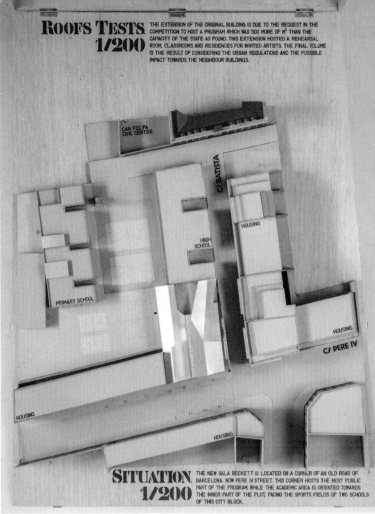

ROOFS TESTS
1/200
THE EXTENSION OF THE ORIGINAL BUILDING IS DUE TO THE REQUEST IN THE COMPETITION TO HOST A PROGRAM WHICH WAS 50% MORE OF M² THAN THE CAPACITY OF THE STATE AS FOUND. THIS EXTENSION HOSTED A REHEARSAL ROOM, CLASSROOMS AND RESIDENCES FOR INVITED ARTISTS. THE FINAL VOLUME IS THE RESULT OF CONSIDERING THE URBAN REGULATIONS AND THE POSSIBLE IMPACT TOWARDS THE NEIGHBOUR BUILDINGS.

SITUATION
1/200
THE NEW SALA BECKETT IS LOCATED ON A CORNER OF AN OLD ROAD OF BARCELONA, NOW PERE IV STREET. THIS CORNER HOSTS THE MOST PUBLIC PART OF THE PROGRAM, WHILE THE ACADEMIC AREA IS ORIENTED TOWARDS THE INNER PART OF THE PLOT, FACING THE SPORTS FIELDS OF TWO SCHOOLS OF THIS CITY BLOCK.

The openings of the bar on the ground-floor corner express the building's willingness to open itself up to the neighborhood and connect with the street. This is the new Sala Beckett's corner of interaction, with lots of doors and a diversity of clientele. The preexisting balcony, which runs the length of the façade, along with the upper cornice, emphasizes the street front. The balcony is preserved intact in the new design, connecting all of the doors of the rooms along this façade and reinforcing the relation of the building's first floor with the Calle Pere IV. The cornice divides the façade in two. Lower down, the façade looks toward the street, the preexisting apertures marking the rhythm. Higher up, the apertures are more in accord with the larger dimensions of the roof structure.

20 GEN. 2011

ALZADO BATISTA.

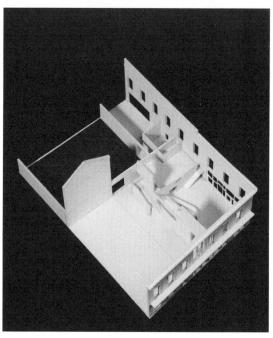

The competition model then served to present the project to the members of the Fundació Sala Beckett and later on to explain it to a wider audience, made up of people from Barcelona's cultural, political, and theatrical milieus.

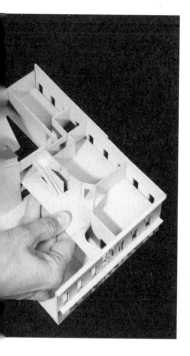
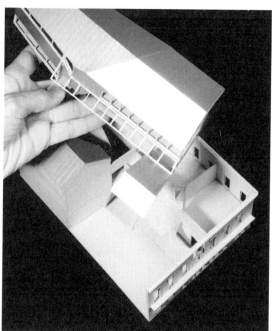
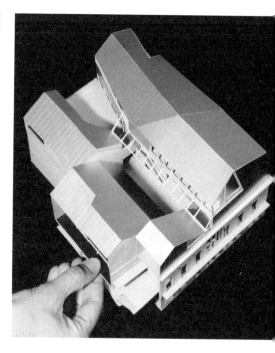

Presentation of the project at Can Felipa, December 2012.

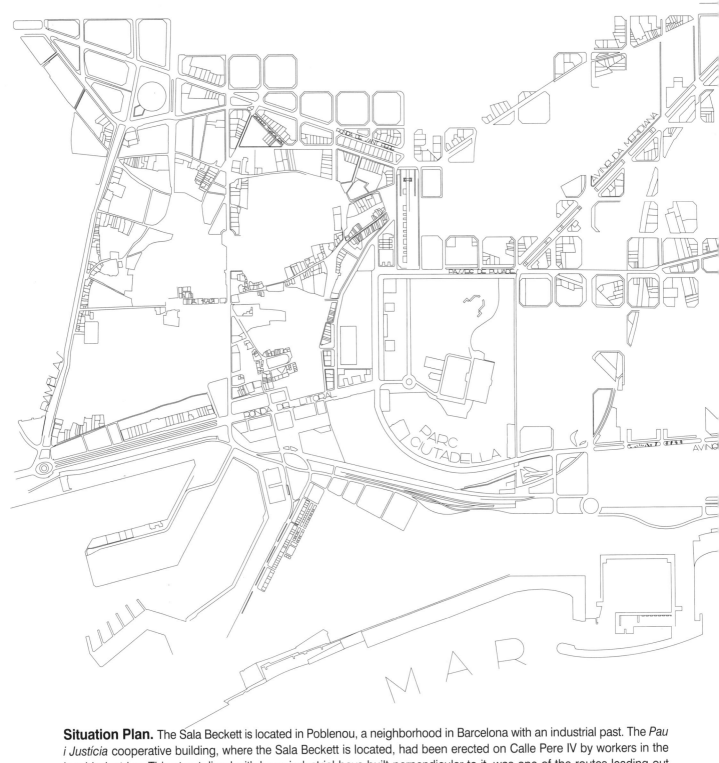

Situation Plan. The Sala Beckett is located in Poblenou, a neighborhood in Barcelona with an industrial past. The *Pau i Justícia* cooperative building, where the Sala Beckett is located, had been erected on Calle Pere IV by workers in the local industries. This street, lined with large industrial bays built perpendicular to it, was one of the routes leading out of the city toward France, along the coastline, and is older than the Eixample de Barcelona. The former cooperative maintains this structure of two large bays with a central passageway serving as a vestibule, similar to so many other buildings in the area, although in this case the vestibule is covered.

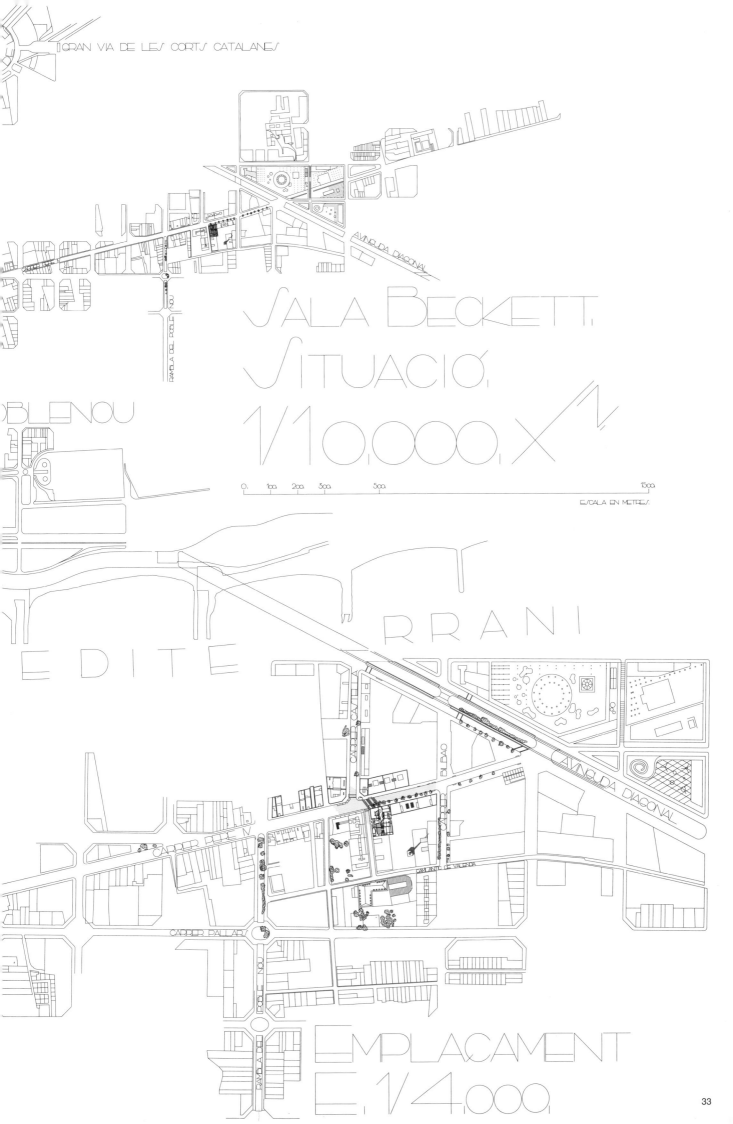

GRAN VIA DE LES CORTS CATALANES

AVINGUDA DIAGONAL

RAMBLA DEL POBLE NOU

SALA BECKETT.
SITUACIO.
1/10.000. X

POBLENOU

0. 100. 200. 300. 500. 1500.
ESCALA EN METRES.

MEDITERRANI

CARRER CAVELLA

BILBAO

AVINGUDA DIAGONAL

CARRER PERE IV

CARRER PALLARS

CARRER ANDREU DE VALENCIA

RAMBLA DEL POBLE NOU

EMPLAÇAMENT
E: 1/4.000.

Members of the *Pau i Justícia* workers'
cooperative at the intersection of Pere IV and Batista
Arxiu Històric del Poblenou

The *Pau i Justícia* Workers' Cooperative
1924

The *Pau i Justícia* [Peace and Justice] Workers' Cooperative was founded in 1897, in the same aim as many other cooperatives that appeared in the Poblenou district in the last decades of the nineteenth century: to collective the savings of its members, so that basic necessities could be purchased at moderate prices, with no need for intermediaries. Over time, the surpluses generated by the cooperative's sales would constitute retirement and health care funds for its members.

These cooperative stores gradually turned into typical meeting places for members of the working class. As the number of members grew, the cooperatives organized themselves in order to expand their premises, where, in addition to the sale of foodstuffs, cultural and recreational spaces were established. Some of them, such as *Pau i Justícia*, became the owners of the buildings in which they were established and expanded them as the number of the cooperative's members increased. The construction of these buildings was carried out by the members themselves, working on Sundays and holidays, their days off from regular employment.

In 1924 *Pau i Justícia* officially inaugurated its premises on Calle Pere IV in Poblenou. The two-storey building was designed by the construction foreman Josep Masdeu, who organized the spaces into two parallel bays, with a central passageway. On the ground floor there was a grocery store; on the second floor —with its independent entrance, signaled by the pediment in the middle of the façade along Pere IV— there was a café and dance hall, with a stage on which weddings, first communions, and other festivities could be celebrated.

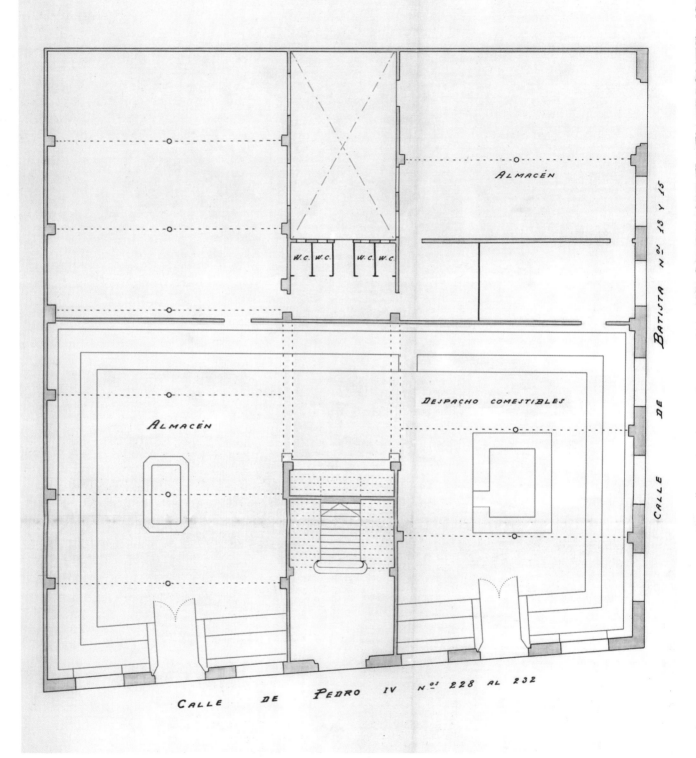

On the ground floor was the grocery store, with two entrances and a large storeroom at the back. The store was spacious, organized into various different sections, and supplied with plentiful natural light, with a resemblance to a market. The countertops were of marble and wood, with a lower shelf made of iron bars on which to place a bag while one was shopping. There were large wood-framed windows, with decorated glass panes, giving onto the two streets, and hydraulic tiles on the floor, with various types of carpet design in the area where one waited to be attended to. The cast-iron pillars and vaulted ceramic ceiling were materials and techniques very common in the construction of the age.

This initial construction, composed of two bays perpendicular to Pere IV, with a narrower bay between them, was expanded in 1935 by means of a third bay toward the back of the lot, perpendicular to the first two and of the same height and dimensions. The ground floor of this new bay would serve to expand the storeroom of the grocery store, while a primary school for the children of the members of the cooperative was installed on the upper floor. The school was entered from Calle Batista, by way of a stairway connecting the school directly with the street.

The three bays had the same dimensions: eleven meters wide and six meters high per floor. Because of the wooden trusses supporting the pitched roof, there were no intermediate pillars on the upper floor, while on the ground floor there was a single pillar in the middle of each bay. The structure was very similar to the rest of the industrial buildings in the neighborhood. What made the cooperative different from an industrial workplace was its decoration with cornices and ceiling roses, hydraulic tiles of different designs, magnificent woodwork, and colored-glass windows.

On the upper floor there was a mezzanine level reached by way of the café. Next to the bar, a wooden stairway communicated with the offices of the various sections of activities: *sardana* [a type of Catalan folk dance], hiking, billiards, chess…

"The use given to the building has much to do with people in very precarious economic conditions, with few resources, who get together and make an effort to organize themselves, in order to ensure their own survival, and this economic effort immediately leads them also to social and cultural activities, not merely economic ones, manifest in all the cooperative's recreational sections: theater, dance, choir, sardanas…*"* Toni Casares. Interview for the film *Scale 1:5*.

FIRST OCCUPATION 2013
CROSS SECTION

GRAPHIC SCALE IN METERS

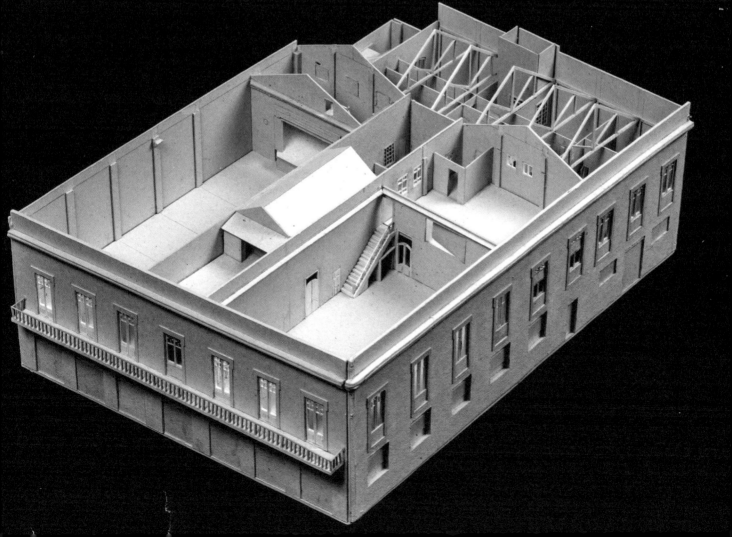

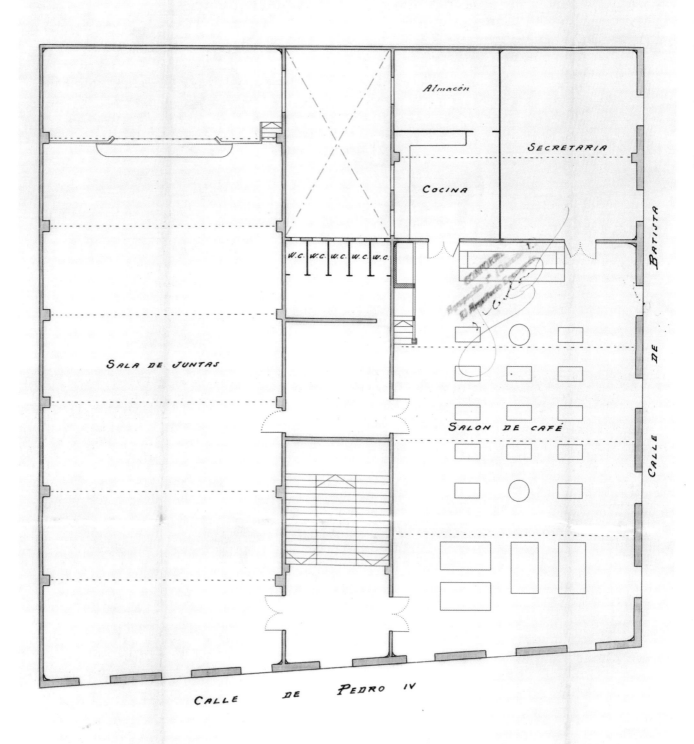

PLANTA PISO

Almacén

Secretaria

Cocina

W.C. W.C. W.C. W.C. W.C.

Sala de Juntas

Salon de Café

Calle de Batista

Calle de Pedro IV

The upper floor was devoted to leisure activities, functioning in complete independence of the ground floor. The stairway led up directly from Calle Pere IV to a small vestibule with a view of the street, which led in turn to a large café or ballroom, designated on the plan as *Sala de Juntas* [Meeting Room]. In the late 1970s the cooperative went into economic crisis: both consumption and leisure habits had evolved, but the greatest change was the disappearance of the spirit of cooperation itself. In the 1997 the cooperative closed definitively.

Following pages: Theater and dance hall on the upper floor in 1924 and 2011
Photos by Arxiu Municipal Districte de Sant Martí and Adrià Goula

State As-Found *January 2011*

In the late 1990s, the cooperative went bankrupt and closed its doors for good, as the building passed into private hands. For a few years a gymnasium operated on the ground floor, while the upper floor remained empty, just as the cooperative had left it. The building was not well maintained and began to fall into disrepair. Finally, the municipality purchased it, but even then it remained abandoned until 2013. During these years of abandonment, the building began to deteriorate seriously. The roof collapsed and rainwater found its way in. The neighborhood residents, many of them former members of the cooperative, watched as the building fell into disrepair, waiting to see what might be done with it and whether it could be salvaged.

"It could well have run into the ground completely, as it was not cataloged heritage. From an esthetic or artistic viewpoint, it was definitely not considered sufficiently important or interesting or original to preserve. The building was deteriorating, it was falling down, and when the municipality bought it, it was thanks to the pressure of local residents and other entities that the decision was made to put it to a cultural use, that is, not to turn it into a supermarket, but to make it a building with a cultural purpose. This owed not only to the architecture of the building, but rather to local memory, to what had been an emotional bond." Toni Casares. Interview for the film *Scale 1:5*.

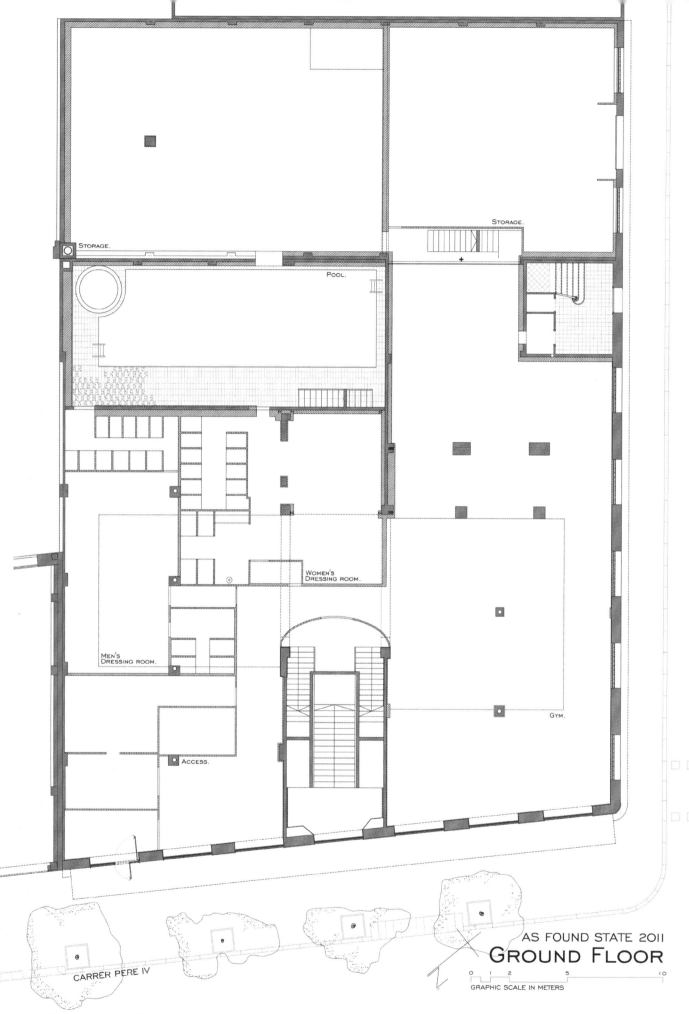

STORAGE.

STORAGE.

POOL.

WOMEN'S
DRESSING ROOM.

MEN'S
DRESSING ROOM.

ACCESS.

GYM.

AS FOUND STATE 2011
GROUND FLOOR

0 1 2   5   10
GRAPHIC SCALE IN METERS

CARRER PERE IV

Ground Floor Occupied by a Gymnasium. One of the bays of the former cooperative store was occupied by a gymnasium, with the other serving to house dressing rooms. A swimming pool had been installed by making use of a former cellar. This level was disconnected from the upper floor, which was reached directly by the wide stairway leading from Calle Pere IV into the café and ballroom.

The gymnasium put an end to the decoration and furnishings of the large cooperative store. The windows were boarded up, the hydraulic tiles were replaced by plastic imitation wood, the cast-iron columns were lined with brick and mirrors, and a pool with Roman decoration made its appearance. All traces of the former store were completely effaced.

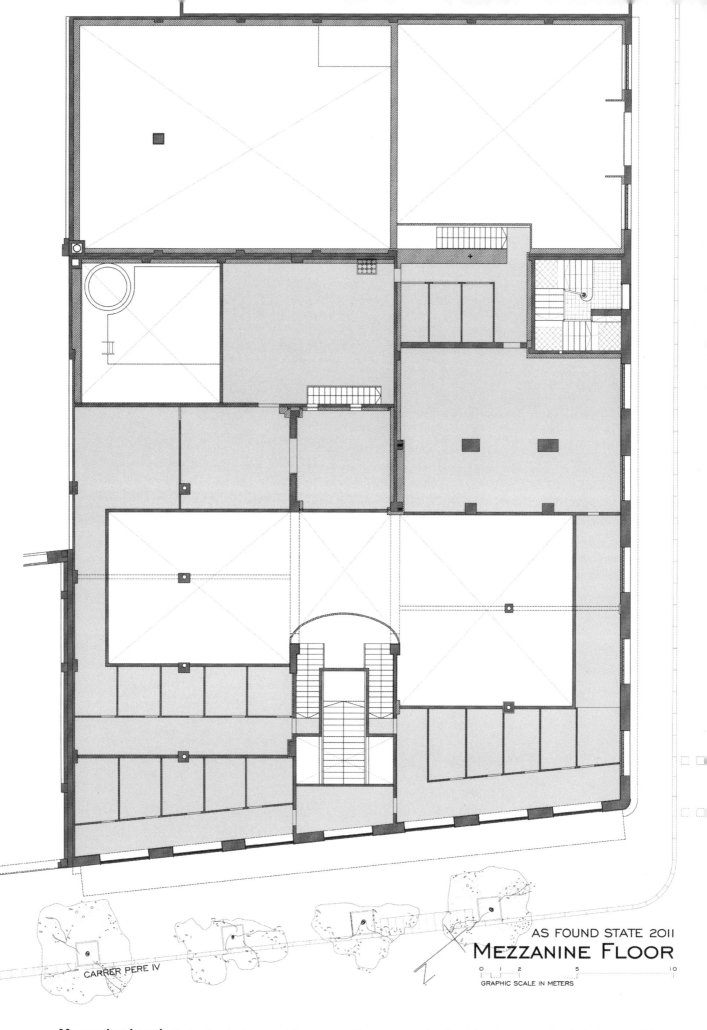

AS FOUND STATE 2011
MEZZANINE FLOOR

CARRER PERE IV

0 1 2 5 10
GRAPHIC SCALE IN METERS

Mezzanine Level. During the last years of the cooperative, a mezzanine level had been constructed all around the ground floor, reducing the original height from six meters to less than three. When the gymnasium was installed, this level was occupied by a long series of little booths.

Stairways were built for this new mezzanine level, spaces without sufficient headspace or light, where the beams made things even more cramped. Since there were no windows looking onto the street on this mezzanine level, the disorienting claustrophobic effect was still more pronounced.

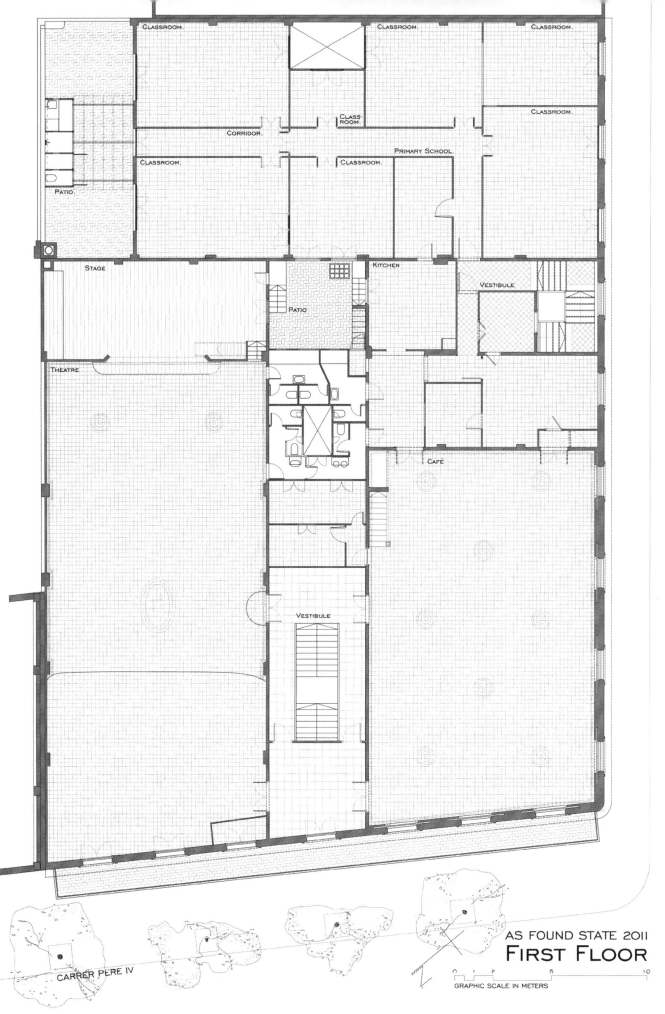

CLASSROOM.   CLASSROOM.   CLASSROOM.

CLASS-
ROOM.

CLASSROOM.

CORRIDOR.

PRIMARY SCHOOL.

CLASSROOM.   CLASSROOM.

PATIO.

STAGE   KITCHEN

VESTIBULE

PATIO

THEATRE

CAFÉ

VESTIBULE

AS FOUND STATE 2011
FIRST FLOOR

CARRER PERE IV

GRAPHIC SCALE IN METERS

First Floor. *"The former use given to this floor of the building was very similar to what we were planning to do. When we first went in, we saw the traces of a bar, of a school, and of a theater. That trio is the Sala Beckett: a bar as meeting place, a school as training space, and a theater as a space of creation. It had already been done for us."* Toni Casares. Interview for the film *Scale 1:5*.

As we climbed a half-hidden stairway to the first floor, we discovered that up there, in an advanced state of disrepair, was the primary school of the children of the members of the cooperative, along with the patio of the actors, the former theater, the café with its kitchen... All the furnishings were abandoned. Time had stood still.

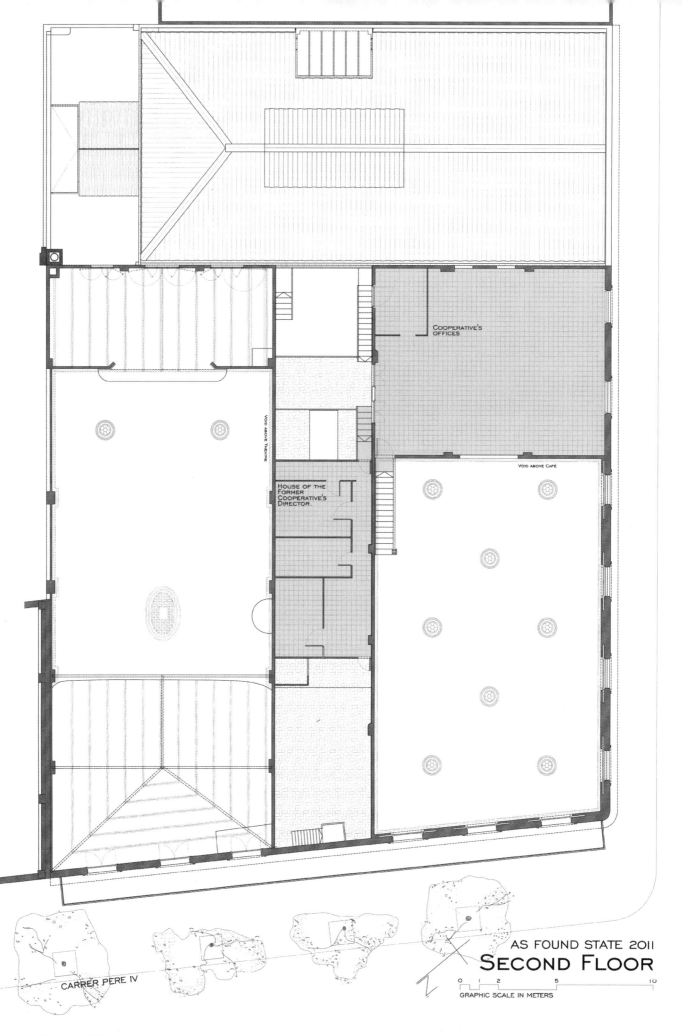

COOPERATIVE'S OFFICES

VOID ABOVE THEATRE

VOID ABOVE CAFÉ

HOUSE OF THE FORMER COOPERATIVE'S DIRECTOR.

CARRER PERE IV

AS FOUND STATE 2011
SECOND FLOOR

0   1   2   5   10
GRAPHIC SCALE IN METERS

Second Floor. In the upper part of the central vestibule there was a small apartment for the chairman of the cooperative, reached by a stairway leading from the exterior patio. It was a space disconnected from the functions of the rest of the building, more in contact with the sky than with the interior. On that same level were the offices of the cultural and recreational sections of the cooperative, reached by a wooden stairway from the café.

The abandonment of a building is an eloquent moment. How is it that we abandon buildings and things? It explains a lot about us as a civilization. And this building was abandoned because the spirit of cooperation had disappeared. It resisted for a few years, empty, and it had a great story to tell.

The cooperative itself was a place of generous dimensions. In a densely-built city like Barcelona, such large rooms are difficult to find, and even today, for us, as architects, deciding to design a room six meters high is no common occurrence. There were still many of the original doors, windows, and paving stones —they can be seen in the photo, beneath a layer of dire— that we thought it would be very good to preserve. Since the original building had been very economical in its construction, these elements gave it a delicate, human dimension.

We were pleased to be inheriting such large spaces, with traces of a very different age, the age of the cooperatives, of the generation of our grandparents: an age not so distant in time, just before our civil war, but which had disappeared completely. And we also saw a future in this atmosphere of abandonment, the traces of former lives that could mix with those of theater people and writers, all working together in the day-to-day activities of the building, writing a new chapter on its walls.

The new Sala Beckett by Flores & Prats

Juan José Lahuerta

The fact that certain Spanish editions of the works of Samuel Beckett have titles like *Detritus* or *Residua* seems almost like a premonition, considering the way Flores & Prats have operated (and not designed) in the new headquarters of this fantastic theater in Barcelona known as Sala Beckett. The Latin term detritus means consumed, eroded; in science it refers to parts separated from a body or sediments of earth and stone; in general use it indicates what is left over, what remains. And as if to come full circle, the detritus is residual, a left over. But the residue also has to do with the work of the alchemists. In fact Residua is an adaptation of the original French title *Têtes-mortes* (Dead Heads), which Beckett used to make reference to the excess in alchemical processes, the remains that could not be utilized.

I don't know if Flores & Prats or Toni Casares, director of the theater, had these references —these... coincidences?— in mind when they decided how to intervene in the ruined sheds of the site of the new Sala Beckett. Certainly, from the outset, they thought about working with debris and left overs, though assigning them a value that has nothing to do with the idea of the useless left overs of the alchemists. Instead, they decided to raise them to a higher status, transforming them into protagonists, inverting processes of sedimentation and shifting layers of debris upward, to the top of the pile: in tune with the spirit of Beckett, detritus and residuals become an indispensable requirement of the work.

In the new Sala Beckett the ruins found by Flores & Prats are assigned civil and moral values that through the redemption of usage value have been transformed into *truth*. Let's remember one very important aspect here: the building of the old Cooperative *Pau i Justícia* that has become Sala Beckett was not listed as protected heritage. The architects could have demolished it to have an empty lot on which to build a totally new theater. Neither the architects nor the theater management were obliged to conserve anything, not even the memory of the place. Yet they have done just that, making an important design decision in ideological terms: this extraordinary project begins with that decision, and the architectural approach of Flores & Prats is thus linked to one of the more provocative ideas formulated by Samuel Beckett in *Detritus*. In a conversation with Georges Duthuit, speaking of the possibilities of art, the Irish writer said he would prefer a condition in which "there is nothing to express, nothing with which to express, nothing from which to express, no power to express, no desire to express, together with the obligation to express."

Flores & Prats could have made tabula rasa of the sheds of the old cooperative and built their own *invention* on the freed-up land, without obstacles. Instead, they sensed another type of *obligation*. In effect, in this project *obligation* opposes *invention*. Faced with crumbling walls, collapsing ceilings, cracked floors, the overlapping of countless restorations accumulated over time, the remains of doors, partitions, windows, railings, moldings, plaster, ceramics —in short, rubble of little value— Flores & Prats did not think about *eliminating* it all, but about conserving it.

Why does the concept of heritage have to be associated with something prestigious and monumental? From the viewpoint of Flores & Prats and Toni Casares the idea of patrimony does not come from pater, it cannot be imposed from above, but arises like a formless, headless mist from time and experience, from what is radically collective, from below, even from the deepest strata. The sheds were not even a ruin as such —since ruins have the prestige of time and thus become timeless— but just a pile of rubble, so ordinary, so worthless as to be able to vanish without any regrets. But for Flores & Prats that rubble imposed the "obligation to express": it represented the bond with the deepest roots of living memory of a working-class neighborhood like Poblenou. The broken floors, crumbling walls, sinking roofs, the fragments of ceramic and glass, the pieces of plastic were all quite worthless in terms of trade value, but very dear —in the affective sense— from the standpoint of usage value, accumulated in an infinite number of layers, latent in every detail, ready to reawaken in collective memory. In short, the (a)patrimonial aspect of the old dilapidated building was defined by its many resident phantoms: the genteel but solid ghosts of the collective identity, which as in old yellowed photographs could not be left homeless. The new Sala Beckett —a theater, precisely so— would become the home of those marvelous phantoms and the voices that do not want to take *their leave and help us to survive* —to continue to be the owners of the city, in spite of it all— in the midst of all these left overs, allowing us in the end to impose the collective on the subjective, the place on the space, memory on invention, truth of things that have usage value over the simulacra of trade value, hands and tools over statistics, in the new but old converted building.

Faced with the old structure, Flores & Prats decided to take two complementary paths. One for the whole and one for the parts, or more precisely the pieces, even the smallest ones: colored glass, tiles, wooden moldings, plaster ceilings, handles… The first path implied clarification of the situation: restoring the building to its original form, based on a system of parallel and crosswise sheds, which had to be reconfigured from top to bottom, in the circulation and the roofing. But clarifying —i.e. restoring typological clarity— does not mean demolition. Flores & Prats do not *make* space, they do not *empty,* or cut, open or remove. They undo and redo, untangling a tangle or a complicated knot, tracing back —to better understand it— through the steps and gestures of the person who created it: they find the threads, unthreading them and threading them again; they undo stitches and restitch them, unlace and re-lace. Clarifying means putting things back where they belong, without eliminating anything: in the end, the sheds, the circulation routes, the roofs present themselves to the gaze, the touch, experience. But there is also the other path, the one that assigns importance not to the container but the content, not to the large but to the very small: true detritus and left overs, the little pieces.

As soon as they entered the building and saw the spectacle of the rubble, Flores & Prats decided to make an inventory of all the materials, all the elements —glass, wood, ceramic, plastic, etc.— still in place or scattered amidst the ruins. The drawings in which they show all the frames of the building —doors, windows, claddings, glazings, etc.— convey the form and size of each, in simultaneous sequences, all on the same scale, and are of particular interest to help us understand the quantities and typological conditions of what seemed like chaos. But besides the annotated drawings, Flores & Prats have also made small-scale models of these objects. The same criterion of cataloguing and reassembly has been applied to the cement tiles and the plaster suspended ceilings. The systematic quality of the panels with the pieces drawn in a scientific way —as in old carpentry manuals or flooring catalogues— is balanced by the flair of the small models —like the pieces in construction games for kids— in an alternation typical of Flores & Prats that has to do —as I have already emphasized in the introduction to their book Thought by Hand— with the physical and mental paradigms of the *bricoleur* as defined by Claude Lévi-Strauss in *The Savage Mind.* By this I mean that Flores & Prats have not catalogued all the elements of the old building, from the doors to the floors to the handles, because they had already thought about the place these things would occupy in a rational process of design of the already known; they have done so for the elements themselves, to care for them, to conserve them, to be able to ask them: "What would you like to be in the new but old building, *your building?*" Doors and windows, glazings and screens, ceiling roses and plaster, tiles of all kinds, cheerfully respond to the query of the architects, immediately indicating the place they want to have in a building that is still theirs and therefore ours, of the neighborhood, of living memory and the theater. The abstract project invents the materials that will be used to achieve pre-set objectives: it transforms means into ends and therefore simplifies, empties and destroys. The work of Flores & Prats, on the other hand, whose first question is addressed to what already exists and which finds all of its pertinence in what already exists, can only spring from the sincere question asked in the field, under the ultimate condition of being "definitively unfinished."

One final consideration: do not imagine that what we are saying can lead to deduction of a link between the work of Flores & Prats and collage seen as a technique of the avant-gardes: in no moment, in my view, do the two architects set out to juxtapose opposite realities, forcing paradoxes; in fact, what they do is to reveal the affinities that still exist among those things that time the destroyer and human use have separated, broken, snapped apart. *Detritus* and *Residues* are revived in their inner harmony, without being simplified in any way, but instead in all their complexity full of questions. The Parthenon, the conclusive myth and epitome of the idea of harmony in our culture, was partially built with fragments from the temples the Persians had destroyed at the Acropolis even before they had been completed. The architects of the Parthenon who took advantage of existing metopes and foundations, which even prior to their placement had been violently scattered by the invaders, did not suffer —to be honest— from the complex of Kant's dove. Neither do Flores & Prats: in an era in which emptiness is rewarded, going against the current, they require and demand density of the air, friction and resistance, to be able to fly.

Inventory *Feb 2011 – July 2011*

Adapting the former cooperative building to the technical requirements of contemporary theater work involved a series of actions that might well have completely effaced the charm of the fragile structure we inherited, destroying its delicate decoration or breaking up the enormous spaces that were a large part of its richness. The design competition left it to each team to decide whether to preserve the building or to tear it down, but we liked everything we saw in it and wanted to make it a participant in the new project.

We wanted to keep and reuse all the elements we could turn to account from the abandoned building: mosaic tiles, doors, windows, wainscoting, lamps, ceiling roses… In order to identify them all, and to know exactly what we had, we spent three months or so in the abandoned building, gathering information, taking measurements, and drawing everything that was still there in great detail: every molding, flashing, and mullion, every design on the tiles, it all interested us alike. We still didn't know exactly how we would end up using these elements, but we had the intuition that everything inside the building should stay there, even if it were to be moved to a different location, in an attempt to lend continuity to its history, through these objects charged with a past. In this way, they might reactivate the place by their presence, bringing along the time already accumulated and adding it to the memories the new occupants would eventually generate.

We decided that each element should be put to the same use it had had in the former cooperative building: the doors would remain doors, the mosaic tiles would remain tiles, the rosettes would continue to serve as decorative elements… There would be no reinterpretation of their function. We were also aware that we were manipulating material that was very common in the city of Barcelona, and that even today, when an apartment or an entire building is renovated, this kind of woodwork and flooring often ends up in the dumpsters installed temporarily in front of construction sites. It is surprising, but still today these elements continue to be invisible. The inventory would be a way of making the contractor understand their importance in the future project.

When the renovation work began, all the elements we had drawn in the inventory were carefully removed and stored away. The fragile building resisted the work of renovation, and when all these elements returned, the culture they carried within them also returned: carpenters who knew how to draw and not only to work with wood, carpenters who understood geometry; very pretty colored tiles, with designs conceived for rooms with borders on the flooring, with cornices at the juncture of wall and ceiling... All these decorative elements had been used for generations, and here, in a building so sparsely decorated, they assumed special importance.

Woodwork *Page 68*

Flooring *Page 78*

Ceiling Roses *Page 82*

23

ESTAT ACTUAL DE LA
NOVA SALA BECKETT
EX COOPERATIVA PAU I JUSTÍCIA
C/ PERE IV 228-232, BARCELONA.

INVENTARI. FUSTERIES EXISTENTS.
P.o1
FLORES & PRATS ARQUITECTES.
SETEMBRE 2011

I/1000.

PORTA Po1
PORTA DE FUSTA I VIDRE
QUANTITAT= 2 UDS. PINTADES MARRÓ

SECRETARIA

TERRA HABITACIÓ

I/100.

ALCAT FRONTAL
D4. MOTLLURA AMPIT.
I/4.

PLANTA

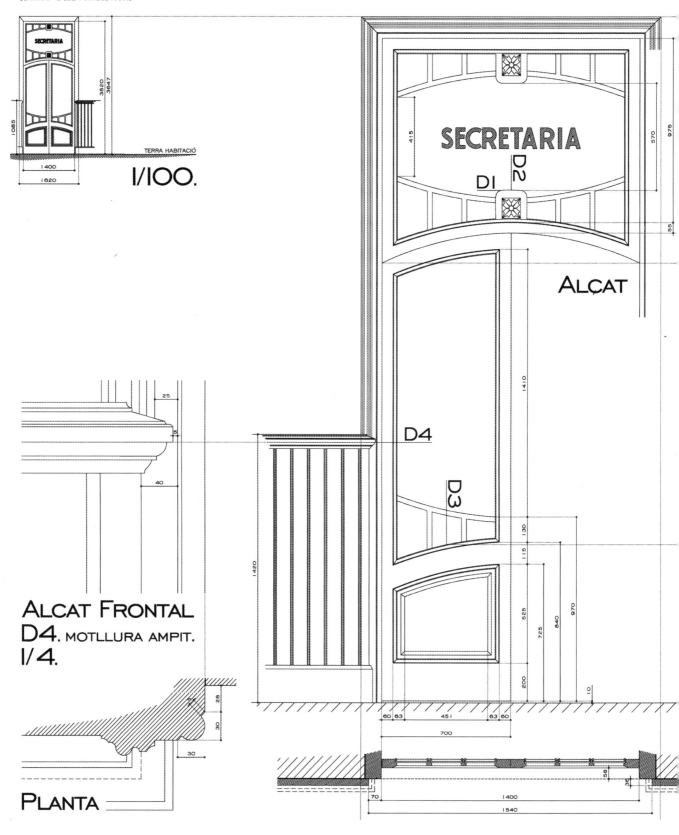

SECRETARIA

ALCAT

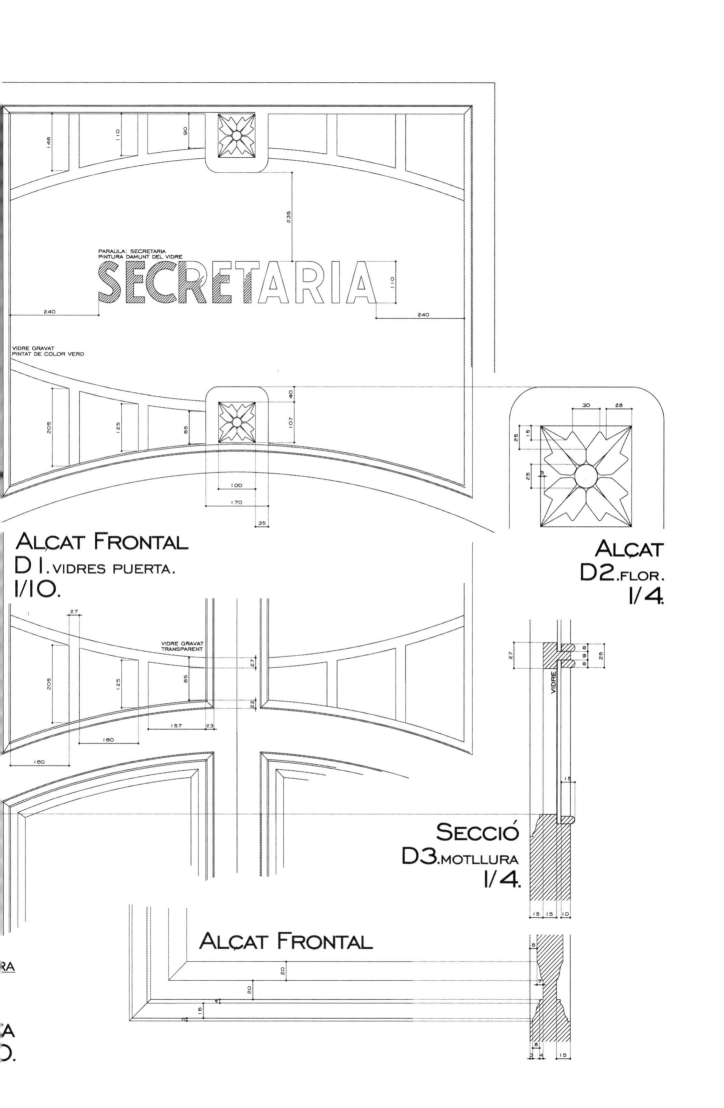

PARAULA: SECRETARIA
PINTURA DAMUNT DEL VIDRE

SECRETARIA

VIDRE GRAVAT
PINTAT DE COLOR VERD

ALÇAT FRONTAL
D1.VIDRES PUERTA.
1/10.

ALÇAT
D2.FLOR.
1/4.

VIDRE GRAVAT
TRANSPARENT

VIDRE

SECCIÓ
D3.MOTLLURA
1/4.

ALÇAT FRONTAL

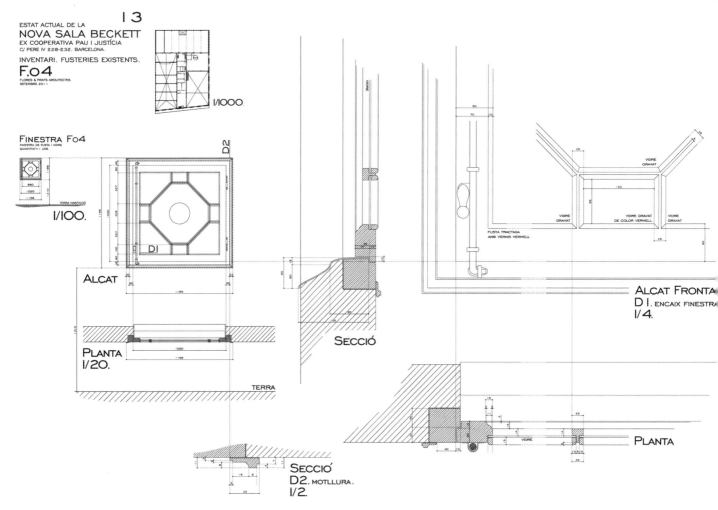

More than a hundred plans were drawn on sheets of DIN A1 paper: every door, window, ceiling rose or hydraulic tile was explained in a separate document. Every drawing had a small general plan that showed the location of the element in the cooperative building, as well as a drawing of the complete element at a scale of 1:100, along with details at larger scales.

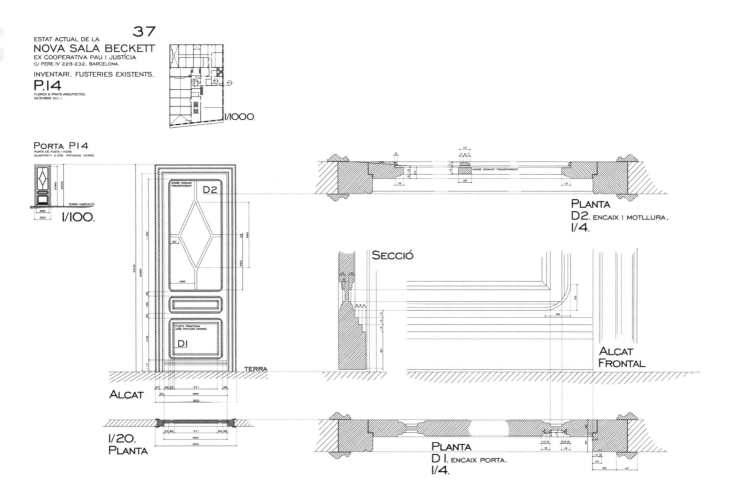

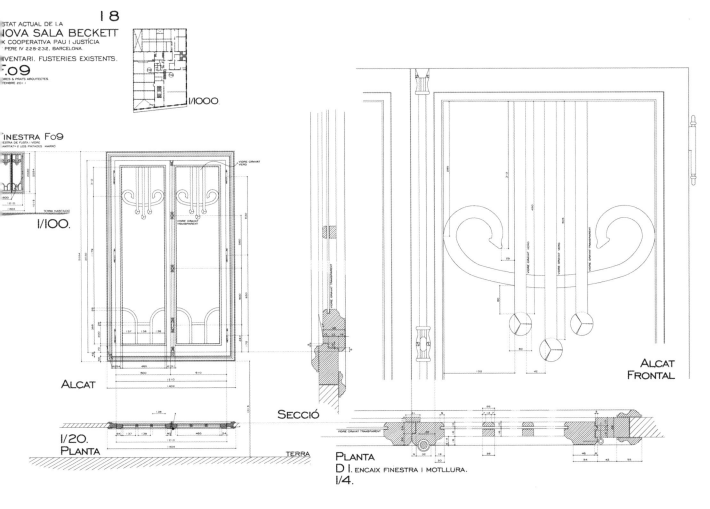

18

Drawing all this material at the same scale served to give us an accurate idea of the elements we had to work with: how many there were, what condition they were in, and how big they were. It served to make them visible, to give them importance as a unit, one by one, ensuring that they would be included in the future project, that they would not leave the place.

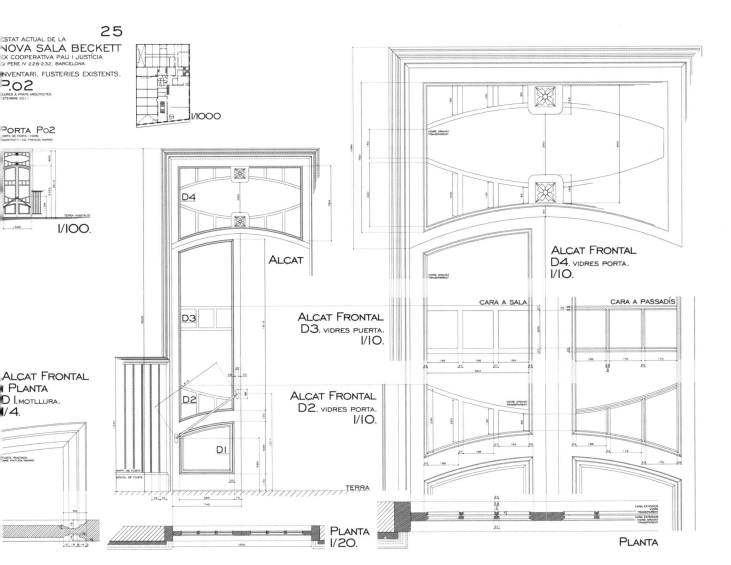

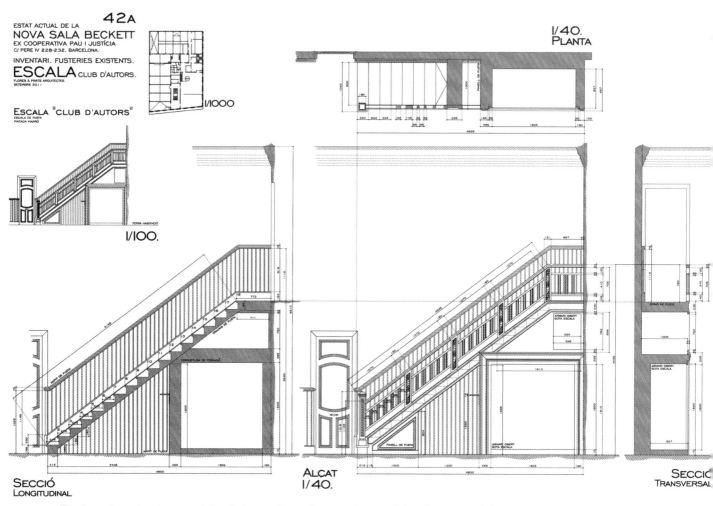

The inventory drawings contained observations about each one of the elements —information about flashings, gutters, interior braces, levers— so that we could understand how they had been constructed, in case we had to renovate, modify, or expand them. By drawing them, we returned to the trades and disciplines that had participated in the construction of the building, and to the culture of construction we wished to incorporate into the new project.

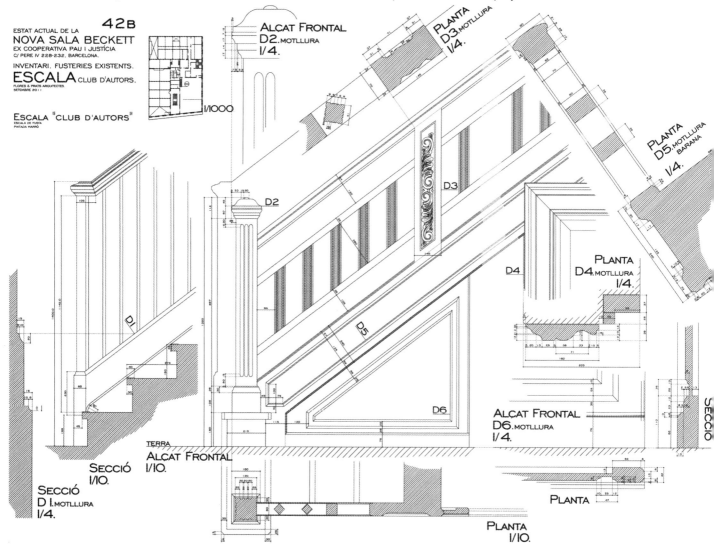

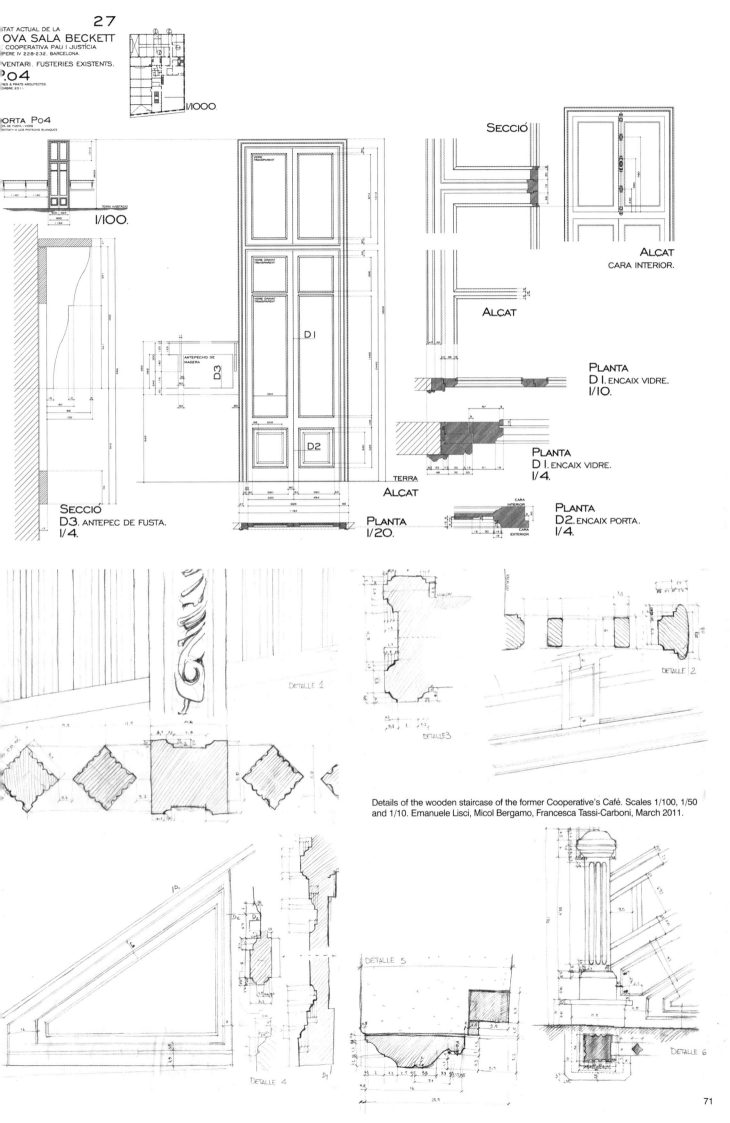

Details of the wooden staircase of the former Cooperative's Café. Scales 1/100, 1/50 and 1/10. Emanuele Lisci, Micol Bergamo, Francesca Tassi-Carboni, March 2011.

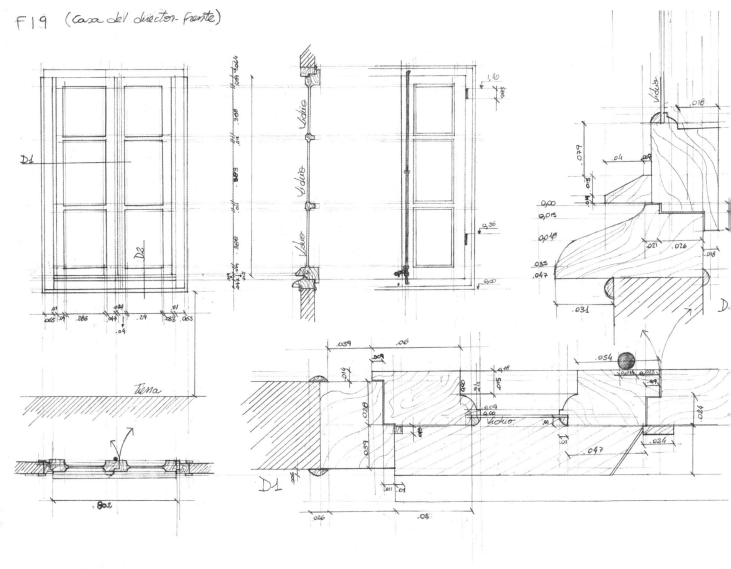

When we drew them, we realized that every door and every window was unique. Each one had a different detail, a bit of circular or rectangular latticework, or different kinds of glass. It was fascinating to see how the carpenter's work was by no means systematic: every day he had had to decide on a new kind of door or window.

By drawing them with such care, we conferred importance on them, so the contractor could understand that they represented a treasure for us. At the first meeting we had with him, we gave him the entire inventory. Seeing the detail of the drawings, he understood that all these elements needed to be cared for, and above all not to be broken.

Many of the elements of the former cooperative building were moved from their original locations. A few stayed where they were, some of them being modified to adapt to new standards or new uses. A door might be replaced by a window, or vice versa, and some floor tiles were moved to accommodate the new circulation through areas that had formerly been isolated. During the renovation process, absolutely everything happened, but in the end, as the director said: "It looks like nothing has happened here."

Surveying the building of the abandoned Cooperative.
Micol Bergamo, Emanuele Lisci, Francesca Tassi-Carboni. Spring 2011.

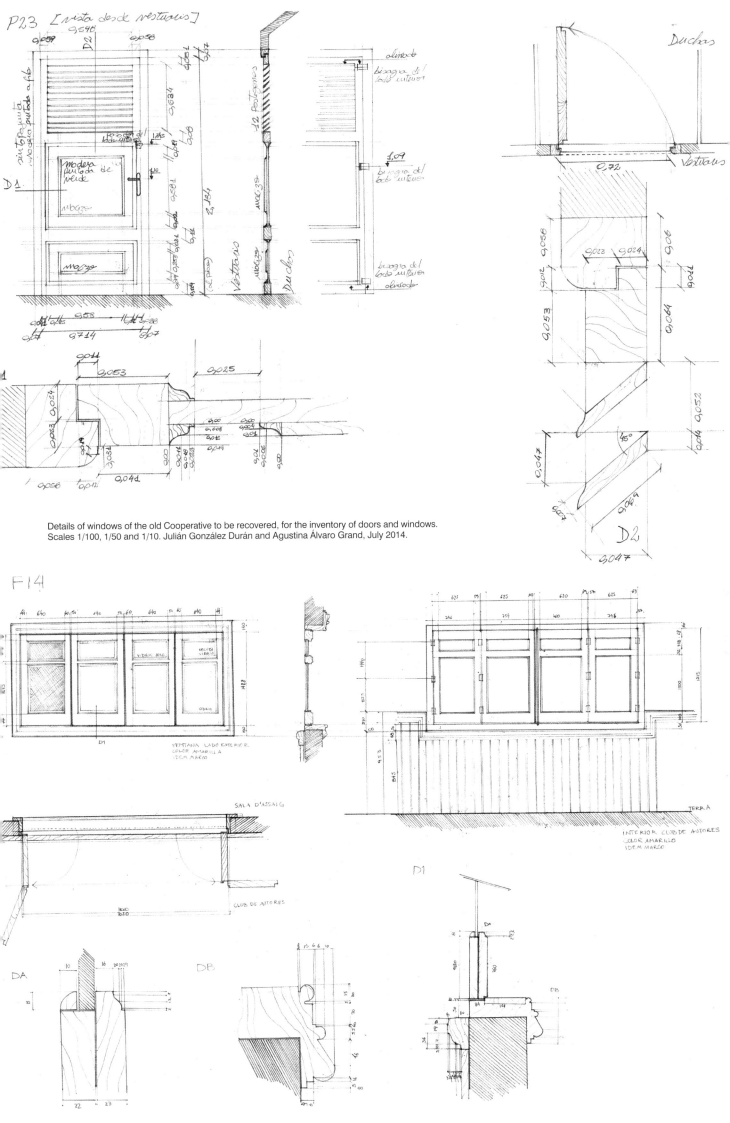

Details of windows of the old Cooperative to be recovered, for the inventory of doors and windows.
Scales 1/100, 1/50 and 1/10. Julián González Durán and Agustina Álvaro Grand, July 2014.

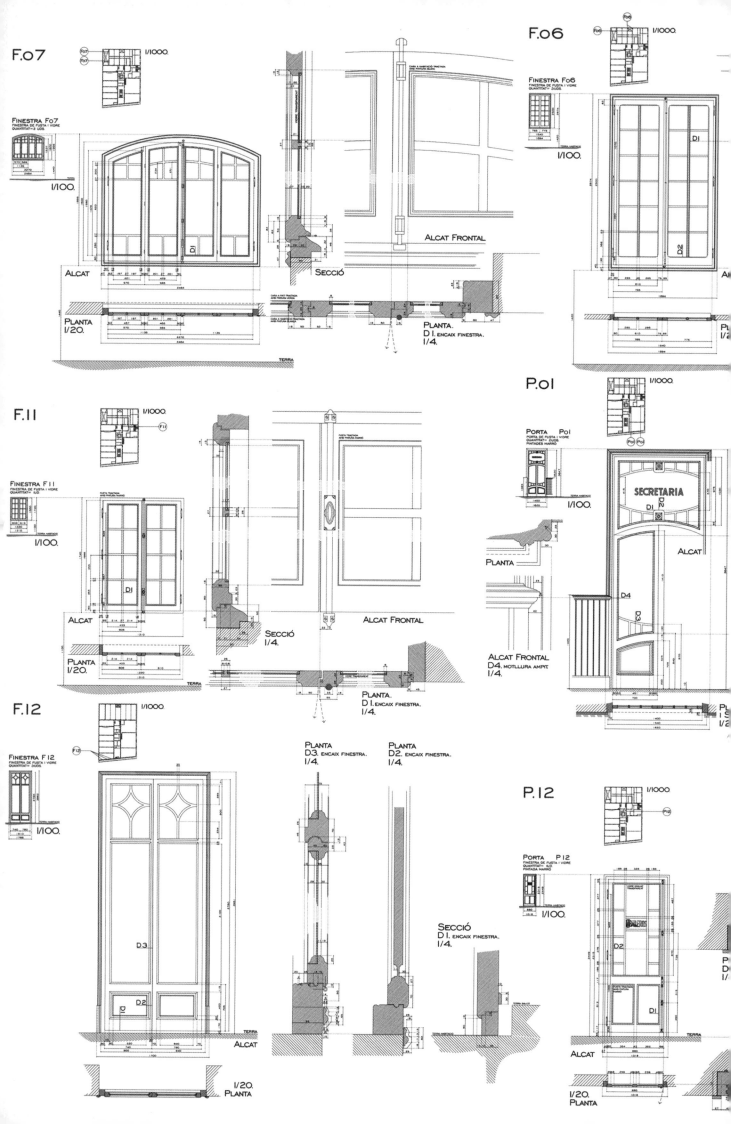

F.07

I/1000.

Finestra Fo7
FINESTRA DE FUSTA I VIDRE
QUANTITAT= 2 UDS.

I/100.

Alcat

Planta I/20.

Secció

Planta.
D1. ENCAIX FINESTRA.
I/4.

Alcat Frontal

TERRA

F.06

I/1000.

Finestra Fo6
FINESTRA DE FUSTA I VIDRE
QUANTITAT= 3UDS.

I/100.

D1

D2

F.11

I/1000.

Finestra F11
FINESTRA DE FUSTA I VIDRE
QUANTITAT= IUD.

I/100.

Alcat

D1

Planta
I/20.

TERRA

Secció
I/4.

Alcat Frontal

Planta.
D1. ENCAIX FINESTRA.
I/4.

P.01

I/1000.

Porta Po1
PORTA DE FUSTA I VIDRE
QUANTITAT= 2 UDS.
PINTADES MARRÓ.

I/100.

Planta

SECRETARIA

D1
D2

Alcat

D4

D3

Alcat Frontal
D4. MOTLLURA AMPIT
I/4.

F.12

I/1000.

Finestra F12
FINESTRA DE FUSTA I VIDRE
QUANTITAT= 3UDS.

I/100.

Planta
D3. ENCAIX FINESTRA.
I/4.

Planta
D2. ENCAIX FINESTRA.
I/4.

D3

D2
D1

TERRA

Alcat

I/20.
Planta

Secció
D1. ENCAIX FINESTRA.
I/4.

P.12

I/1000.

Porta P12
FINESTRA DE FUSTA I VIDRE
QUANTITAT= IUD.
PINTADA MARRÓ

I/100.

D2

D1

Alcat

I/20.
Planta

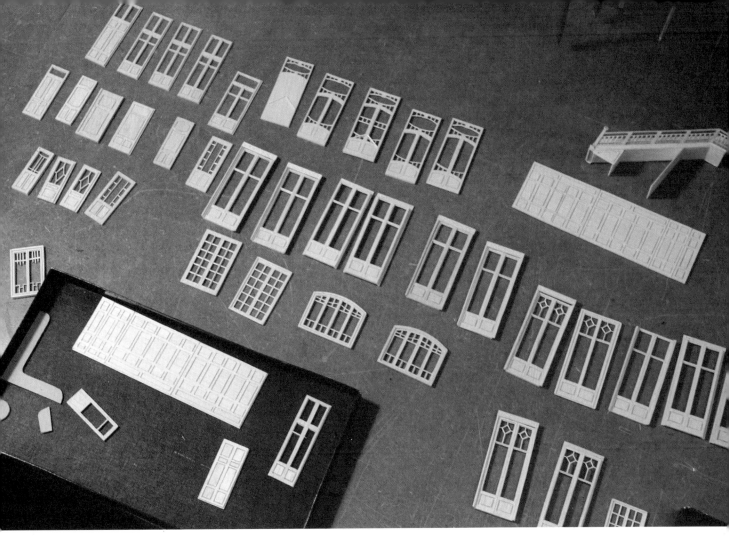

Once all the doors and windows had been drawn, they were converted into little models on a scale 1:50. Having a physical model was also a way of knowing that nothing had been forgotten. It was a very intuitive approach. Each element was labeled to identify its corresponding place in the inventory drawings, where we could appreciate all its qualities: whether it had colored glass panes, and the type of moldings or mullions. Later on, when we began to design the new circulation of the building, the doors and windows found their new places in the plans and then in the models on a scale 1:50.

ESTAT ACTUAL DE LA
NOVA SALA BECKETT
EX COOPERATIVA PAU I JUSTÍCIA
C/ PERE IV 228-232, BARCELONA.

INVENTARI. PAVIMENTS EXISTENTS.
SALES 1, 2, 3, 4, 5 I 6.

SALA 2
FLORES & PRATS ARQUITECTES
SETEMBRE 2011

RAJOLA S.02
MOSAIC HIDRÀULIC
QUANTITAT= TEXTURA
CENTRAL 494 uds
19.8 M²
SENEFA 85 uds
13 m/L
GRIS 89 uds
13.6 m/L

1/1000

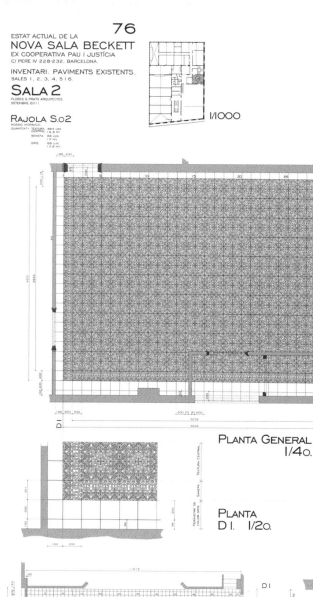

PERÍMETRE DE
COLOR GRIS

SANEFA

TEXTURA CENTRAL

PLANTA GENERAL
1/40.

PLANTA
D1. 1/20.

PERÍMETRE DE COLOR GRIS   SANEFA   TEXTURA CENTRAL

TEXTURA CENTRAL
1/2

SANEFA
1/2.

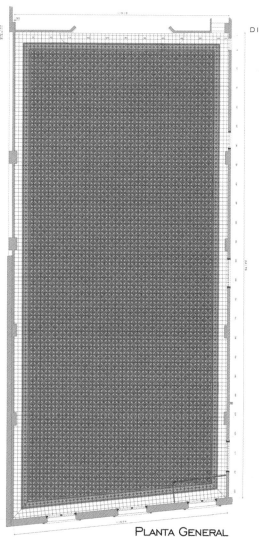

D1

PERÍMETRE DE COLOR GRIS   SANEFA   TEXTURA CENTRAL

PLANTA GENERAL
1/100.

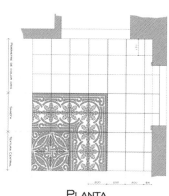

PLANTA
D1.
1/20.

1/1000

ESTAT ACTUAL DE LA
NOVA SALA BECKETT
EX COOPERATIVA PAU I JUSTÍCIA
C/ PERE IV 228-232, BARCELONA.

INVENTARI. PAVIMENTS EXISTENTS
SALES 1, 2, 3, 4, 5 I 6.

SALA 6
FLORES & PRATS ARQUITECTES
SETEMBRE 2011

RAJOLA S.06
MOSAIC HIDRÀULIC
QUANTITAT= TEXTURA
CENTRAL 5479 uds
219 M²
SENEFA 660 uds
132.4 m/L
GRIS 881 uds
146.2 m/L

TEXTURA CENTRAL
1/2.

SANEFA
1/2.

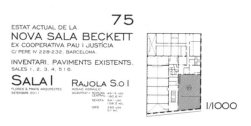

ESTAT ACTUAL DE LA
NOVA SALA BECKETT
EX COOPERATIVA PAU I JUSTÍCIA
C/ PERE IV 228-232, BARCELONA.

INVENTARI. PAVIMENTS EXISTENTS.
SALES 1, 2, 3, 4, 5 I 6.

SALA 1   RAJOLA S.01
FLORES & PRATS ARQUITECTES
SETEMBRE 2011

1/1000

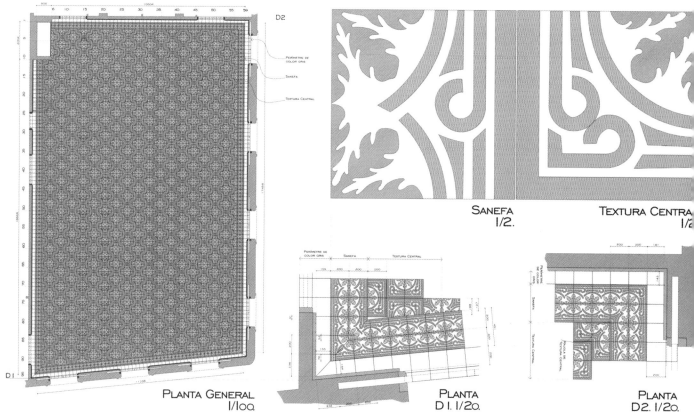

SANEFA
1/2.

TEXTURA CENTRAL
1/2

PLANTA GENERAL
1/100.

PLANTA
D 1. 1/20.

PLANTA
D2. 1/20.

In the case of the hydraulic tiles, the plans were divided by room, since each room had tiles of different designs. When we drew them, we observed the logic of the borders at the corners and the sectioning that had been done to fit them into irregular geometries. Then we calculated the area of each type of tile, of the central design, the length of the border…

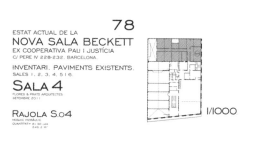

ESTAT ACTUAL DE LA
NOVA SALA BECKETT
EX COOPERATIVA PAU I JUSTÍCIA
C/ PERE IV 228-232, BARCELONA.

INVENTARI. PAVIMENTS EXISTENTS.
SALES 1, 2, 3, 4, 5 I 6.

SALA 4

RAJOLA S.04
MOSAIC HIDRÀULIC
QUANTITAT= 61.30 UDS
245.2 M²

1/1000

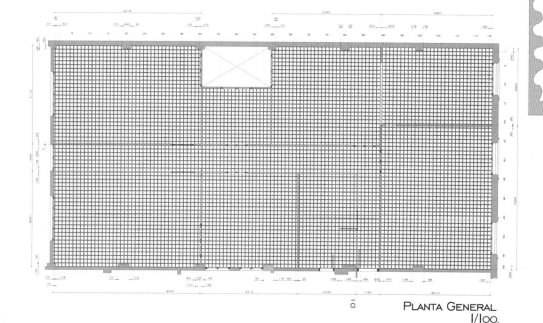

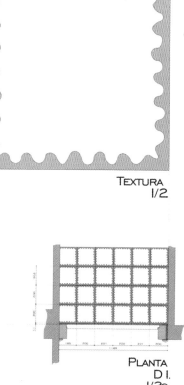

TEXTURA
1/2

PLANTA GENERAL
1/100.

PLANTA
D 1.
1/20.

ESTAT ACTUAL DE LA
NOVA SALA BECKETT
EX COOPERATIVA PAU I JUSTÍCIA
C/ PERE IV 228-232, BARCELONA

INVENTARI. PAVIMENTS EXISTENTS.
SALES 1, 2, 3, 4, 5 I 6.

SALA 5
FLORES & PRATS ARQUITECTES
SETEMBRE 2011

1/1000

RAJOLA S.o5
MOSAIC HIDRAULIC
QUANTITAT= 478 UDS.
29 1,7 m²

PLANTA GENERAL
1/40.

PLANTA
D 1. 1/20.

TEXTURA
1/2.

ESTAT ACTUAL DE LA
NOVA SALA BECKETT
EX COOPERATIVA PAU I JUSTÍCIA
C/ PERE IV 228-232, BARCELONA.

INVENTARI. PAVIMENTS EXISTENTS.
SALES 1, 2, 3, 4, 5 I 6.

SALA 3
FLORES & PRATS ARQUITECTES
SETEMBRE 2011

1/1000

RAJOLA S.o3
MOSAIC HIDRAULIC
QUANTITAT= TEXTURA 977 UDS.
CENTRAL 39 M²
SANEFA 84 UDS.
12 B. m/L.
GROS 58 UDS
11 B m/L

SANEFA
1/2.

TEXTURA CENTRAL
1/2.

PLANTA GENERAL
1/40.

PLANTA
D 1.
1/20.

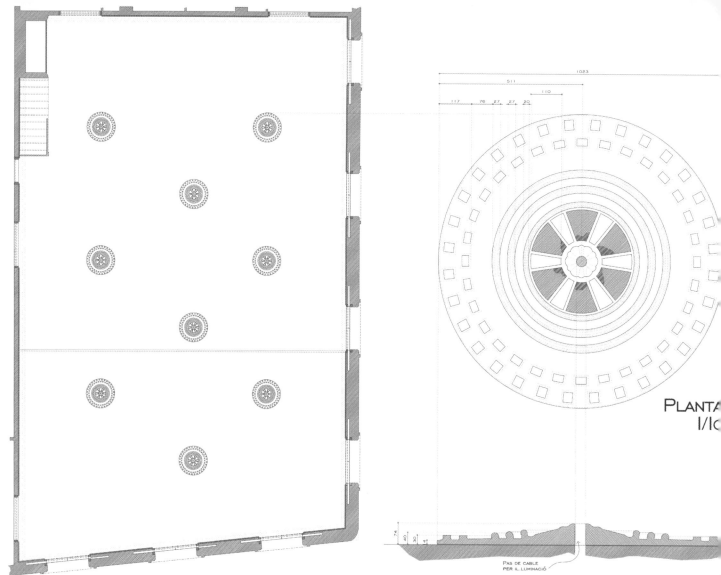

PLANTA GENERAL
1/100.

PLANTA
1/1[

SECCIÓ
1/1[

PAS DE CABLE
PER IL.LUMINACIÓ

Three of the ceiling roses of the former theater, which had survived the rain and the collapse of the roof, were salvaged and used as surface decorations, now on walls instead of ceilings, placed in such a way that the light passes tangent to them, bringing out the reliefs.

First Occupancy *July 2013 – July 2014*

Once the competition project had been drawn up, and while we were still waiting for the funds to start the works, the Sala Beckett team decided to move temporarily into the building of the former cooperative.

They occupied the second floor of the building for a year. They would go in by the side door on Calle Batista: the stairway of the former school led directly up to the first floor. The abandoned ground floor, with the remains of the former gymnasium, was not seen at all.

They experienced some discomfort in working there. The hallways were cold and noise filtered from one room to another, because the old doors did not close tightly. They were able to adapt, however, and discovered that the charm of the building helped to lessen these inconveniences. As for the noise, the students and professors who participated in various workshops found it positive to hear other activities going on in the distance.

We were well aware that in updating the thermal and acoustical conditions of the old building we would run the risk of ruining it: this was one of the challenges of the project. Thanks to the experience of this initial occupancy, the Sala Beckett team discovered that certain imperfections could be tolerated for the sake of a building with more charm. It was necessary to work together to strike a balance between technical demands and the intangible value of the building we had inherited.

The yearlong occupancy provided us with more information about how the building could contribute to the new program, even as it helped us to think about how to incorporate these new uses into the former cooperative building without causing it to disappear.

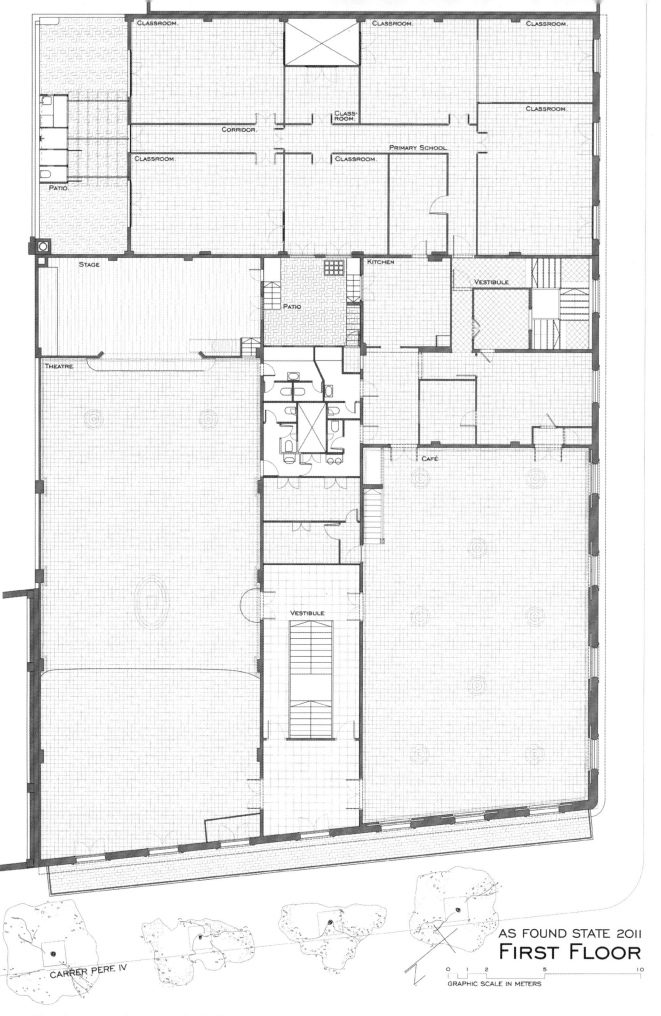

CLASSROOM.   CLASSROOM.   CLASSROOM.

CLASS-
ROOM.

CORRIDOR.

CLASSROOM.

PRIMARY SCHOOL.

CLASSROOM.   CLASSROOM.

PATIO.

STAGE   KITCHEN

VESTIBULE

PATIO

THEATRE

CAFÉ

VESTIBULE

The changes made were minimal, affecting mainly the central part of the floor. The two large halls were recovered for public use: the former café became a rehearsal room and the former theater was restored to its original function. In the central part, the restroom area was redistributed: some new dressing rooms were added and the spaces were provided with natural light and ventilation. The former kitchen was reorganized to function as a kitchen and dining area for Sala Beckett staff, while the classrooms at the back of the floor were converted into offices and spaces for acting classes.

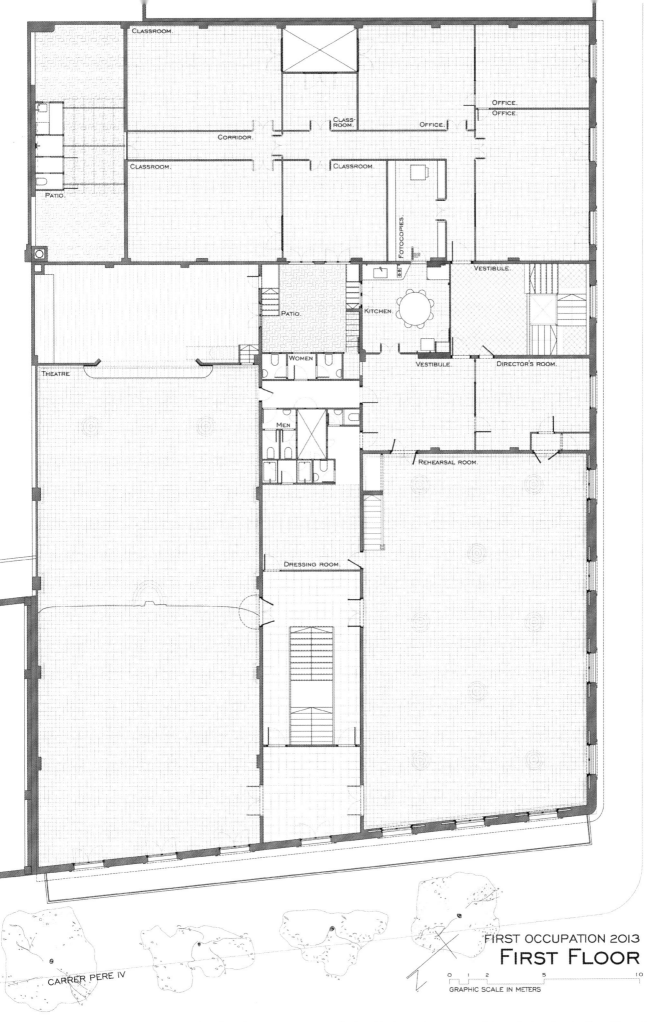

CLASSROOM.

CLASS-ROOM.

OFFICE.
OFFICE.

CORRIDOR.

CLASS-ROOM.

OFFICE.

CLASSROOM.

PATIO.

CLASSROOM.

CLASSROOM.

FOTOCOPIES.

VESTIBULE.

PATIO.

KITCHEN.

WOMEN

VESTIBULE.

DIRECTOR'S ROOM.

THEATRE

MEN

REHEARSAL ROOM.

DRESSING ROOM.

The stairway leading up to the first floor issued onto a vestibule with three doors, one of them belonging to the office of the director. This room also had three doors, allowing the director to enter on one side and leave on the other, to appear and disappear. The rooms with multiple doors functioned very well for the circulation of the Sala Beckett team and of the guest actors working there. The final design would incorporate these changes in the circulation, offering possibilities of entering spaces by surprise and leaving them without being seen, while at the same time never having to take the same route from one point to another.

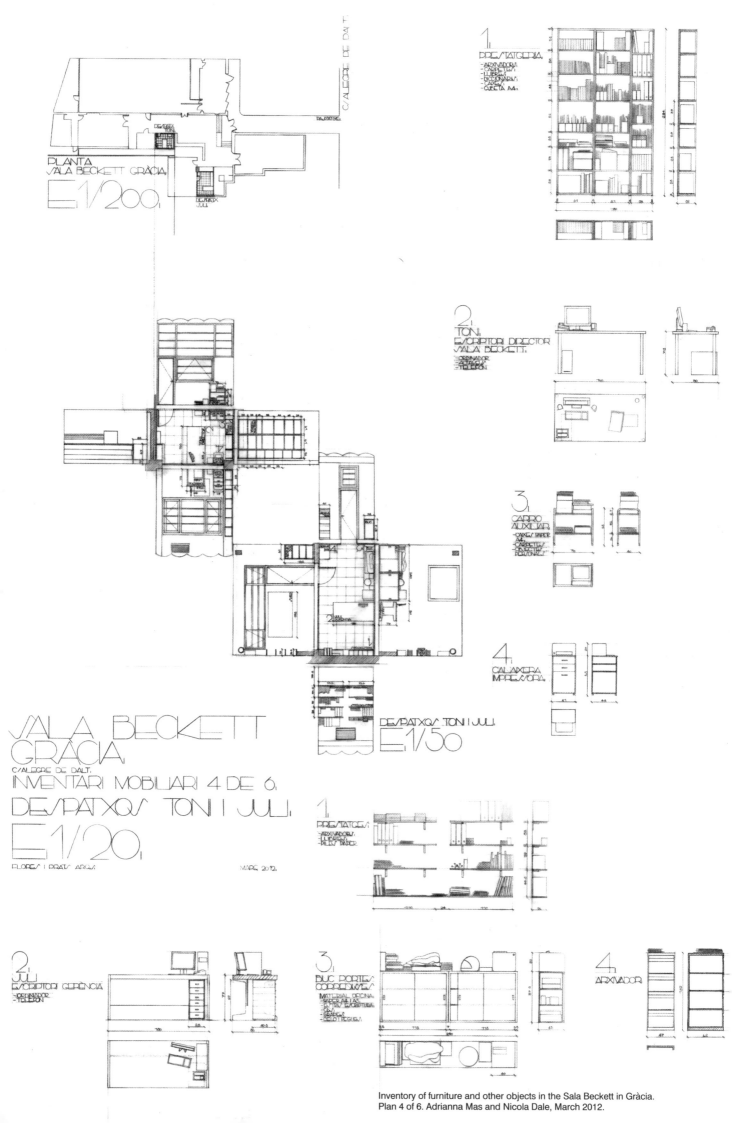

Inventory of furniture and other objects in the Sala Beckett in Gràcia.
Plan 4 of 6. Adrianna Mas and Nicola Dale, March 2012.

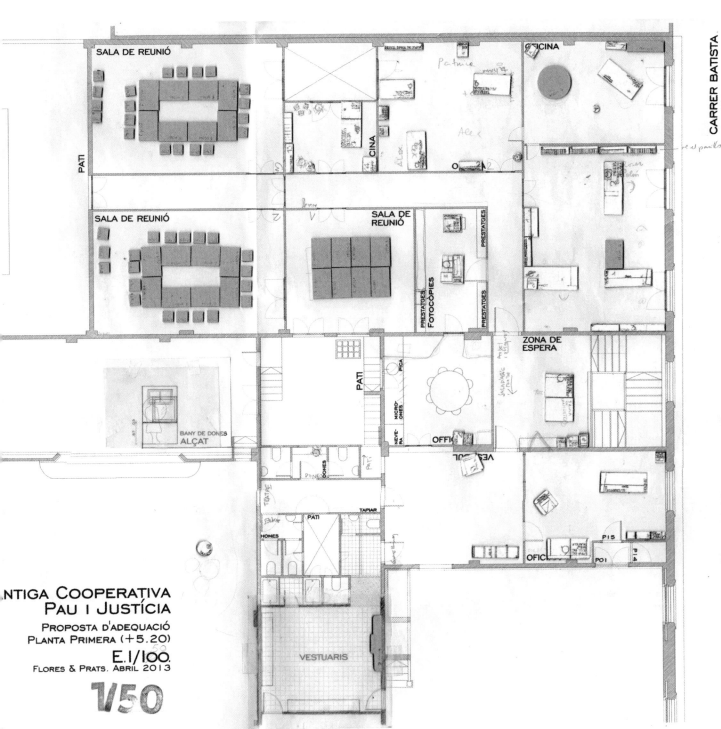

Proposal for distributing furnishings and objects from the former Sala Beckett in Gràcia on the first floor of the *Pau i Justícia* building in Poblenou. EP + RF, April 2013

The Sala Beckett in Gràcia: An Inventory of Furnishings

Before the Sala Beckett moved from its former premises in the Gràcia neighborhood, we visited the space to draw up an inventory of all the existing furnishings that might be reused in the new building. We made scale drawings (1:20) of all these elements in the different areas: administration, coordination, library, offices, rehearsal rooms, etc. The result was six plans on DIN A0 paper full of furniture and other objects of various kinds that could be reused.

It was a way of getting to know how the Sala Beckett worked and how much space was needed for each activity. The office area was the most densely furnished: tables filled up the rooms, with almost no storage space, either for files or for theater props. These drawings were a good way of understanding how the personnel of the Sala Beckett functioned and how they were to be distributed in the new temporary premises where they were going to move for a year.

The drawings were also useful in talking with them and helping to organize the move. In the course of several meetings, we decided where each piece of furniture from Gràcia would go when it was taken to Poblenou. When they found themselves beginning to work in the more generous spaces of the cooperative building, all those familiar furnishings helped them to appropriate the new spaces more readily.

Serveis

H

D

Colors. The first occupancy gave us the opportunity to try out some things directly in the building, such as the application of new colors in some of the rooms. In the last years of the building's use as the premises of the cooperative, a very severe tone of brown had been applied to doors and wainscoting. We changed these brown parts for a more lively, "theatrical" red, giving the doors and walls a more cheerful look.

Indication of colors for the dressing rooms on the first floor of the former Cooperative building. RF, June 2013

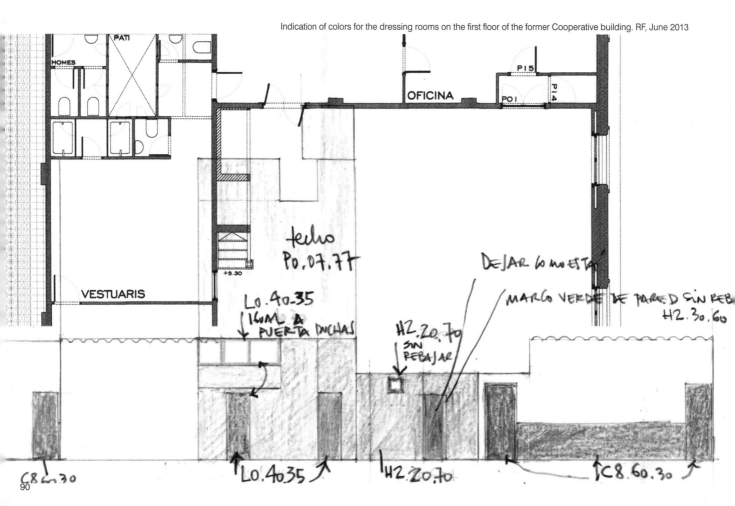

We also tried out ways of painting the new walls so that they would work well with the old ones, which we intended to leave as intact as possible, with traces and remains of their former painted surfaces. Before actually painting the walls, we tested the new colors directly on photographs of the spaces. The palette of new colors was based on those already existing on various elements in the building —doors, window frames, flooring—, which we used as a guide.

Colors for the first-floor dressing rooms on top of a photo
of the construction site by Adrià Goula. RF, June 2013

Serveis
d'Assaig
Sala
Vestuaris

Sala
d'Assaig

1

3 2

3 2 Sala d'Assaig

Lettering. Another test we performed, whose results were later incorporated into the final design, dealt with ways of indicating the names of the rehearsal rooms and classrooms. The building had gone through a lot: there was writing and graffiti on the bar, on the doors… We wanted to join in taking direct action on the walls, even though we were working in a preexisting building. If the director of the Sala Beckett put a certain value on the traces and histories left on the walls, we thought the new occupation of the building should leave yet another trace. Understanding things in this way encouraged us to devise some templates and then paint the names of the rooms directly onto the doors and walls.

While all of this was going on inside the building, its external appearance continued unchanged. The painted sign on the lateral façade of the building and the red on the door of the former school were the first indications that the building was being occupied again. This door was the only entrance for the public during the time the Sala Beckett team temporarily occupied the former cooperative. The door issued directly onto the square stairway that led up to the first floor, where there was activity again. The ground floor remained empty. As the Sala Beckett team occupied the former cooperative building, we continued designing the definitive renovation on the basis of this initial occupancy: how to incorporate new colors, how to install new elements without affecting the walls as they were, how to deal with noises and weather conditions, how to organize connections and circulations for the actors, the staff, and the public…

Summer Workshop 2013. That year the eighth edition of the Sala Beckett's Summer Workshop was held in the former cooperative building: a week of seminars, workshops, and dramatized readings with professors and students from different countries. All in all, more than a hundred people were going to put the building to the test.

We were very interested to learn their impressions: to see whether the ruinous state of the building was acceptable and whether the dressing rooms and the open circulations were sufficient for this temporary occupancy. The director passed on the comment heard most often among the participants during those days: "Don't touch anything! It's perfect the way it is!"

"I have to admit that I look more to the past than to the future. For example, I am the kind of person who, when I can't sleep, when I have insomnia, rather than worrying about what will become of me in x number of years, which has never concerned me at all, I go back over my childhood instead. I must have had a very happy childhood and I always go back to the past. I am the kind of person who gives more importance to the past than to the future. I see the future as a blank: there is nothing there; while the past, on the other hand, is loaded with stuff. Which is why, if I have to fix my gaze on a place, I do so looking backwards rather than forwards. Which is why, when I am often asked: What are your hopes, what are your dreams? I really don't have many, but on the other hand I am very interested in the past. Among other reasons, also, because I believe that humankind, that is, that people are basically stories and fictions. And where I find these stories and fictions is in what I imagine having happened in places.

For example, when I was younger, in the village we used to spend the summer, I loved to go into the abandoned houses and imagine the families that had lived there, to imagine what might have happened… For example, when I go around the city and see party walls with bathroom tiles visible: that is fascinating. There are stories scattered over the walls, memory... It's not even memory, because after all I am inventing stories from all these remains. So that when I walk into a place like the former cooperative building, what excites me is what might have happened, the emotions of the people who lived there, the quarrels, the love affairs: all that stimulates my imagination, more than what is going to happen. And I'm sure that has a lot to do with theater, obviously, because you imagine stories, because what we are really made of, are stories, fictions, accounts: that is what defines us as persons." Toni Casares. Interview for the film *Scale 1:5*.

CONFEZIO

Water colors of the as-found state of the walls of the former *Pau i Justícia* cooperative building.
Augustina Álvaro-Grand and Valentina Tridello, Spring 2014.

"What is heritage? Heritage, for me, is the remains, the traces that allow us to imagine who were are. In other words, they are spaces that tell us more or less made-up stories —because the stories are never real, because history is always a construction— that allow us to explain ourselves, despite the fact that the projection we make of an old wall is a completely invented projection. But they help; they directly kindle the imagination; they are places to seize onto in order to construct stories." Toni Casares. Interview for the film *Scale 1:5.*

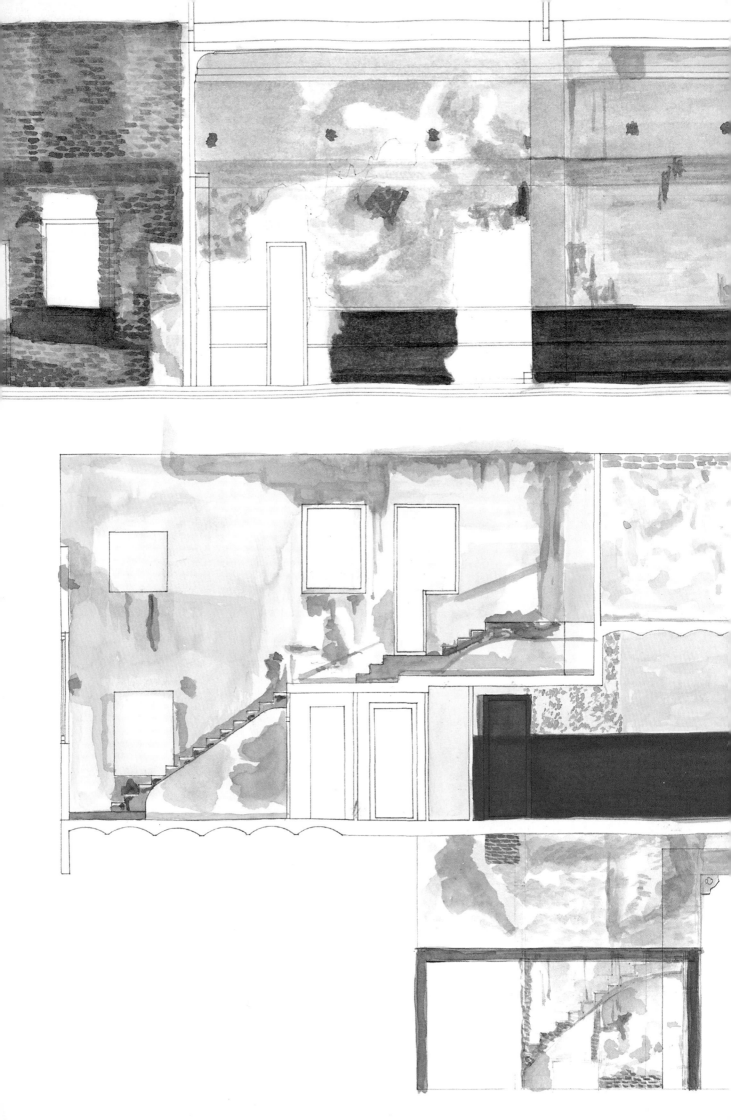

Model of the construction project, developed from the competition proposal. Budget: 8 million euros.

From 8 Million to 2.5 Million
January – July 2014

After winning the architecture competition in January of 2011, we worked on the new project for two years, defining the work that needed to be done. In line with the requirements of the competition, the project had a budget of eight million euros.

Shortly after completing the work plans, we received the news —in the midst of a severe economic crisis (2011-2012)— that there were no funds for the construction of this new theater. But the director of the Sala Beckett, Toni Casares, was unwilling to go without a new home for the Sala Beckett, so he asked what the minimum budget might be for a project that would allow work to begin again. In order to figure this out, we had to go back to the drawing board, considering with Toni what the essential was for the Sala Beckett in order for it to function. The first decision was to modify the project, so that it would fit into the existing building, eliminating parts of the program that could be abandoned, as important as they might be: the artists' residences, the two big rehearsal halls located under the great canopy on the upper level of the old building, and the storage area and heating/air conditioning installations in the basement.

We spent a few months fitting this smaller program into the building as it was, with the minimum transformation necessary to incorporate a theater program in decent conditions. We had to be sure that the program would not fragment the marvelous spaces we had inherited. Although we were working with less surface area, we did not want to destroy the charm and generosity of the building. We had become familiar with its qualities by drawing it, just as the Sala Beckett team had done so by occupying the premises for a year in 2013.

Every new set of plans was immediately quantified in economic terms. First we designed a project with a budget of one million euros. Then Toni thought we could obtain a little more money, so we designed again at 1.5 million euros, and so on successively until we were sure of obtaining the definitive amount of 2.5 million euros, which allowed us to make better use of the existing building. This budget allowed us to undertake all of the modifications, visible and invisible, that the building required: structural reinforcement, acoustical improvements, a theater with capacity for 250 at street level, the construction of new circulations, new apertures for natural light, etc.

Model of the second version of the project, the one finally constructed. Budget: 2.5 million euros.

The theater director's dreams and ambitions had to be trimmed to a budget that amounted to 30% of the original one, which meant he had to accept far fewer possibilities to create activities in the future project. Nevertheless, moving from premises of 700 square meters to a building with a surface area of 3,000 square meters, at a central location —on a corner of Pere IV in the heart of Poblenou, one of the most culturally and socially active neighborhoods in the city— was challenge in itself. In the end, it meant a large expansion of the Sala Beckett's plan of activities, as the advantages of the new location were made the most of.

The New Sala Beckett. This new project reuses all the existing spaces, without adding any new ones, concentrating on the two floors of the original building. Nevertheless, the program is distributed in a way very similar to that of the competition project: the ground floor remains devoted to activities for the general public —bar/restaurant, main performance hall—, along with the dressing rooms attached to the hall, offices, areas for technicians, and storage space. The upper floor continue to serve the program of theatrical training and creation, except that now the training part —previously on three floors— has been reduced to just one.

The combination of two levels of dressing rooms —on the ground floor and on the mezzanine level— remained as the competition project, as do the office areas on several levels, looking onto Calle Pere IV, where they enjoy the plentiful natural light along that facade. Also preserved were two fire exits —one a stairway at the corner of Pere IV and the wall of the neighboring construction, the other the square stairway of the former primary school— and the Authors' Club, which straddles the bar and the Theatre Downstairs.

The most significant change, apart from the loss of added height and a basement level, was that the main performance hall would not have the height indicated in the competition project, since we had to make use of the floor slab of the former primary school, rather than demolishing it for extra height. So that hall was replaced by the present one, slightly sunken below ground level (1.20 meters, or seven steps), just enough to make room for five meters of free space below the spotlights. Another result of this change is that the two performance halls, on the ground floor and on the second floor, now partially overlap. Careful attention has been given to insulating them from each other, so that performances can be given in both simultaneously.

In July of 2014, the new project was approved by the city council and construction began.

The new Sala Beckett is organized around a central lobby. This double-height space is responsible for keeping all the activities together, from one end of the building to the other, from the entrance on Pere IV to the acting classrooms at the back. Two large gaps in the floor slab let natural light into the ground floor. The central patio of the upper floor, larger now than in the former cooperative building, is another source of natural light, and helps to extend the circulation around itself, leading with ease into the midst of the acting classrooms at the back.

Whereas the former cooperative building functioned as three autonomous units, with no communication among them —grocery store on the ground floor, café and theater at the front part of the first floor, and primary school at the back—, and with independent entrances and circulations, in the new Sala Beckett, everything works together: everything is connected to everything else, so that actors and playwrights, spectators and students, and members of the permanent staff all mix together. Every day, out of these encounters, new projects and new fictions are born.

The main entrance is by way of Calle Pere IV. On arriving, visitors encounter the box office, where they can pick up tickets purchased previously or ask about a workshop or seminar, and from there they enter to sit down on the red sofa or go into the bar a have drink while waiting for the show to begin. The Theater Downstairs is slightly lower than the lobby. This generates a feeling of attention and concentration on the performance to be presented, but the difference in level is not so marked as to disconnect the hall from the atmosphere of the lobby and the street outside.

On the upper floor, the café of the former Cooperative has been converted into a rehearsal hall and the former theater is now the Theater Upstairs of the Sala Beckett. The acting classrooms are located in the former primary school, occupying the same area and same rooms.

Central Lobby. We wanted someone coming into the building early in the morning to take part in a workshop, or arriving in the evening to enjoy a night of theater to be welcomed as if they were entering a big house, a place where interrelating with others would become easier. The lobby is a space flooded with natural light, to which all of the activities in the building are directed. Music and voices can be heard, and people can be seen suddenly appearing and disappearing, hinting at the existence of hidden rooms and passages. It is a space onto which many doors open and, when you move around in it, you realize that the building is full of countless intercrossing vistas, so that it is easy to encounter other people in it.

Watercolors painted in situ and attached to the model of the building, to remember important information that the project should incorporate.

There are also spaces adjacent to the circulations, where you can pause to talk or to sit down alone and do some work. The building is waiting for you to occupy it. This lobby is not a space that was anticipated in the original program, but it has become the center of the new Sala Beckett, a genuine social relations platform, where encounters or work sessions can take place unexpectedly, multiplying interactions and creating new ones. Theatrics are not limited to the spaces specifically devoted to the scenic arts. There is theater everywhere in the building.

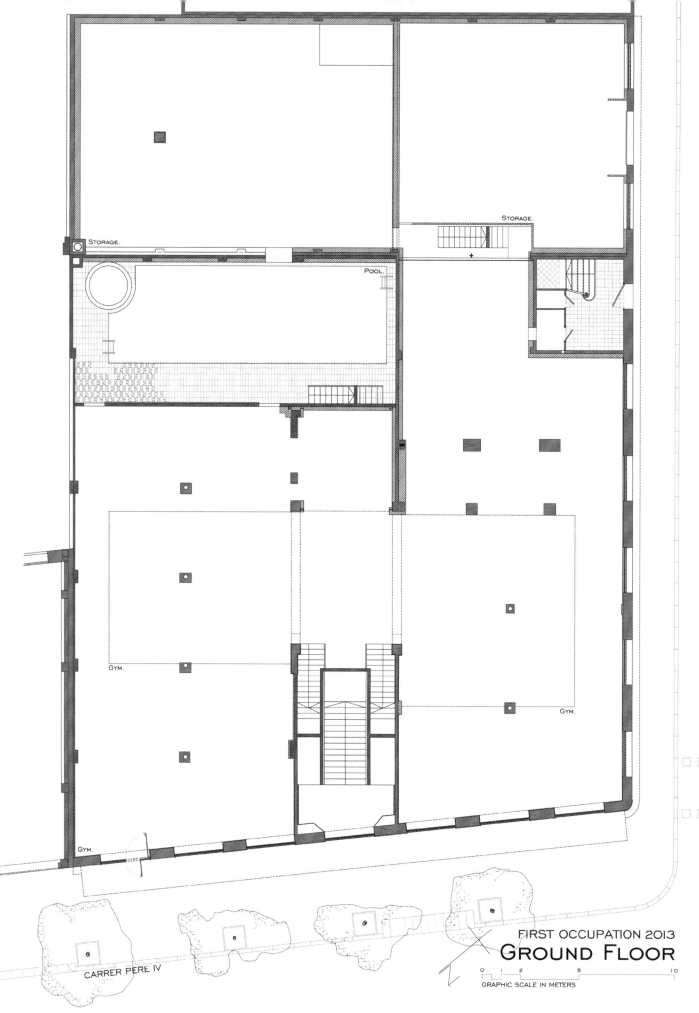

STORAGE.

STORAGE.

STORAGE.

POOL.

GYM.

GYM.

GYM.

FIRST OCCUPATION 2013
GROUND FLOOR

0   1   2   5   10
GRAPHIC SCALE IN METERS

CARRER PERE IV

The central stairway to the upper floor that we found in the preexisting cooperative building, apart from not being original to it, prevented it from having a clear connection to Calle Pere IV. One of the changes proposed in the project was to eliminate this stairway and construct a new one closer in, not in the middle of the lobby, but rather to one side. As one enters the building by way of this new main entrance, the stairway is no longer an obstacle: the lobby extends all the way to the back of the building, where the entry to the Theater Downstairs is located.

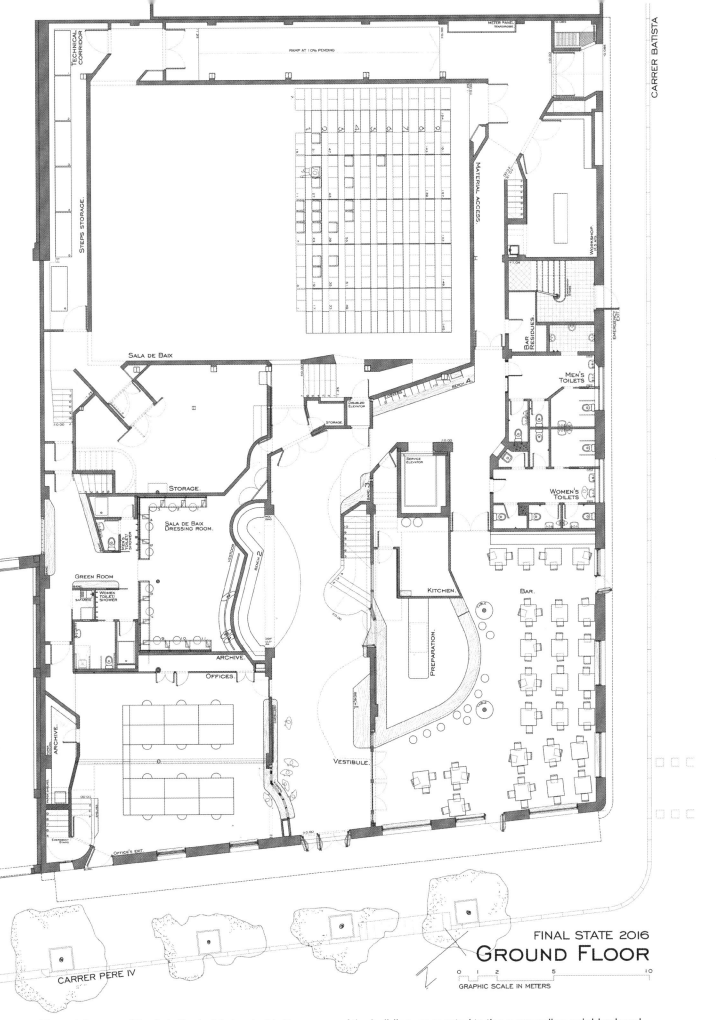

CARRER BATISTA

CARRER PERE IV

METER PANEL
WARDROBE

TECHNICAL
CORRIDOR

RAMP AT 10% PENDING

STEPS STORAGE.

MATERIAL ACCESS.

WORKSHOP

BAR
RESIDUES.

SALA DE BAIX

EMERGENCY
EXIT

MEN'S
TOILETS

DISABLED
ELEVATOR

STORAGE

WOMEN'S
TOILETS

STORAGE.

SERVICE
ELEVATOR

SALA DE BAIX
DRESSING ROOM.

MEN'S
TOILET
SHOWER

KITCHEN.

BAR.

GREEN ROOM

WOMEN
TOILET
SHOWER

PREPARATION.

ARCHIVE.

OFFICES.

ARCHIVE.

VESTIBULE.

EMERGENCY
STAIRS

OFFICE'S EXIT.

FINAL STATE 2016
GROUND FLOOR

0 1 2   5   10
GRAPHIC SCALE IN METERS

The public area of the Sala Beckett is located in the corner of the building, connected to the surrounding neighborhood. It can be entered off Pere IV or Batista, by way of the lobby or of the bar. The actors and Sala Beckett staff have a second entrance by way of a side door on Pere IV, while a third entrance off Batista is reserved for technicians and theater material. This separation of the circulations and zones of movement of general public, actors, and staff, which is a key element in the smooth functioning of the center, has been maintained since the competition project.

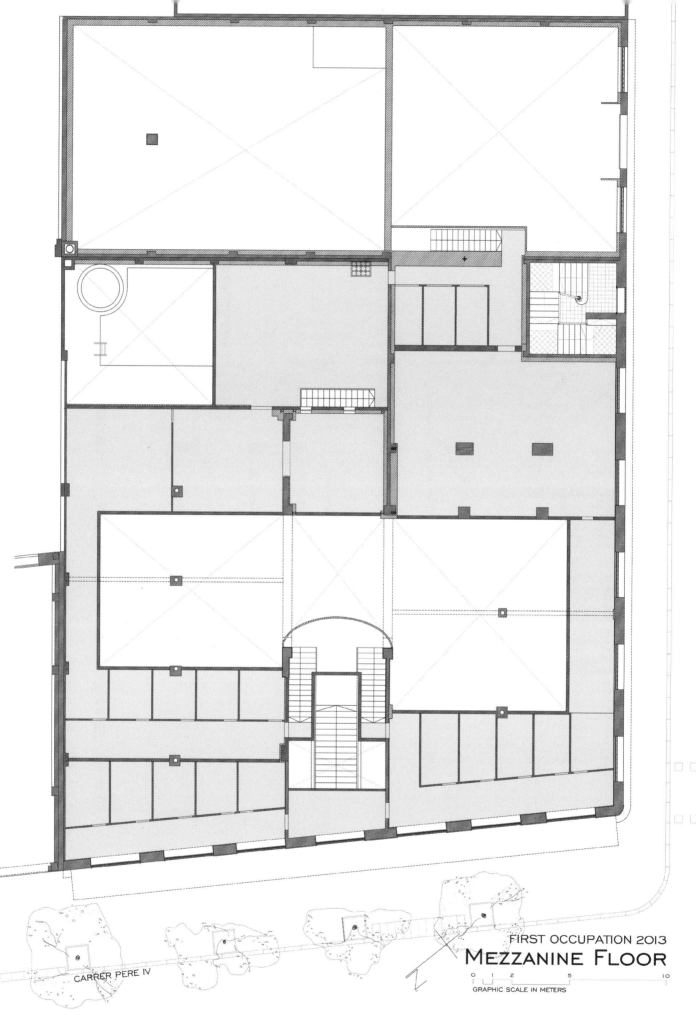

CARRER PERE IV

In the final years of the building's occupation by the Cooperative, some mezzanine spaces were constructed that fragmented the ground floor, reducing the generous dimensions of the original space, with its height of almost six meters. In the new project, most of these mezzanine spaces have been eliminated, including all those constructed along the main facade side and in the central lobby, so that the original height has been restored.

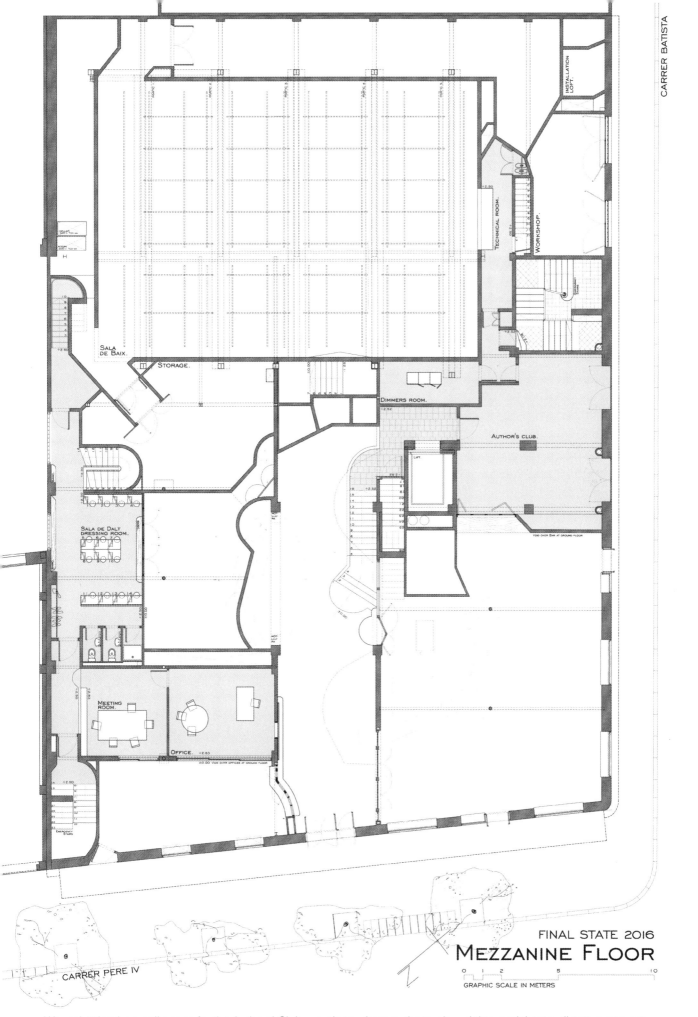

SALA
DE BAIX.

STORAGE.

TECHNICAL ROOM.

WORKSHOP.

INSTALLATION LOFT.

DIMMERS ROOM.

AUTHOR'S CLUB.

LIFT.

VOID OVER BAR AT GROUND FLOOR

SALA DE DALT
DRESSING ROOM.

MEETING ROOM.

OFFICE. +2.83

2.0.00 VOID OVER OFFICES AT GROUND FLOOR

EMERGENCY STAIRS

FINAL STATE 2016
MEZZANINE FLOOR

0 1 2   5   10
GRAPHIC SCALE IN METERS

CARRER PERE IV

We maintained a small space for the Authors' Club —a place where authors, playwrights, and theater directors can get together, located as a bridge between the Theater Downstairs and the bar— and a surface for dressing rooms and office spaces located along the interior patio at the back. The dressing rooms receive plenty of natural light from this patio and the mezzanine spaces of the offices from the double-height lobby space.

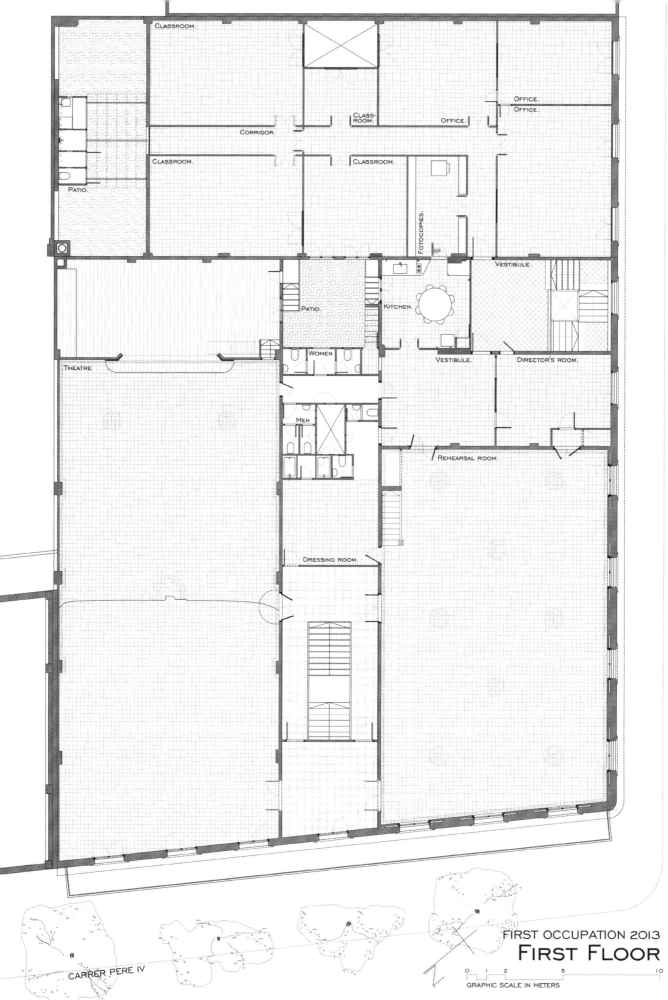

CLASSROOM.

CLASS-
ROOM.

OFFICE.

OFFICE.

OFFICE.

CORRIDOR.

CLASSROOM.

CLASSROOM.

CLASSROOM.

PATIO.

FOTOCOPIES.

VESTIBULE.

PATIO.

KITCHEN.

WOMEN.

VESTIBULE.

DIRECTOR'S ROOM.

THEATRE.

MEN.

REHEARSAL ROOM.

DRESSING ROOM.

CARRER PERE IV

FIRST OCCUPATION 2013
FIRST FLOOR

0 1 2 5 10
GRAPHIC SCALE IN METERS

On the first floor, the theater of the former cooperative building was very elongated, stretching to the facade along Calle Pere IV. The central passageway was occupied by the restrooms of the theater and café and by the entrance stairway from the ground floor. The school, in the back bay, was reached by way of a square stairway leading up from Calle Batista and a narrow L-shaped corridor that distributed the classrooms on either side.

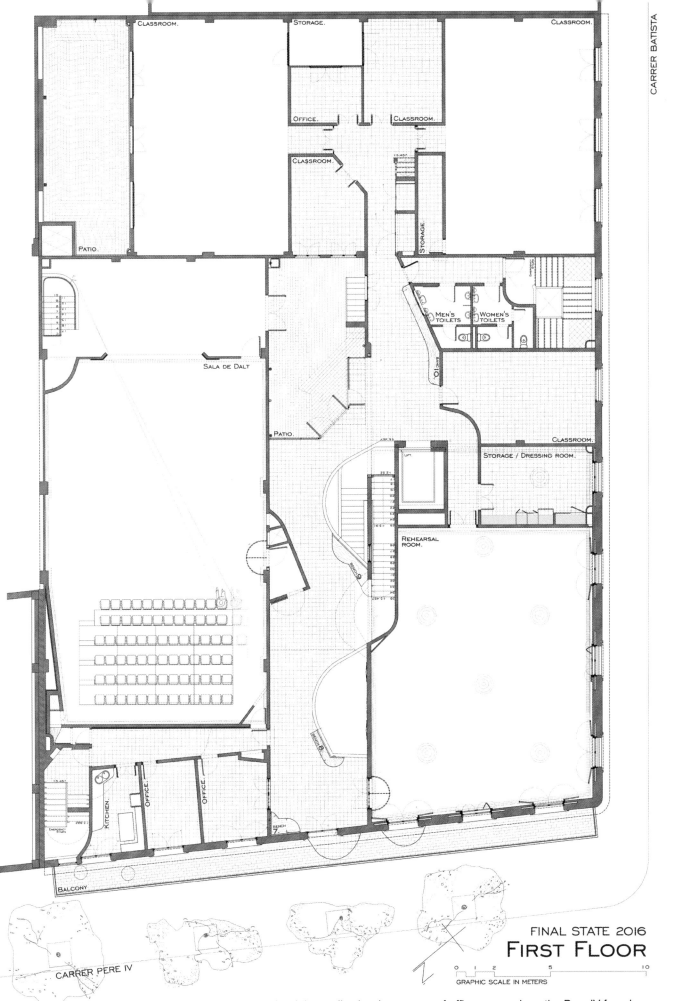

CARRER BATISTA

CLASSROOM.

STORAGE.

CLASSROOM.

OFFICE.

CLASSROOM.

CLASSROOM.

STORAGE.

PATIO.

Men's
TOILETS

WOMEN'S
TOILETS

SALA DE DALT

PATIO.

CLASSROOM.

STORAGE / DRESSING ROOM.

LIFT.

REHEARSAL
ROOM.

KITCHEN.

OFFICE.

OFFICE.

BALCONY.

CARRER PERE IV

FINAL STATE 2016
FIRST FLOOR

0 1 2   5   10
GRAPHIC SCALE IN METERS

The new Theater Upstairs reuses the old one, but it is smaller, leaving a zone of office space along the Pere IV facade, with plenty of natural light, which serves as a sound buffer between the hall and the street. The former café has been converted into a rehearsal hall, while the classrooms of the former primary school are now acting classrooms. The lobby connects all these programs to the ground floor. In order to achieve this, the former restrooms in the middle of the upper floor were eliminated, and the former patio has been enlarged to make for more natural light.

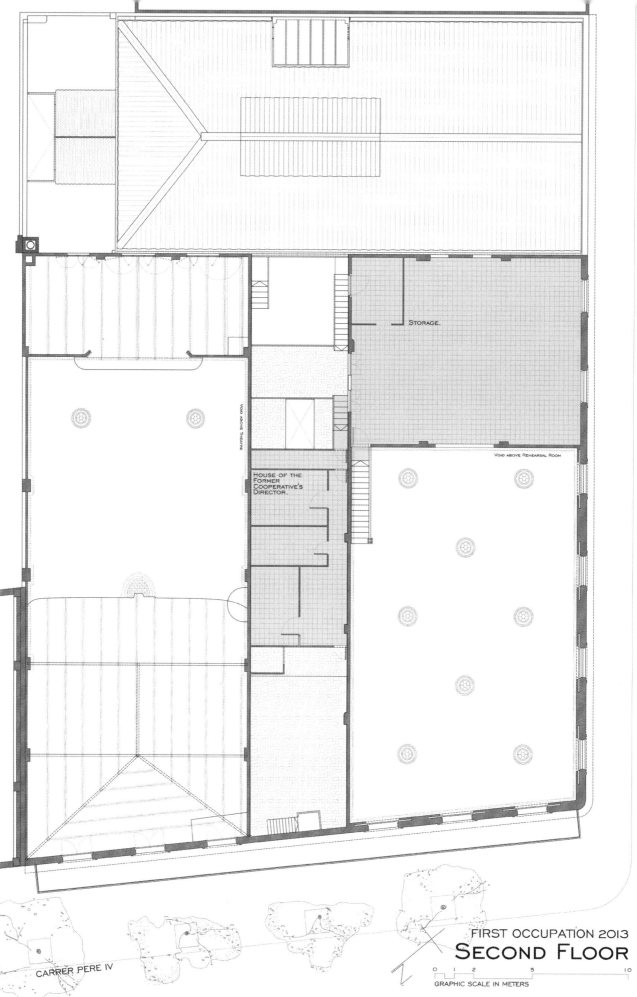

STORAGE.

VOID ABOVE THEATRE

HOUSE OF THE FORMER COOPERATIVE'S DIRECTOR.

VOID ABOVE REHEARSAL ROOM

CARRER PERE IV

FIRST OCCUPATION 2013
SECOND FLOOR

0 1 2   5   10
GRAPHIC SCALE IN METERS

The former offices of the sports section of the Cooperative, connected to the café by a wooden stairway and a window, are now yet another dramaturgy classroom. The wooden stairway was moved to the back of the building and the entrance to this new space was also moved to the back, so that the former entrances can serve a new zone of the theater.

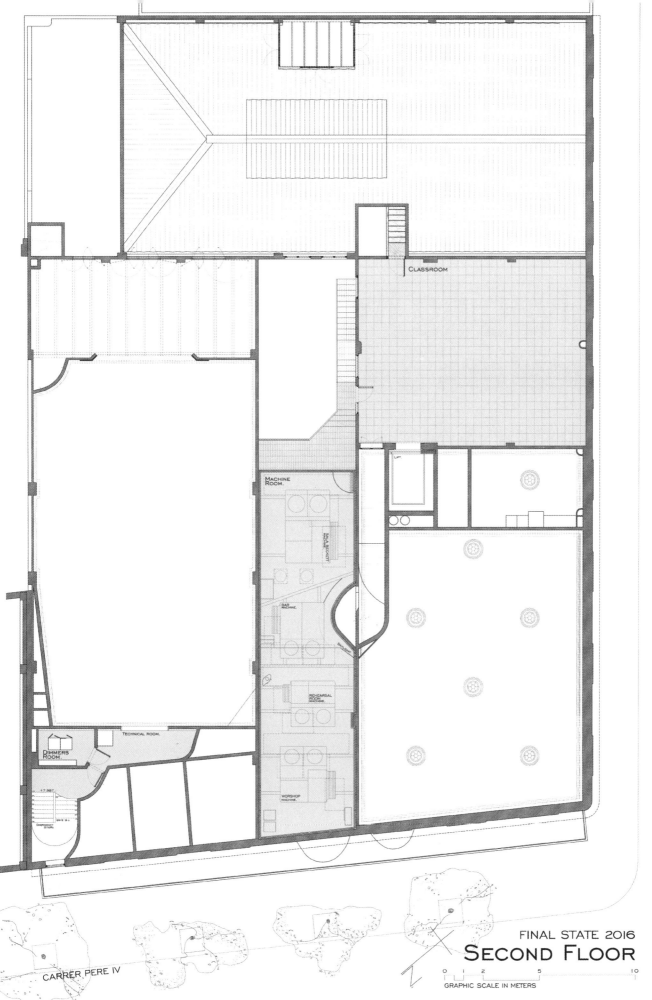

CLASSROOM.

MACHINE
ROOM.

SALA BECKATT

BAR
MACHINE.

BALLOON.

REHEARSAL
ROOM
MACHINE.

TECHNICAL ROOM.

DIMMERS
ROOM.

+7.997

WORSHOP
MACHINE.

EMERGENCY
STAIRS

LIFT.

CARRER PERE IV

FINAL STATE 2016
SECOND FLOOR

0 1 2   5   10
GRAPHIC SCALE IN METERS

The former residence of the director of the Cooperative, located above the central lobby, is now a machine room containing the heating and air conditioning equipment for the two performance halls, the rehearsal hall, and the bar. The stairway leading up to this space, which begins in the patio, has been modified to connect with the new dramaturgy classroom. As a result, one can enter by way of the wooden stairway from the other classrooms and leave by the patio stairway for a rest break or a smoke.

Construction Sept 2014 – June 2016

Marks made with red tape on the ground floor of the building, before work on the definitive project began, July 2014.

Drawing on a 1:1 Scale

During the final design stage, the director of the Sala Beckett was concerned that some of the elements of the lobby and the bar were too close together: the counter too close to the façade, the stairway too close to the bench…

The ground floor had been stripped of the remains of the gymnasium, and we had access to the building. We decided to draw the outline of the bar, the stairway, and the long bench with red tape directly on site, so that we could have a more direct experience of the dimensions. It helped us better to understand the scale of these elements in relation to the building as a whole, and also to test the distances that worked best between them.

A few weeks after drawing with red tape, work began in earnest.

Red marks
on the state as found..

Red marks
on the final state.

CARRER BATISTA

September 2014. The work began with the removal of all the elements that were not be used in the final design, such as the attic structures on the ground floor and the central floor slab on the upper floor, as well as other minor elements that were eventually to be salvaged, but that needed to be stored outside of the building while it was reinforced structurally, such as doors, windows, hydraulic tiles, rosettes, moldings, railings, and wooden stairs.

This initial work was the most strenuous: the machinery seemed to be speeding up the definitive ruin of the building by the hour. Its construction was very economical, and we were afraid the walls would not stand up to so much shaking. Decades of neglect had allowed constant rainwater into the interior of the building, and all the elements of the metallic structure that were removed looked very rusty.

When the floor slab of the former central lobby had been demolished (it was very deteriorated by the successive stairs and restrooms of the former theater and café, and the new project called for its replacement), the center of the building was transformed into a great void, allowing more light to enter in this central part. When it was left without the doors and without the intermediate floor slab, the thirteen-meter heights of the lobby were fully visible, as well as the slender nature of the construction: just 15 centimeters thick, in spite of being so many meters high. It began to be difficult to recognize the former cooperative during visits to the site.

"I believe all this is part of working with the spaces, making it possible to give a different dimension among the levels, simply so that you do not forget the structure of the house. So that, when you are up there, you know that you have this center down here. I believe that these are things —I don't know if they are taught in architecture school— that emerge spontaneously: in a certain way, this respect allows you to perforate and turn it over, but without any desire to implant yourself, or to make it a project that is signed and sealed." Miralda, speaking of the project for the "Casa de la Prensa" in his interview for the film Scale 1:5.

GRAPHIC SCALE IN METERS

The former cooperative functioned with three independent programs: a commercial one on the ground floor and a leisure program and a school on the upper floor, each one with its own entrance from the street. The new Sala Beckett, on the other hand, was to function as a unit. The design was intended to make the three original units function together, effacing the disconnections between them.

FINAL STATE

The connection is achieved in the central lobby by combining light and circulation, by means of a skylight above the new stairway that communicates the two levels. The new intermediate structure is of reinforced concrete, used to buttress to two high walls of the lobby, and at the same time it contains two large apertures to let in light and provide views.
In the final section, the structural and acoustical reinforcements made in the upper part of the existing floor slab can be seen, so that the outline of the ceramic vaulting is not lost from below, and can be seen in the offices, dressing rooms, and bar.

Comparing the two longitudinal sections —initial and final state—, you can see the 25-centimeter increase in the floor slab of the upper floor. We were very eager for this increase to be absorbed by means of the total renovation of the building. Since two of the three stairways are new, we made them reach the new level of finished flooring, and to the third we added two steps of the same artificial stone. In this way, it is impossible to see the increase of floor level, except on the balcony: there, the level of the flooring was not increased, so that the cantilever would not have to support more weight. Our solution was to transform the change of level into low benches. That is where the reinforcement made to the building can be appreciated.

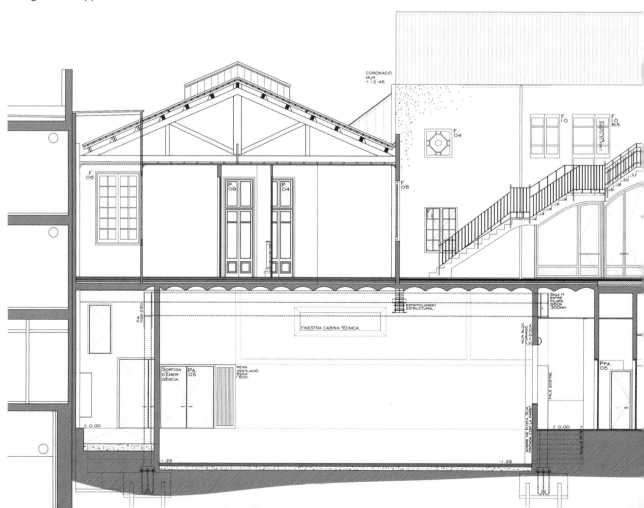

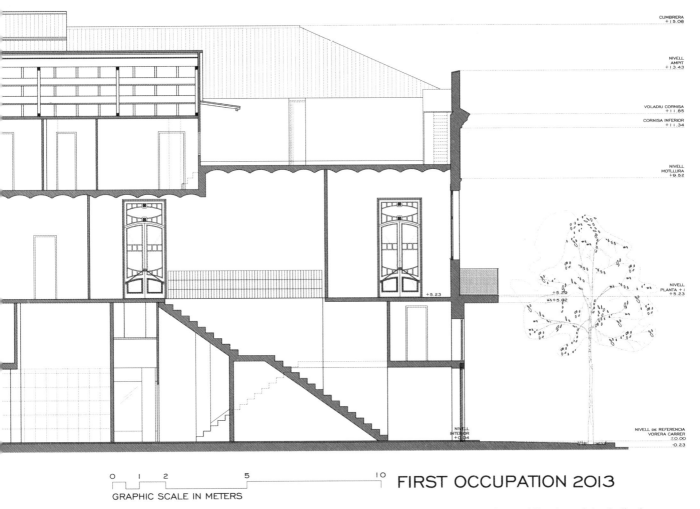

O I 2   5   IO
GRAPHIC SCALE IN METERS

FIRST OCCUPATION 2013

Above the layer of acoustical insulation the bases began to be laid for the various sections of flooring of the halls. In the theater spaces, such as the upstairs theater, the rehearsal halls, and the two acting classrooms, wooden flooring was put down: a base of wooden planks over which two layers of plywood were laid. In the other spaces —offices, other classrooms, and vestibules— the hydraulic tiles salvaged from the same floor were laid down, but in different arrangements or forming different designs.

LONGITUDINAL SECTION
FINAL STATE

As the floor slab of the central lobby was being demolished, the doors, windows, flooring, rosettes, and other elements recorded in the inventory were removed, so that they could be stored away until they were brought back to the site and reincorporated in their new positions. The doors and windows were protected with numbered wooden panels with the inventory code on them. The door and window frames that remained were also protected, so that they would not be knocked or battered during construction.

In the case of the flooring, the tiles were raised and cleaned on the underside, in an attempt to remove the mortar that still adhered to them from their original installation. This cleaning was done with a carbon fiber polisher, which is not aggressive, ensuring that the pieces would not break in the process. The tiles were classified and then piled up on different palettes, numbered according to the room they came from, in accordance with the inventory.

The upper floor needed to be reinforced structurally in order to meet new standards, and also acoustically, in order to ensure that no noise filtered through between the ground-floor and upper-floor performance halls, so that theater activities could be held in both of them simultaneously. The structural reinforcements were made above the floor slab structure, with connectors between the lower trusses and metallic mesh on the upper part.

Once the connectors were welded to the joists, the entire floor was concreted. A layer of elastic material was placed over this concrete in order to separate it from the follow layer of concrete, eight centimeters thick, which served as acoustical insulation, detached from the perimeter walls, in order to avoid the transmission of sound by mass. The bases of the flooring of each room were installed over these layers.

At the back of the ground floor, the original flooring was excavated, in order to reach the level of the Theater Downstairs, located 1.20 meters below the level of the lobby and the street. This level guaranteed a free height of five meters from floor to lighting grille.

When we dug down, we immediately encountered natural soil, a trace of the not-so-distant past is this part of the city that was once farmers' fields.

In order to obtain the free breadth of the main hall, we had to tear down a wall of the original building, holding it at the level of the ceiling. This was achieved by means of frames that covered the entire span, with pillars located on the outside of the walls of the hall. In this way, the frame structure affects only the ceiling of the hall, but the surrounding walls remain free of structural elements.

The pillars of these frames required deep foundations, since the ground on which the new Sala Beckett is located is not very firm through the first several meters below ground, owing to the proximity of the sea. As a result, each pillar is supported on a pile cap, which assembles micro-piles reaching fourteen meters deep, where they rest on solid ground.

The main hall had to allow for different seating configurations and relations between audience and stage, so that productions could be staged with a single audience in front, or the audience divided on two sides or on four sides around a central stage.

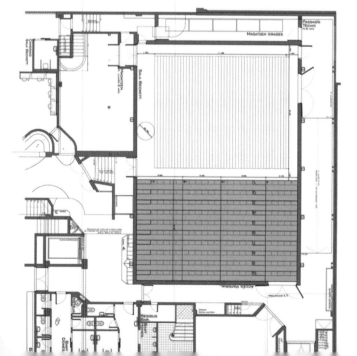

SALA BECKETT OPCIÓ 1
MIDES INTERIORS   ÀREA NETA ESCENA
19.70 x 13.95 = 274.82 M²   11.45 x 9.30 = 106.50 M²   AFORAMENT: 210 PLACES

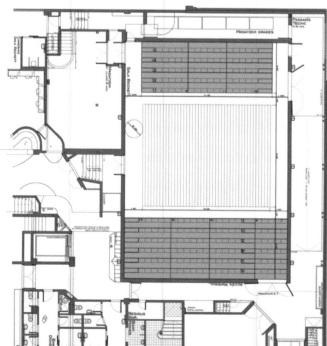

SALA BECKETT OPCIÓ 2
MIDES INTERIORS   ÀREA NETA ESCENA
19.70 x 13.95 = 274.82 M²   10.95 x 8.45 = 92.53 M²   AFORAMENT: 206 PLACES

Thus, the minimum width of the hall is determined by these configurations, the most critical being that of the audience on the two long sides, with a strip of four meters of audience, seven meters of stage, and four meters of audience, making for a total width of fifteen meters.

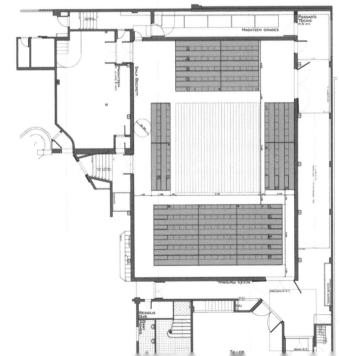

SALA BECKETT   OPCIÓ **3**
ES INTERIORS   ÀREA NETA ESCENA
70 x 13.95 = 274.82 M²   16.70 x 4.75 = 79.50 M²   AFORAMENT: 208 PLACES

SALA BECKETT   OPCIÓ **4**
MIDES INTERIORS   ÀREA NETA ESCENA
19.70 x 13.95 = 274.82 M²   7.45 x 7.25 = 54.00 M²   AFORAMENT: 206 PLACES

Model on 1:25 scale used to study the proportions of the hall, the entrances, the height of the seating, and that of the ceiling: how to make the most of the space between frames for the air conditioning, lighting, and fire safety installations, etc.

In the new Sala Beckett, the two theaters are polyvalent, allowing multiple arrangements of audience and stage. In these kinds of halls, the ceiling also needs to be polyvalent, allowing spotlights to be placed in every direction and position, so that they allow for different ways of the lighting to adapt to the changes in configurations between the audience and the actors.

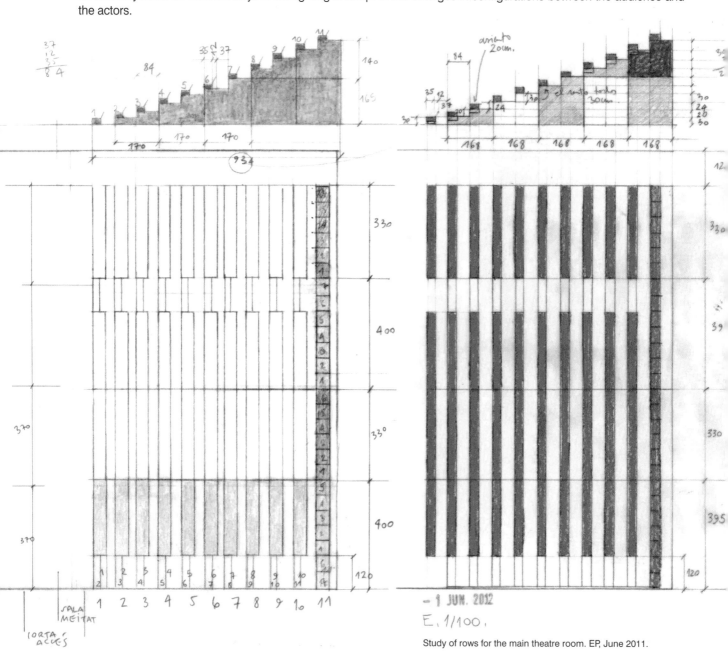

Study of rows for the main theatre room. EP, June 2011.

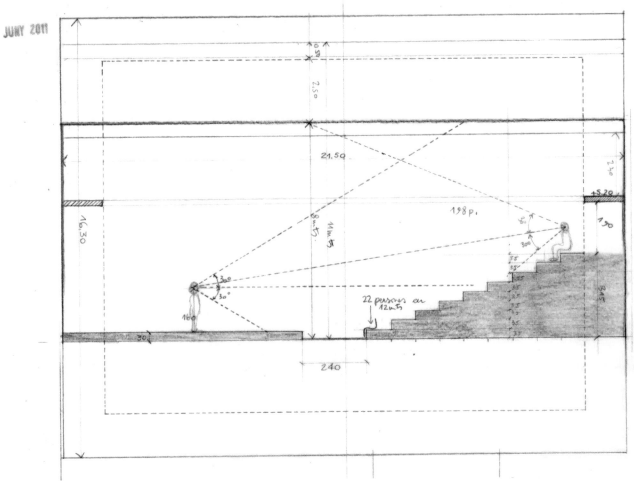

Another aspect that needed to be tested out with drawings and models was the height of the seating, arranged so that it would allow a good view from the highest seats, but not so high that spectators would be left out of the visual radius of the actors. This guarantees a good visual relation between actors and audience.

Théâtre des Bouffes du Nord, Paris.

While we were developing the project, we visited Les Bouffes du Nord, the theater renovated by Peter Brook in Paris in 1974. We had read *The Open Circle* by Andrew Todd and Jean-Guy Lecat and we wanted to visit their theater and see a play directed by Peter Brook. We saw *The Suit* and it was a very exciting experience, because of both the work and the place, the two of them functioning together. It was probably after this visit that we decided that the theater of the Sala Beckett should be everywhere in the building. When you leave the play, the walls inside and outside the performance hall function in continuity: you continue to feel you are in the same place. We later made an axonometric drawing entitled "Theater Everywhere in the Building."

Théâtre des
BOUFFES DU NORD
Saison 2011 2012

THE SUIT
DU 3 AVRIL AU 5 MAI 2012

Can Themba, Mothobi Mutloatse et Barney Simon

Adapté, mis en scène et en musique par
Peter Brook, Marie-Hélène Estienne et Franck Krawczyk

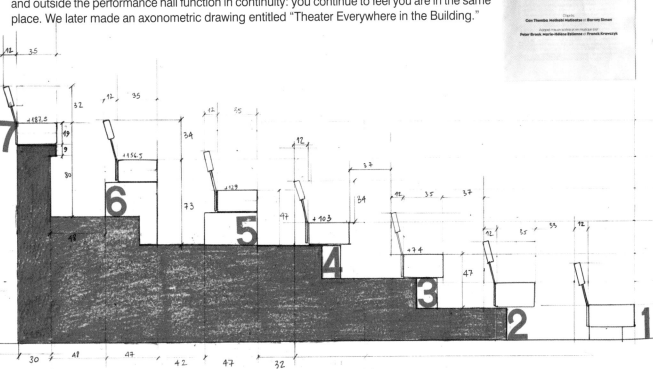

In Les Bouffes du Nord, the relation between stage and audience is designed to ensure that both are part of the same situation. During the intermission, we were able to measure the seating, in order to obtain data from a good reference that would serve when we turned our attention to this subject for the new Sala Beckett.

Section of the rows at Bouffes du Nord, Paris. EP, May 2012.

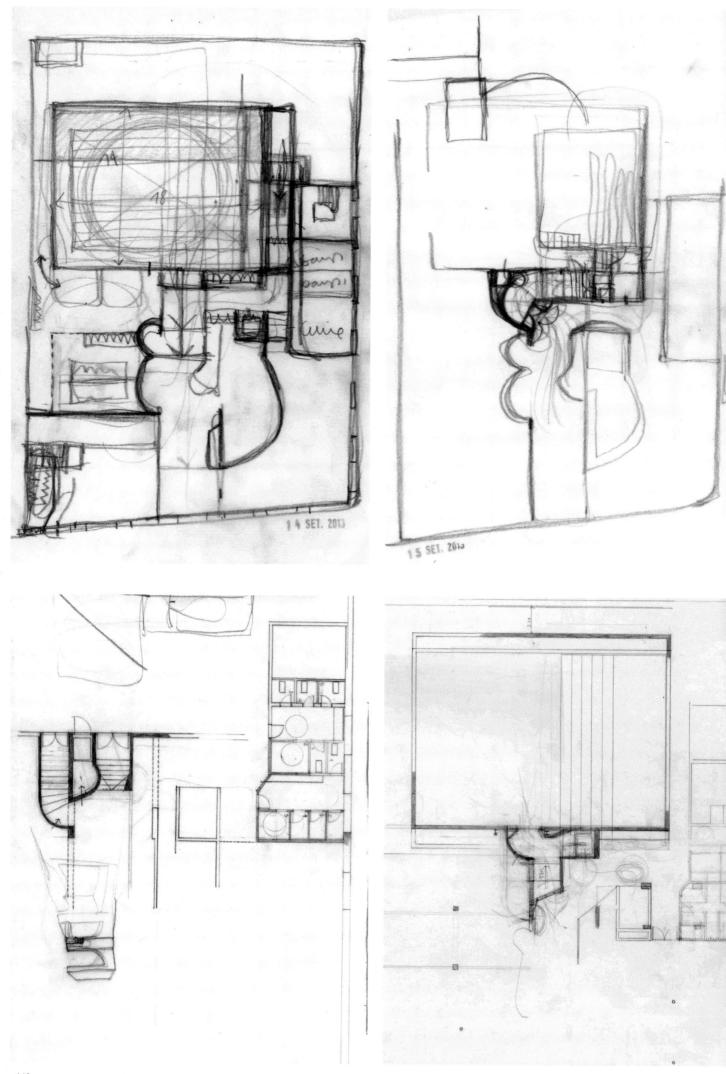

1 4 SET. 2013

1 5 SET. 2013

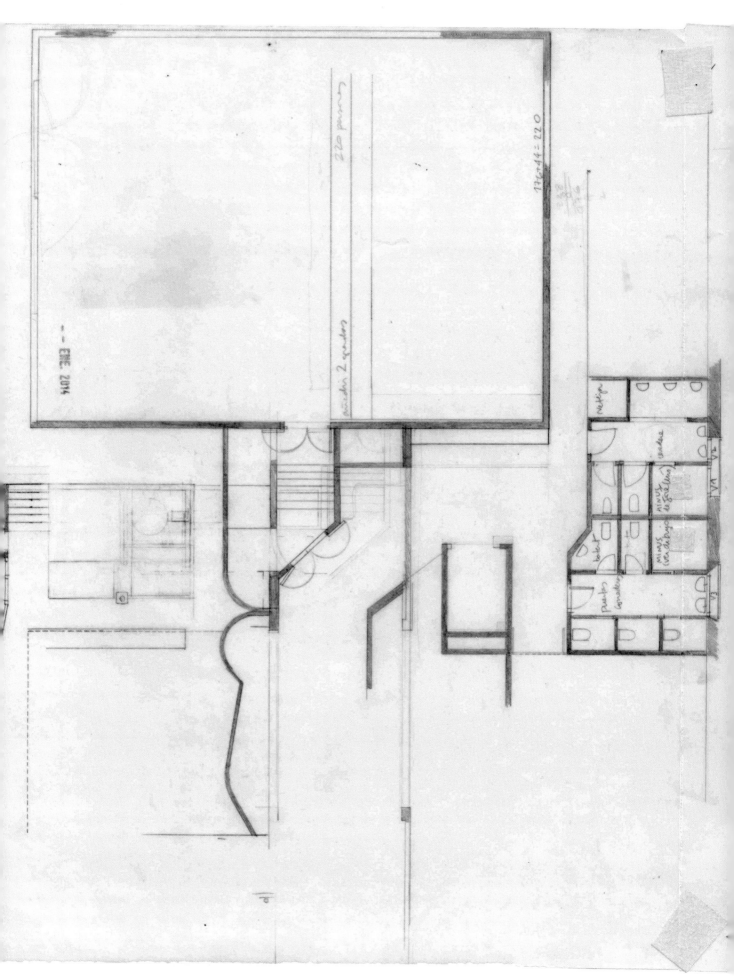

The 1.2-meter drop in level from the lobby to the Theater Downstairs required a small stairway of seven steps and an elevator platform. In one of our first drawings (top left) we tried to resolve the difference in level by means of a frontal ramp, but it projected too far into the lobby, to the middle of the red sofa. The following test drawings seek to make use of the arrangement of the stairway and the elevator in order to create an entrance that slows down the arrival to the hall, avoiding the frontal access with a change of direction that requires one to slow down before beginning to descend.

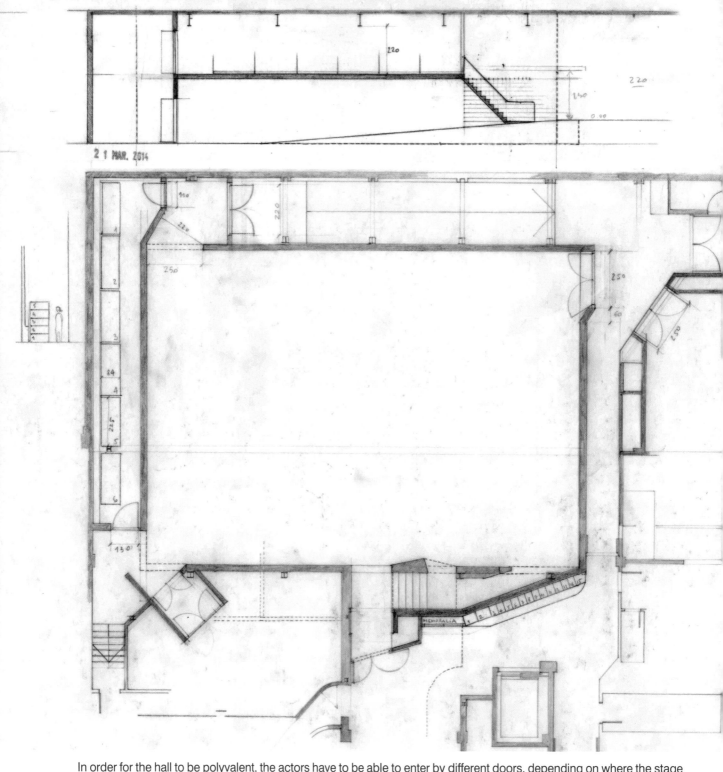

In order for the hall to be polyvalent, the actors have to be able to enter by different doors, depending on where the stage is (which varies for each performance, depending on the play and the director), but without being seen by the audience. In the Theater Downstairs, we wanted to prevent these access points from being visible from inside, leaving them out of the audience's range of vision, and since it was a new hall, we were able to define some entrance chambers on the perimeter, so that the actors enter directly, without opening or closing a door. With these chambers, the outside world disappears during the performance, and the spectator feels trapped in another world, forgetting the lobby and the bustle of the main entrance.

There is a theatrical quality about entering the hall: first you see a window through which you catch a glimpse of who is inside, of the audience already seated, or of how the stage is arranged. As you descend, there are two ways of going in, creating a certain ambiguity, so that the entrance is not direct and this space becomes a small room outside the hall, an intermediate space backstage, behind the scenes.

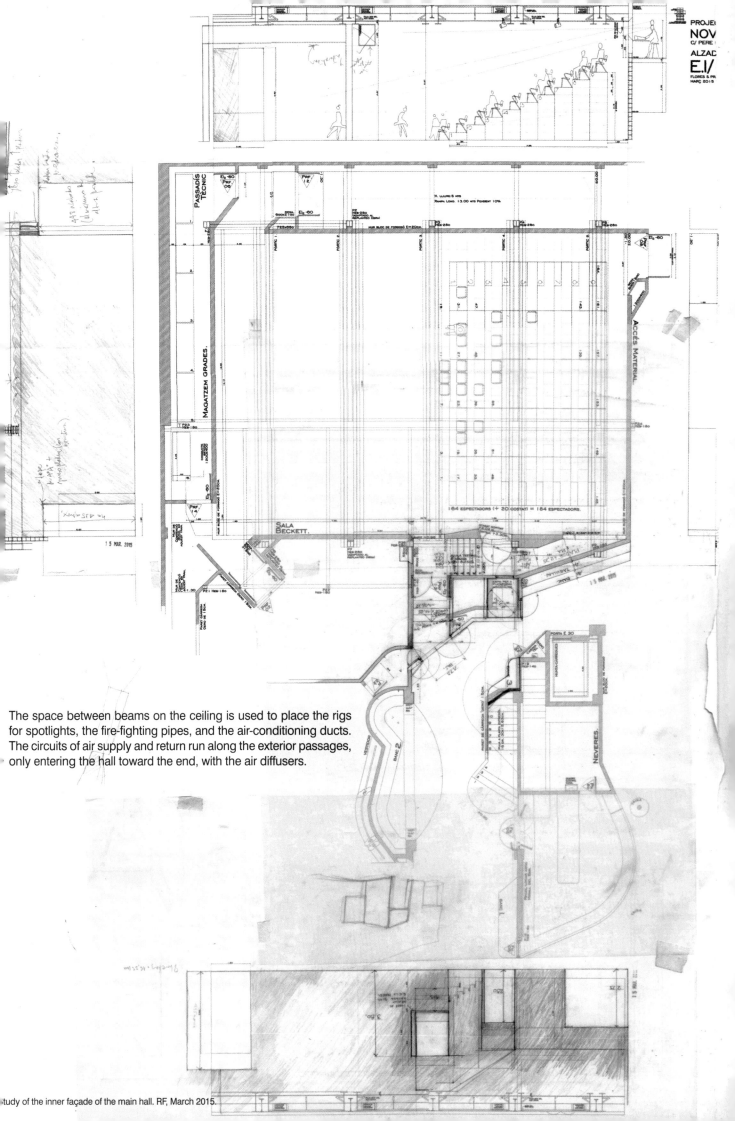

The space between beams on the ceiling is used to place the rigs for spotlights, the fire-fighting pipes, and the air-conditioning ducts. The circuits of air supply and return run along the exterior passages, only entering the hall toward the end, with the air diffusers.

Study of the inner façade of the main hall. RF, March 2015.

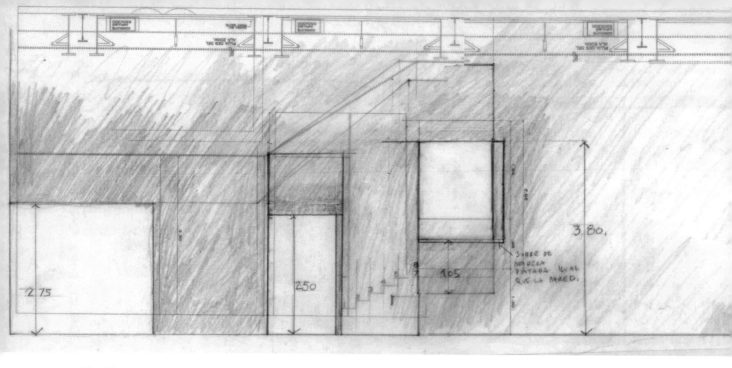

The Theater Downstairs is the only space in the entire Sala Beckett painted black. This is because it is the only hall built from scratch, which did not begin as a preexisting space in the *Pau i Justícia* cooperative, since it required a width that the original spaces did not have. This hall has wooden flooring and a free height beneath five-meter beams. It can be entered by way of all four corners.

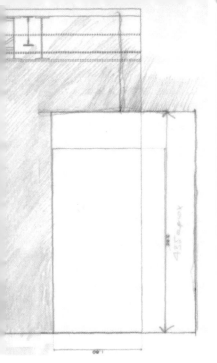

The seating used in this hall can be stored in the surrounding spaces. The seating itself is neither fixed nor retractable, allowing performances to use any one of the four walls to arrange the stage, including the entrance wall with a balcony and two doors of different sizes that can be the beginning of a stage play.

The theater of the former cooperative had a raised stage that was of no interest to the Sala Beckett, which works on a horizontal plane in terms of the relation between performance and audience. So the stage was eliminated, but the proscenium was maintained, since it offers different ways of organizing the hall, as were three windows facing east, for the natural light they provide. The hall had flooring of hydraulic tiles, but the Sala Beckett wanted wooden floors in the theaters, so that stage props could be easily affixed. The tiles from this hall are now in the central lobby and the bar downstairs. The ceiling of the hall collapsed at the outset of the renovation process, so it needed to be replaced. The walls, on the other hand, preserve their original colors and all the signs and traces of various occupancies.

"I believe that the value of salvaging spaces resides in the fact that what remains of the building can be of use to you for something. Since you are going to make a space which proposes, basically, to create and tell stories, once the renovation is finished, you have a lot already done, which is the emotion. The spectator who enters here is already predisposed, because the walls seem to be inviting you to imagine, to create stories, fictions. If it were all a pristine white wall, the creator, the actor of the play you have come to see has to draw you out: 'Hey, abandon the prose of your day to day life and enter into the poetry I am proposing.' It would be a much greater effort. Here, on the other hand, the spectator sits down, looks at the walls, and is already... imagining, already entering onto a terrain that is no longer everyday life."
Toni Casares. Interview for the film *Scale 1:5*.

The rehearsal hall (the café of the former cooperative) also changed its original flooring of hydraulic tiles for wood, but in this case the reed and plaster ceiling escaped the ruin of the building and could be used as we found it, with just some repair of broken parts. This ceiling has very fine acoustical qualities, being a flexible structure that absorbs sound well. For the air conditioning of the hall we made use of the preexisting ceiling roses, which originally served for ventilation. We placed the heating and air conditioning pipes above this ceiling, between the roof trusses, and ran the air ducts into

the rosettes, which now serve as air diffusers. The return is by way of two grilles placed discreetly at either end of the hall. Thus, the installations have minimal impact on the space, giving priority to the traces of the former cooperative, which find maximum expression in this hall. The hall has windows at the corner of the building and a balcony where one can rest between rehearsals. We have prepared these windows both acoustically and climatically, incorporating a second window with wooden shutters to make the hall darker.

In the classrooms, the flooring was removed, the floor slab was reinforced, and then divisions were built in accordance with the new distribution. In the two acting classrooms, the tile flooring was replaced with wood, and the leftover yellow tiles removed to the lobby on the upper floor.

We also changed the position of doors and wooden railing of the former school, all placed in the same part of the building, but in accordance with the new geometry regulating these rooms, now devoted to theater instruction. The soft colors of the classrooms are the same as in the former cooperative building.

SALA BECKETT.
ESTAT ACTUAL. PLANTA PRIMERA.
PAVIMENTS DE L'ANTIGUA COOPERATIVA PAU I JUSTÍCIA.

NOVEMBRE 2017.
FLORES & PRATS ARQS.
DIBUIXAT PER I. MARTINEL.

E. 1/50.

ESCALA GRÀFICA EN METRES.
0 1   5   10   15

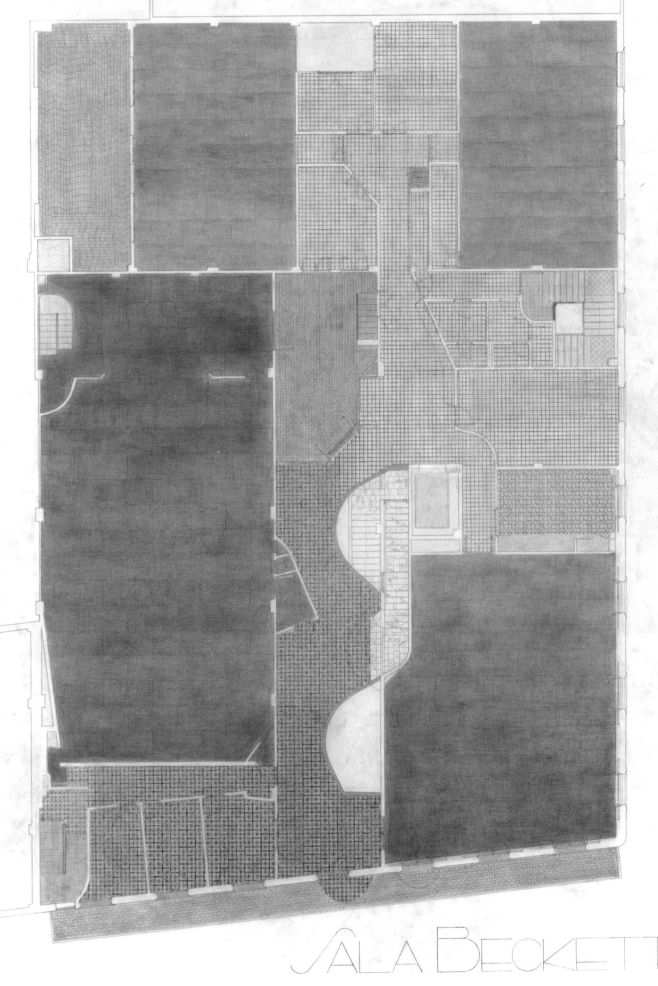

SALA BECKETT.

PROJECTE
PAVIMENTS HIDRÀULICS A PLANTA PRIMERA.

FLORES & PRATS ARQS. NOVEMBRE 2017.
DIBUIXAT PER MJ. CRISTIANO I I. MARTINEL.

E.1/50

ESCALA GRÀFICA EN METRES
0 1   5   10   15

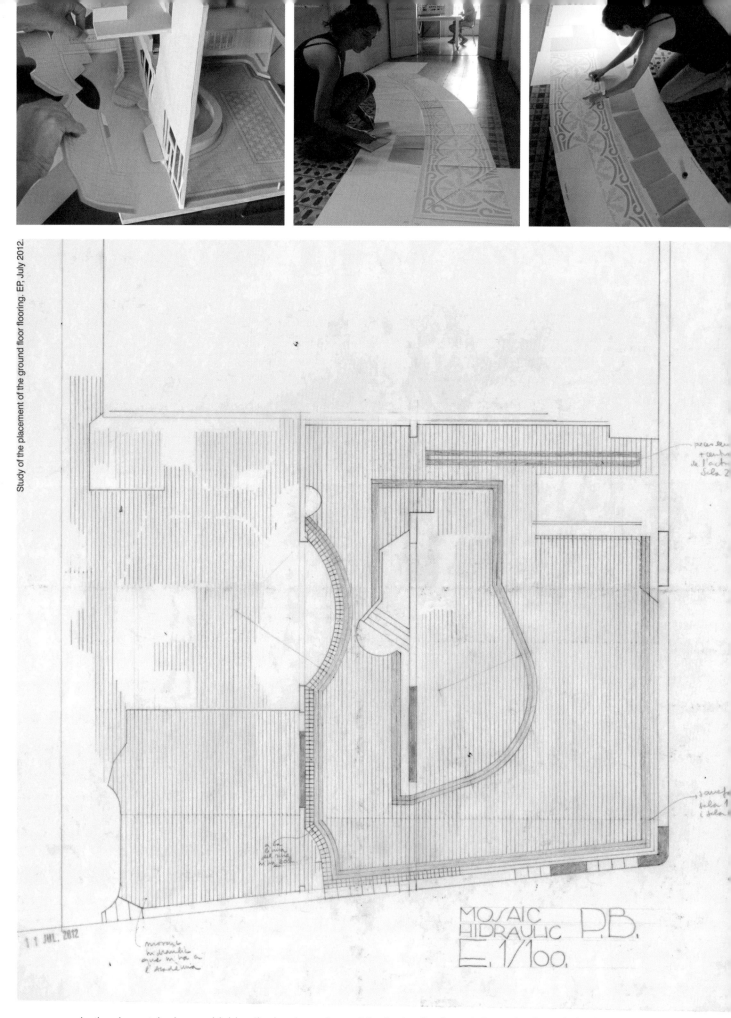

MOSAIC HIDRAULIC P.B.
E. 1/100.

In the downstairs bar and lobby, the border pattern of the hydraulic tiles reinforce the flow of circulation around the kitchen core and the stairway, incorporating some curved stretches. Since these borders were originally placed at right angles, we tried out patterns in the studio, with 1:1 scale prints, to ensure that arranging the tiles in curved patterns would not interrupt the continuity of the design.

SALA BECKETT.

PROJECTE

PAVIMENTS HIDRÀULICS A PLANTA BAIXA.

FLORES & PRATS ARQS. NOVEMBRE 2017.
DIBUIXAT PER I. MARTINEL.

E. 1/50.

ESCALA GRÀFICA EN METRES

0 1   5   10   15

The flooring downstairs is of hydraulic tiles, most of which came from the former theater on the upper floor. We designed some carpets in the cloakroom area and in the middle of the bar, drawing on the idea of the carpeting in some of the waiting areas of the former grocery store, which we had seen in old photographs.

About 20% of the original tiles were lost in the process of renovation, owing to breakage during removal and subsequent handling. When we designed the relocation of the tiles, we took this into account, so we had enough for all the rooms, without having to purchase new pieces.

Final state of the flooring of dressing rooms and ground floor offices.
Majo Cristiano and Inès Martinel, 2017.

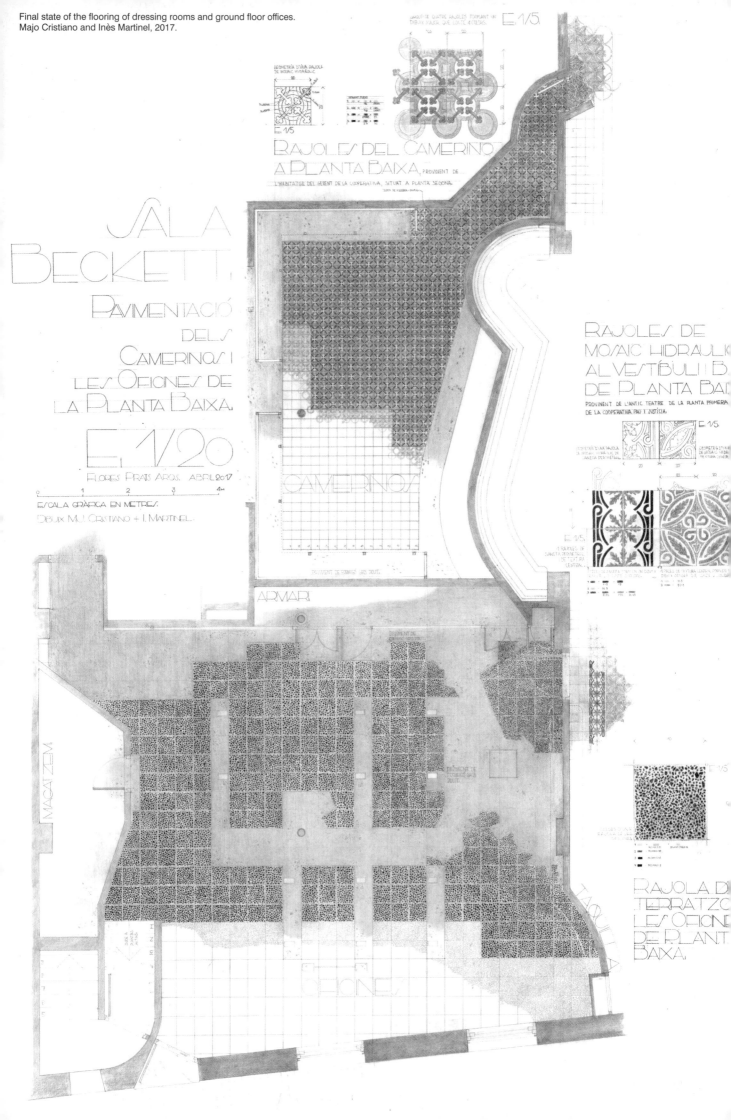

This plan shows the flooring of the ground-floor offices and dressing rooms. The offices are the only space where the terrazzo flooring that existed in some areas of this level has been maintained. The parts that broke or through which electrical wiring passes have been filled in with polished concrete. The hydraulic tiles in the dressing rooms were salvaged from the residence of the director of the cooperative, that is, from the second floor, where the machine room now is. In this space we also found an iron pillar with its original capital, hidden behind some brick cladding and partly concealed by the mezzanine spaces that cut the heights in half.

Since the theater rooms on the upper level have wooden flooring, the tiles have been used for the common areas. In the classrooms, the yellow tiles were used for the part of the lobby leading toward the patio. In the offices and central lobby the ones from the former café were used, except that the original design, based on crosses, was modified to create long bands that lead from the façade to the central patio.

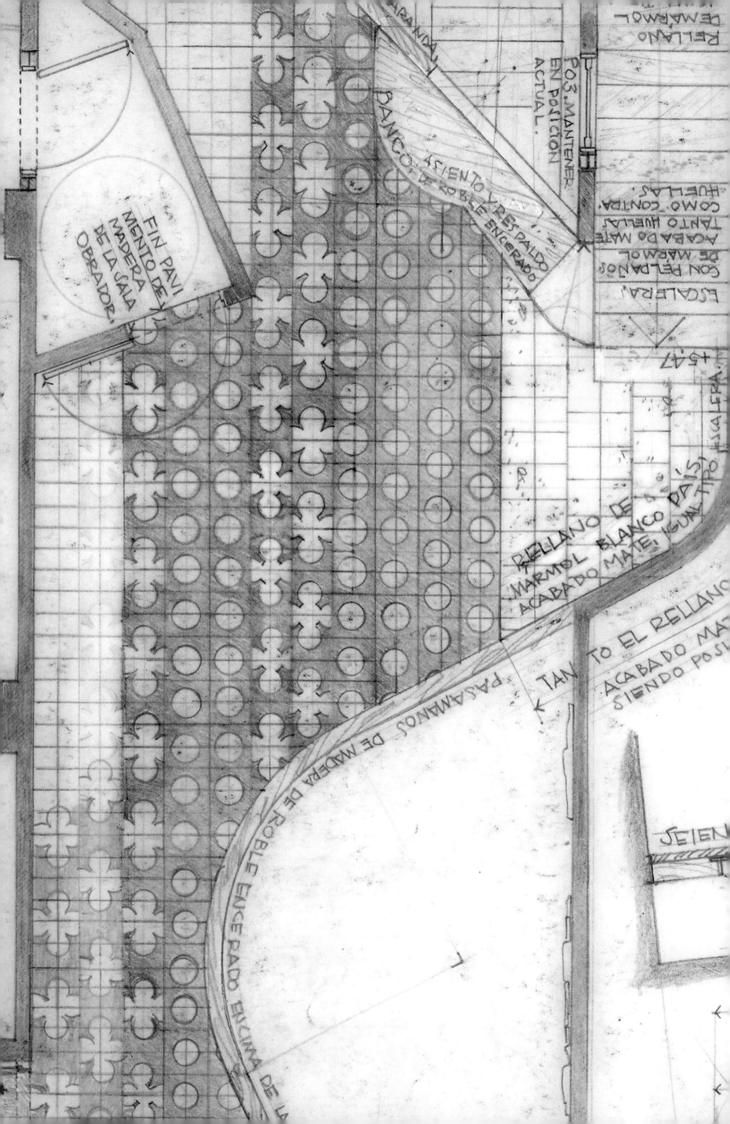

FIN PAVI
MENTO DE
MADERA
DE LA SALA
OBRADOR.

BANCO SIENTO Y RESPALDO DE ROBLE ENCERADO

BARANDA
EN POSICION
ACTUAL.

P03.MANTENER
EN POSICION
ACTUAL.

RELLANO
DE MARMOL

ESCALERA:
CON PELDAÑOS
DE MARMOL
ACABADO MATE.
TANTO HUELLAS
COMO CONTRA
HUELLAS.

+5.47

RELLANO DE PAIS,
MARMOL BLANCO PAIS,
ACABADO MATE

TANTO EL RELLANO
ACABADO MATE
SIENDO POSI

PASAMANOS DE MADERA DE ROBLE ENCERADO ENCIMA DE LA

SEIEN

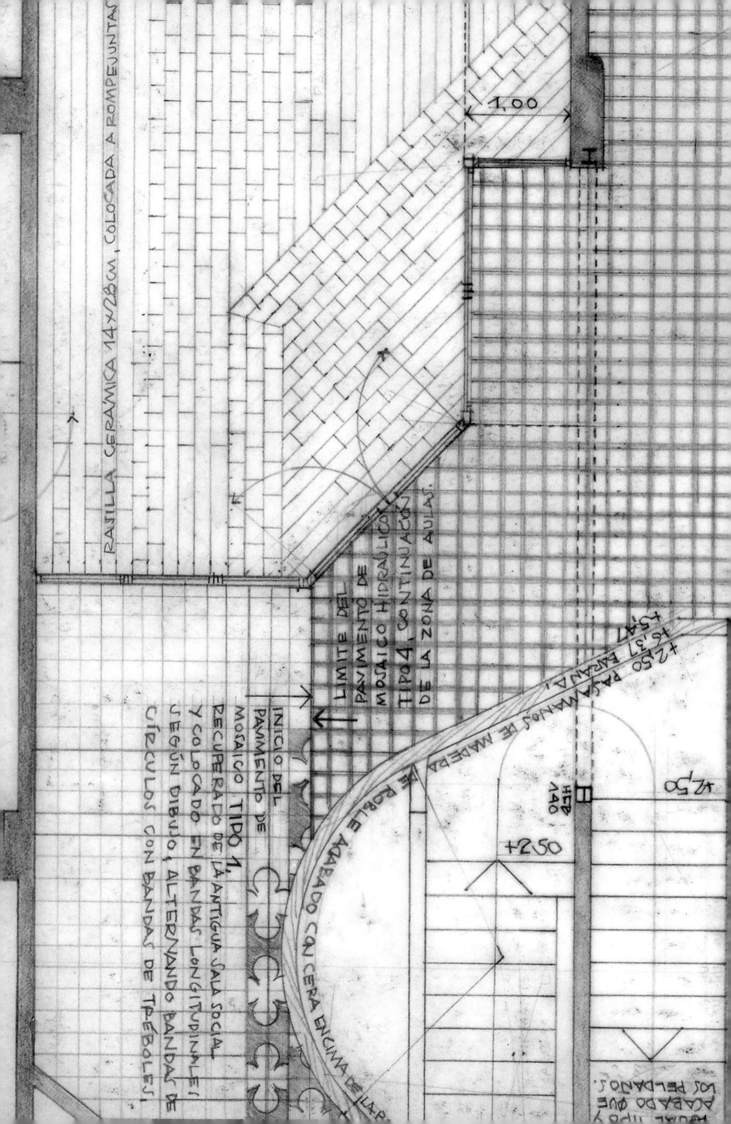

RASILLA CERÁMICA 14×28CM, COLOCADA A ROMPEJUNTAS

PAVIMENTO DE MOSAICO HIDRÁULICO
TIPO 4, CONTINUACIÓN
DE LA ZONA DE AULAS.

LÍMITE DEL

INICIO DEL
PAVIMENTO DE
MOSAICO TIPO 1,
RECUPERADO DE LA ANTIGUA SALA SOCIAL
Y COLOCADO EN BANDAS LONGITUDINALES
SEGÚN DIBUJO, ALTERNANDO BANDAS DE
CÍRCULOS CON BANDAS DE TRÉBOLES.

ACABADO CON CERA ENCIMA DE LA P.

PASAMANOS DE MADERA DE ROBLE

+2.50
+6.37 BARANAL.
+5.37

+2.50

HEB
140

+2.50

IGUAL TIPO Y
ACABADO QUE
LOS PELDAÑOS.

1.00

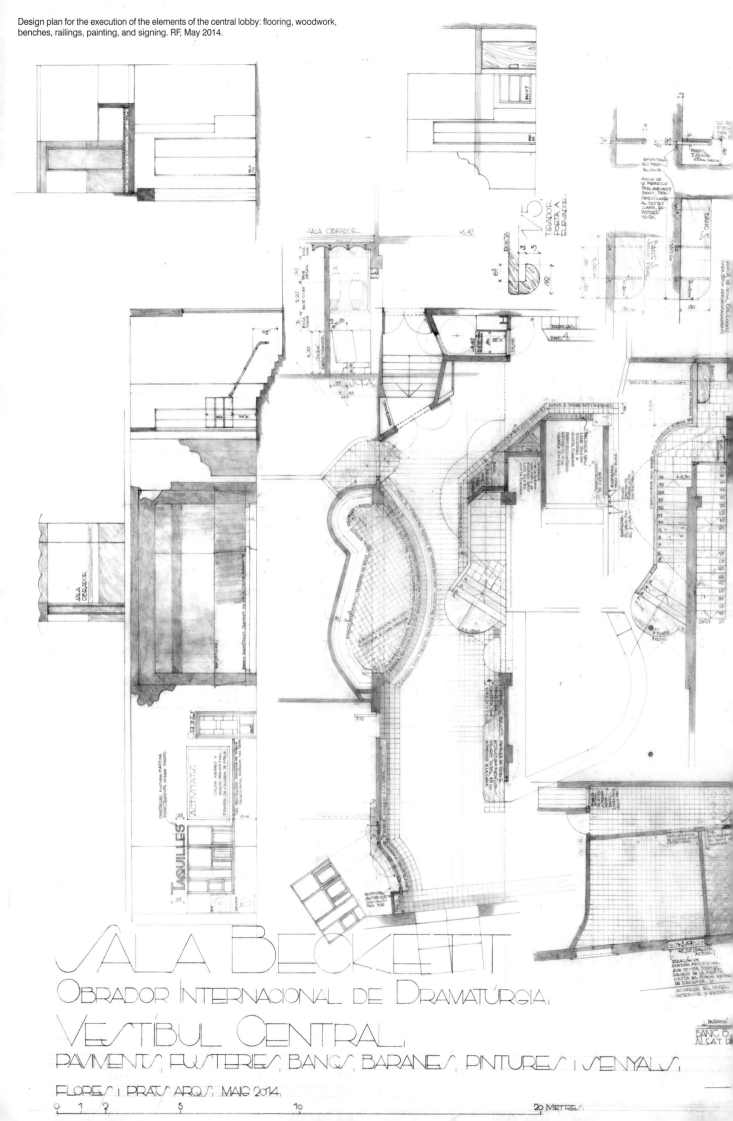

SALA BECKETT

OBRADOR INTERNACIONAL DE DRAMATÚRGIA.

VESTÍBUL CENTRAL.

PAVIMENTS, FUSTERIES, BANCS, BARANES, PINTURES I SENYALS.

FLORES I PRATS ARQS. MAIG 2014.

0 1 2   5   10   20 METRES.

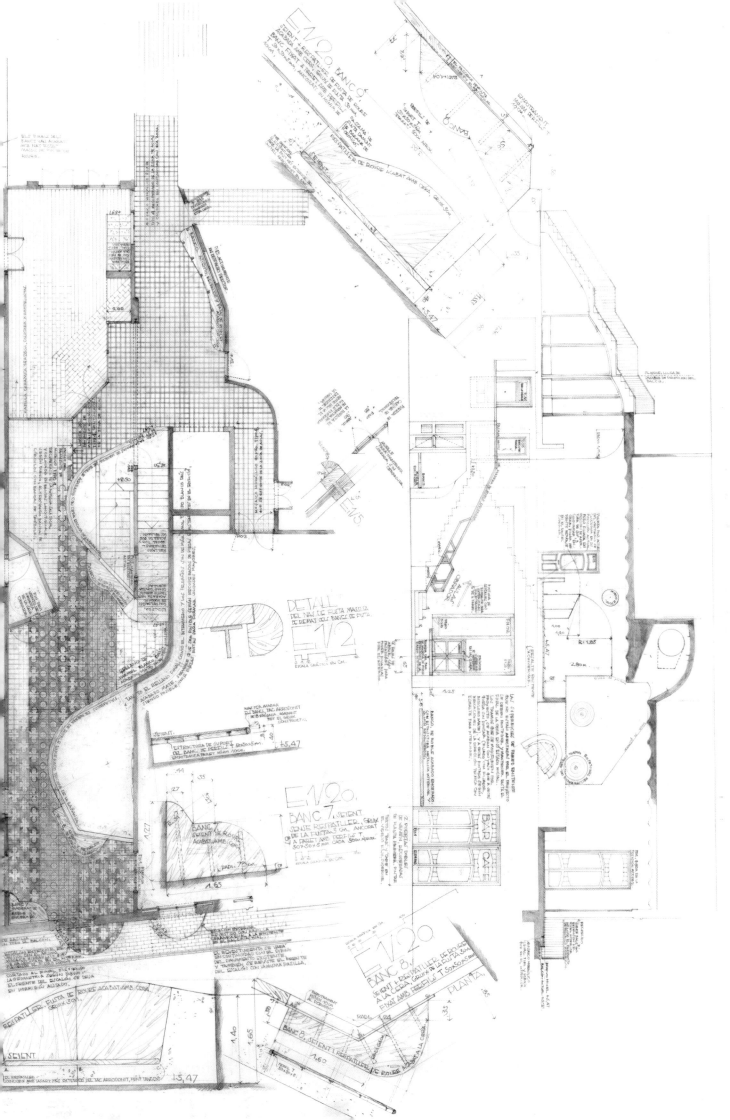

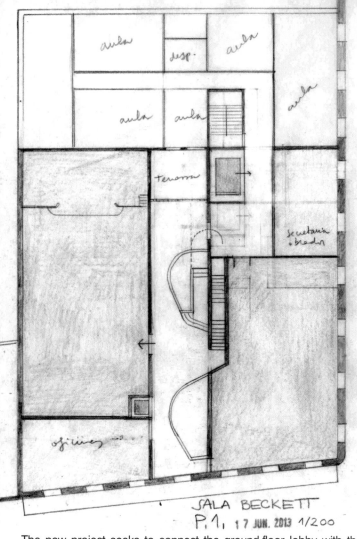

SALA BECKETT
P.1, 17 JUN. 2013 1/200

The new project seeks to connect the ground-floor lobby with the upper level and the classrooms at the back, without it being noticed that one is ascending six meters and moving forty meters deep into the building. Studies of the upper floor. EP + RF, June-November 2013.

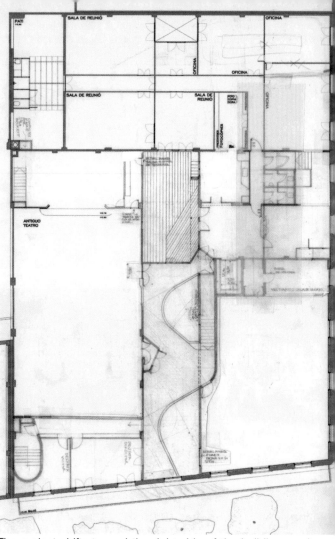

The project shifts toward the right side of the building, no longer remaining symmetrical, and centers the responsibility of this connection on one of its two master walls. We stretched this wall back to connect the Calle Pere IV with the classrooms at the back of the lot, expanding the upper-floor patio to double its original size, so that it becomes a central source of natural light of the floor, helping the flow of circulation backwards in a natural way.

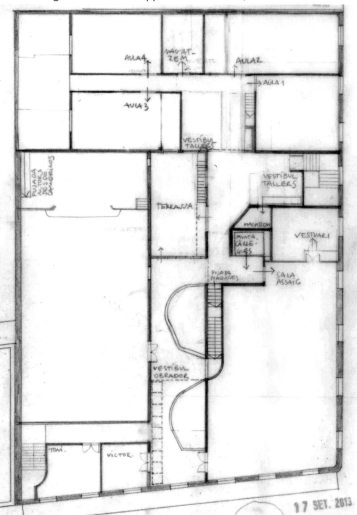

17 SET. 2013

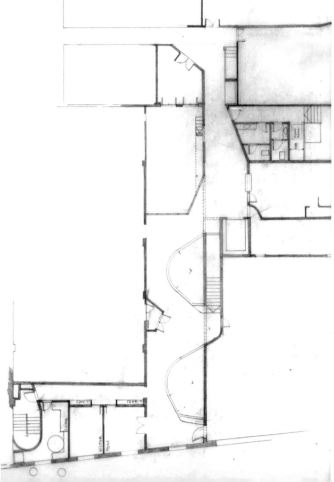

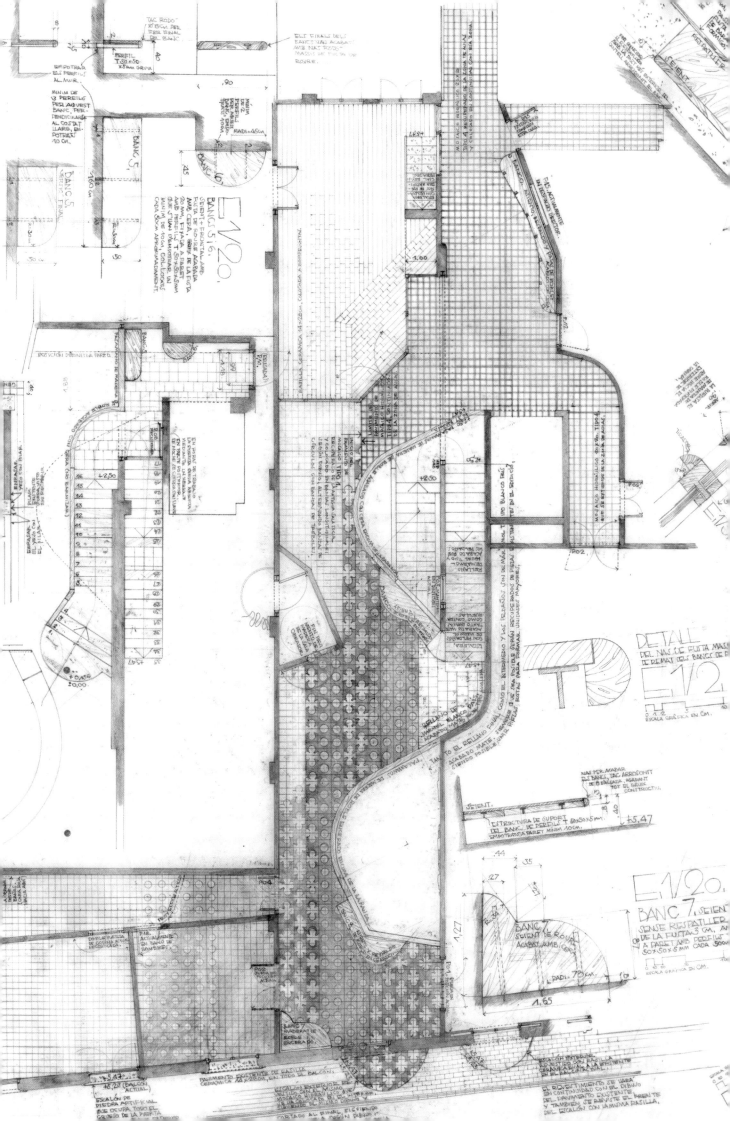

The Two Sides of a Wall. The Sala Beckett gravitates around a very long wall that crosses it lengthwise. Working along this wall to articulate the new program implied certain direct actions on it: incisions to leave space for a new stairway, to allow people to cross at different moment, to let in natural light, and to give a sense of depth. The various incisions activated the wall, which has now become the central axis of the building, with people and light moving from one side to the other, suddenly appearing and disappearing like people in a play.

Paret de
Circulació i Llum.
Sala Beckett

res Prats i Arqs. - Dibux i. Martinel.   Maig 2017.

1/50.

0 1 2   5   10 METRES

The wall that formerly separated spaces now assumes a different dimension: two tall storeys, more than twelve meters high. This gives it a new responsibility: instead of being seen in elevation, it begins to be seen foreshortened, and above all to function in section. The circulation seems to gravitate around the thickness of the wall, along its axis, turning it back and forth. The wall becomes active in a new way, beginning to contain the views it receives, the light that crosses it, the circulation on either side of it, the air running through its cracks…

The state of ruin in which we found the building allowed us to work freely, handling the remains of broken wall and floor slabs and imagining a future for these fragments, accelerating the actions of time in order to create, in a very brief lapse, what a very long period of time had done before us. So it was necessary to insert lintels in walls fifteen centimeters thick, so that the building would survive: to adapt it and manipulate it, in order to salvage this heritage.

The central lobby was the only part of the upper-floor slab we were unable to maintain: the former theater restrooms and the hollow of the former stairway made it very difficult to salvage. Replacing this structure with reinforced concrete gave us the freedom to design new apertures in it, connecting the two levels with a geometry that envelopes the entire building.

The incisions in these slabs can be added to the incisions in the old walls, allowing gazes to combine the old with the new, without separating what has come later from what came before. The preexisting building is brought up to date by carrying its state of ruin into the future, so that, in the end, it can participate with the full weight of its history in an active way in the final building.

The central lobby now functions on two levels. On entering, one looks up and sees that the natural light has been captured by the vault on the upper floor. The sound of voices reach one from up there, as one sees people appearing and disappearing through the great openings, as one sees that illuminated skylight but not the source of the light itself. Attracted by the mystery of how that light that make the skylight function conceals itself, we climb six meters to the upper floor, almost without realizing it. The skylight pierces the wall and gathers in light from the other side, opening up in a half-vault that adds its silhouette to those of the openings, capturing the attention of whoever looks up at it from below on entering.

The Sala Beckett functions from early in the morning, and the final activity of the day are the theater performances. The natural light inside the building is of importance, accompanying as it does the various sessions of theater instruction, creation, and exhibition. The new occupancy is conceived as a continuous articulation amidst different activities, in both plan view and section. One enters the building as one enters a large home, where one is welcome. The passage from the street to the most private zone of the classroom is made in a continuous way, with variations of light and dimensions that signal the passage from the most public zone, near the street, toward a more reserved and private space.

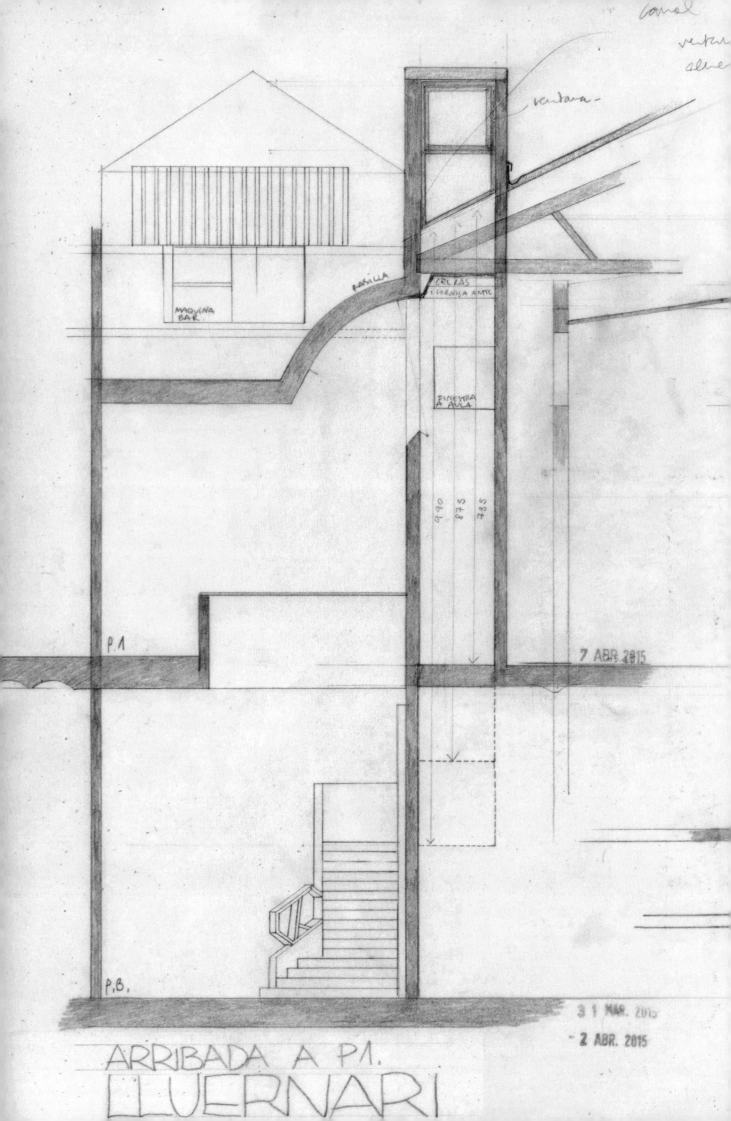

ventana.

MAQUINA
BAR.

PASILLA

CELRAS
I CORNISA ANTE

FINESTRA
A AULA

990 875 735

P.1   7 ABR. 2015

P.B.

3 1 MAR. 2015
- 2 ABR. 2015

ARRIBADA A P1.
LLUERNARI

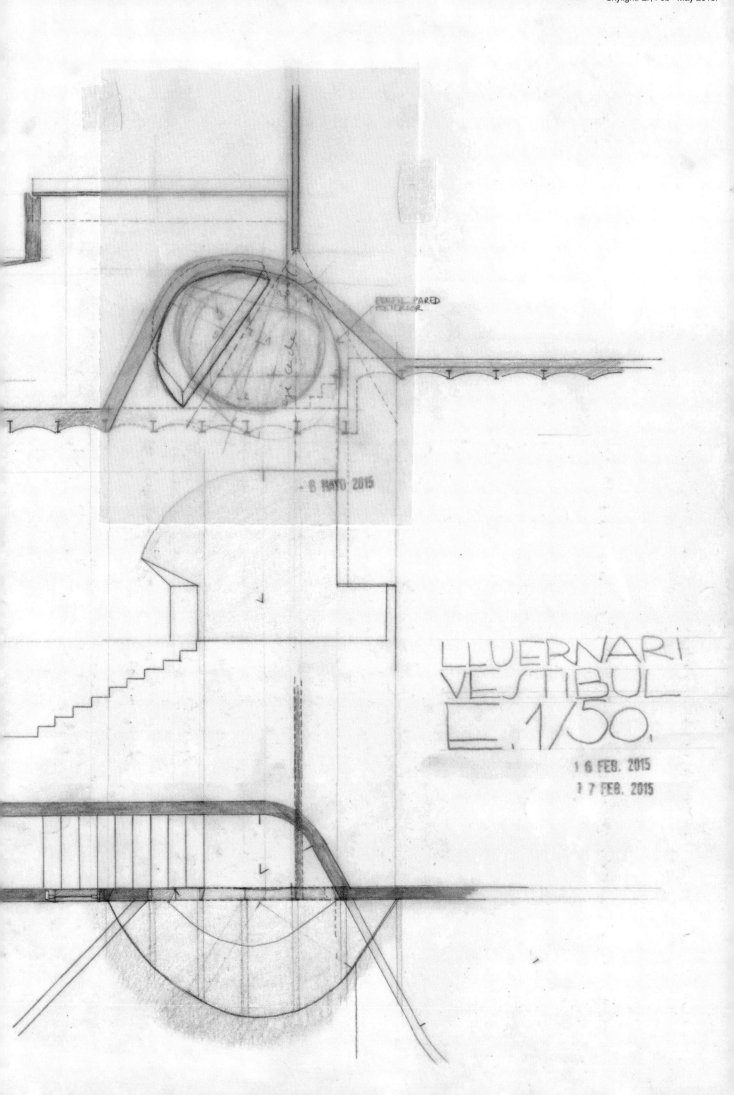

PERFIL PARED POSTERIOR

- 6 MAYO 2015

LLUERNARI
VESTIBUL
E. 1/50.

1 6 FEB. 2015
1 7 FEB. 2015

BAR CAFE

SECCIÓ
VESTIBUL
24 JUL 2014

PLANTA
LLUERNARI

LL
VE

ARRIBADA
ESCALA
A P1.   24 JUL 2014

Above the skylight, which is the most delicate part of the building, are the heating and air conditioning installations of all the classrooms and the bar. Initially the skylight opened directly toward the south from the central lobby, but the density of installations required us to move it to the other side of the wall. Studies of the skylight and machine room floor, above the lobby. EP, June 2014–July 2015.

CLIMATE CONDITIONING ON TOP OF SKYLIGHT SHELL.

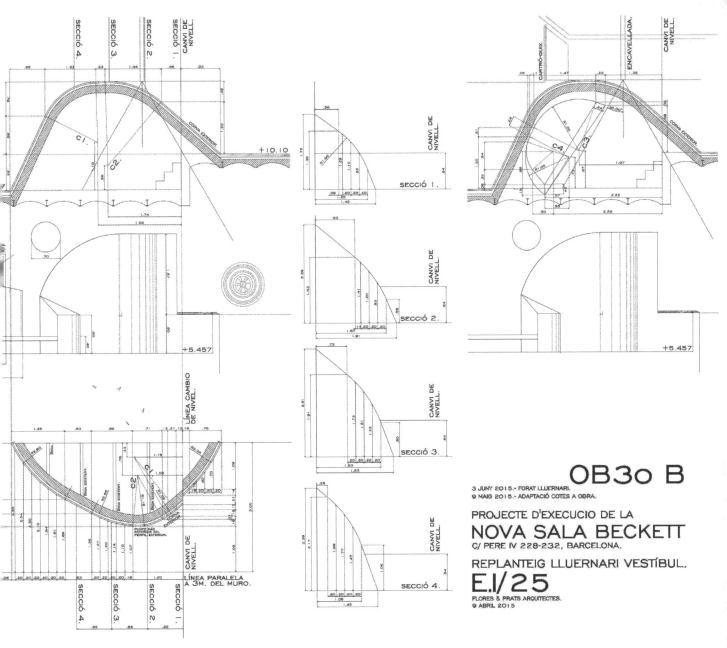

OB3o B

3 JUNY 2015.- FORAT LLUERNARI.
9 MAIG 2015.- ADAPTACIÓ COTES A OBRA.

PROJECTE D'EXECUCIO DE LA
NOVA SALA BECKETT
C/ PERE IV 228-232, BARCELONA.

REPLANTEIG LLUERNARI VESTÍBUL.
E.I/25
FLORES & PRATS ARQUITECTES.
9 ABRIL 2015

The sections of the drawing indicate the outlines of the formwork whereby the masons gave shape to the dome. The construction of this irregular quarter sphere was done against one wall of the lobby. At first it closed in a dark space, until the aperture in the shape of a crescent moon was opened up, letting light pass through from the other side of the wall. In the early morning the sunlight fills this fragment of sphere as if it were water in a recipient.

Breaking up the light and making it pass several times through the same wall reminds us of the ruin we inherited: it recalls the entries of certain houses in Italy, where the air circulates, where everything is exposed to the elements. You go inside,

but the air from outside is already there… The Sala Beckett preserves this character of being an open place, unprotected and fragile, with the exterior in the interior. The emotion of the ruin has remained with it.

The Discipline of the Existing, after the Sala Beckett

Ricardo Flores, Eva Prats

The new Sala Beckett is the union of two stories of very different of origins, which combined to form a new project, each one of them contributing the best of itself. On the one hand, that of the former *Pau i Justícia* cooperative in Poblenou, an abandoned building that retained a strong dose of poetry, in an advanced state of deterioration, but still very present in the memories of the neighborhood's residents. And on the other, that of the Sala Beckett, a drama center with a long presence in the city, highly respected and supported by the theater milieu, which was obliged to change its premises and move into this building in a different neighborhood. The competition to renovate the building and adapt it for use as the new Sala Beckett introduced our studio into this story, as we were able to work for what we believe a project of adaptive reuse should be.

The Cooperative. Our direct and steady observation for several months of the state in which we found the *Pau i Justícia* cooperative building largely influenced our response to a program that, at the beginning, had nothing to do with the previous use of the building, but which at the same time had so many affinities that it was able to fit in perfectly into the preexisting structure, in a sort of "second-hand" way. The former cooperative building had very large rooms combined with compact little pocket spaces, so that you could suddenly open a door and disappear, only to reappear in another hidden circuit of rooms that you never even imagined existed. An ideal place for theater.

But it was not only the physical presence of the former cooperative building that impressed us, affecting our reactions and our designs. It was not only the visible, but also the invisible —what was still alive amidst these ruins—, that made us wish to capture what we had in front of us, in order to leave it as part of the new project. All of the social and cultural activities that had taken place there until just recently: parties, celebrations, dances, and representations, all the *ghosts* of the people who had animated and participated in those spaces were still present in the atmosphere of the large rooms. The former cooperative was an enormous house full of memories, a container of stories that it was our responsibility to care for, so that they would not flee the place. We had to carry them forward to connect them with the new project.

The competition raised a first issue which, for us, was the key to the entire subsequent development of the project. Although the building had played such an active role in the history of the neighborhood —the site of social, cultural, and political activities for the greater part of the twentieth century, and one of the few buildings still remaining in the city that bore witness to the workers' cooperative movement as a fundamental force in the social and civic development of our culture—, in heritage conservation terms it was not protected. In other words, it could be demolished, and a new building could be erected in its place. At the time of the competition, therefore, the decision whether to preserver it or not was by no means a minor one, and especially because, in its advanced state of deterioration, it would have to be transformed into a drama center with the technical specifications —acoustical, climatic, and structural— required by a functioning contemporary theater. As a result, the decision to preserve the building, in its fragile physical state, was key: indeed, it was the beginning of the project.

But what we had in front of us was simply too striking, in an emotional sense, to allow it to be lost. It had to made use of as the basis of the new theater: we realized we couldn't tear it down but had to salvage it, to accept the existing ruin as a starting point. And we wanted to salvage everything: the physical heritage but also the emotional legacy. All of the stories that still floated around in those spaces, telling of people who had spent their time there, had to be a part of the future Sala Beckett. All our efforts were therefore devoted to maintaining those memories as part of the building, where they would form the basis of the new project.

Sala Beckett. Before moving to Poblenou, the Sala Beckett had been working for years in a much smaller space in the Gràcia neighborhood of Barcelona, doing remarkable theater and earning a reputation as a touchstone in the theater world, both national and international. So moving the Sala Beckett from Gràcia to Poblenou was another of the important themes of the project. How to remove it from where it was and take it to a new place, without disruption? How to change building and even neighborhood without the theater losing its aura, it magic, in the process?

We thought it would be helpful for the new premises to have a feeling of being inhabited, of being "in use" and previously occupied, and to achieve this we had to keep the *ghosts* of the former cooperative in the building, where they would be sure to give a friendly welcome to the new occupants and their new stories.

But the *ghosts* of the cooperative were all over the place: in the peeling plaster on the walls and in the overlapping layers of colors that could still be seen, if only fragmentarily; in the scattered furnishings and in the decorated tiles on the walls of the former kitchen; in the floor tiles, with their different designs in each room (flowers, leaves, fishes, or raindrops); in the doors and windows, with their latticework, designed and painted differently on every wall; and in the dimensions of the spaces, the six-meter heights of the rooms and the doors more than four meters tall, with colored glass and signs above them. All of this evoked another age and a different way of doing things, a different way of using space and, most definitely, of spending time.

Inventory. So that, to begin with, in a more intuitive than a reasoned way, we began to draw everything we saw, as a way of becoming familiar with it and keeping it in order, so that it could eventually become a part of the future project. We called it the Inventory: we gathered together all of elements that had been salvaged from the ravages of time,

including those that had fallen to the ground, but could be reconstructed —like the rosettes on the ceiling of the former theater, now on one of the walls of the lobby—, and we drew them with intensity, getting to know them thoroughly, one by one, and discovering in the process that each element had a particular character, that each one was different —its dimensions, its geometry, its structure—, which revealed the craftsmanship and manual skill with which it had been fabricated. Everything was of interest to us, and we explored the history of the place, because through that we were able to understand what had happened there, how things worked, and how the spaces were used. This was fundamental to really getting to know the building, and it helped us to begin designing something from that point on, as we thought about how to use all the time and heritage accumulated in it.

Nevertheless, behind the decision to draw up an inventory there was also our concern about salvaging material that, even today in the city of Barcelona, when a building is renovated, it is very common to see brought down to the street and piled up with actual trash in large containers set up in front of the site. It is surprising but, again, material that represents a significant period of time and a widespread building culture in the city during the years of the development of the *Eixample*, still remains "invisible" even today. The inventory was our way of making the contractor understand the importance of all these elements for the future project.

Ruin. But time had also acted with violence on the physical structure of the building before we arrived, and that also influenced our way of approaching it. When we entered the building it was open to the elements: the outside was inside, with wind and rain where we weren't expecting them. It was possible to see the sky and the sunlight: a feeling of unprotectedness pervaded the atmosphere. And nevertheless, those great empty spaces we found in the old structure, which generated surprising new conditions of scale and allowed for vistas that would not normally have been possible all at once through a succession of levels, were such attractive spatial qualities that they encouraged us to stay and work directly from them, without giving them up. At the same time, it was precisely the fragmentary character of some of the spaces and construction elements that gave us the freedom to go in and participate in the specific moment of the ruined building —the moment when everything seems half-built— and to move forward again from there, as from a starting point. It was a possibility that the former cooperative building, especially because it was not protected as a heritage site, opened up to us.

This unfinished, fragmentary character of the building gave rise to a very specific issue in the project we wished to undertake: an attempt to make the former cooperative building move a step forward and become a new place even better than it was before. It was a question of understanding how to treat and to retouch these walls that we liked so much, but that we had to modify in order to adapt them to the new program. What to touch and what to leave alone, what aspects of the existing building to incorporate and what to abandon, in favor of the new drama center: these were the key issues of the project. It was a task that involved a great deal of intuition, but intuition based on experience. We progressed on the basis of reactions to what we saw in front of us, in a direct, completely empirical way, while at the same time our memories dredged up unconscious affinities with solutions or references from our past, which found a place in the new project.

What most interested us at that moment was to use as much as possible of what we had inherited, attempting not to divide up its qualities: the former cooperative building was a place with generous dimensions, and we were eager to maintain those large spaces, difficult to find in other parts of Barcelona. So we used the strengths of the place as a sort of force of inertia, which allowed us not to start from zero or to invent for ourselves, but rather to respond to the ruin in front of us, so that it would make us react and progress. Its material substance and the weight of its history, the physical and emotional reality it contained, were what opposed resistance to the assaults of the project, forcing us to work both with and against it, until we had struck a balance, where what is added is not new, but rather a modification of what we had in front of us. To work as if it were ours, to design on top of it, to make it part of the project and then to continue designing in order to transform it from within, out of its own constructive, geometrical, programmatic, and emotional logic. Now it is difficult to say what is new and what used to be there before: it is a new generation of a preexisting building.

Making the most of the qualities of the precarious building we had inherited, we left it more open than we found it. An enormous void, full of light and new colors, has been inserted into the former cooperative building, so that now everything faces in that direction, activated by that center, transforming the preexisting building into a place with more energy than before. Students enter the lobby in the morning and the light greets them strongly from above: everything —the students and the space— revolves around that central void, which is on a scale of another age, back when the building was a ruin. And in the end it is like having the ruin there again: a place exposed to the exterior, to the limits between inside and outside, where it is possible to look through spaces, connecting lines and profiles of floors and walls that were originally on different planes. All the best of what the former cooperative building possessed and preserved for us has been captured in the new Sala Beckett.

Temporal Centrifuge. The overlaying of times and periods in the building as we found it made it difficult to distinguish what period each element belonged to, which was part of its charm: it allowed everyone who saw it to reconstruct, in a personal and partial way, the history of what the place had been. This condition of being open to different interpretations allowed us to approach its different histories without distancing ourselves, without separating ourselves mentally or physically from what was in front of us, but instead moving backwards or forwards in time, in order to be able to connect with that moment that most interested us about the former cooperative, in order to build our own version of its history, which was to be that of the new Sala Beckett. In this way, the new actions performed on the building join previous ones at the same level of importance, in a continuous timeline, without hierarchies, so that it is impossible to know what came first and what came later. The building presents itself as a temporal centrifuge that allows everyone who visits it to participate in this reality, where one's own memories feel an affinity with what is there. Now, everyone who looks at these walls remembers some concrete moment in his or her past, activating the space in a unique way as memory rises up to participate in a new reality. The building contains everything at once: the time of the former cooperative, the time of abandonment, and the time of the new Sala Beckett.

Plan and section of the main staircase.
Inès Martinel, March 2017.

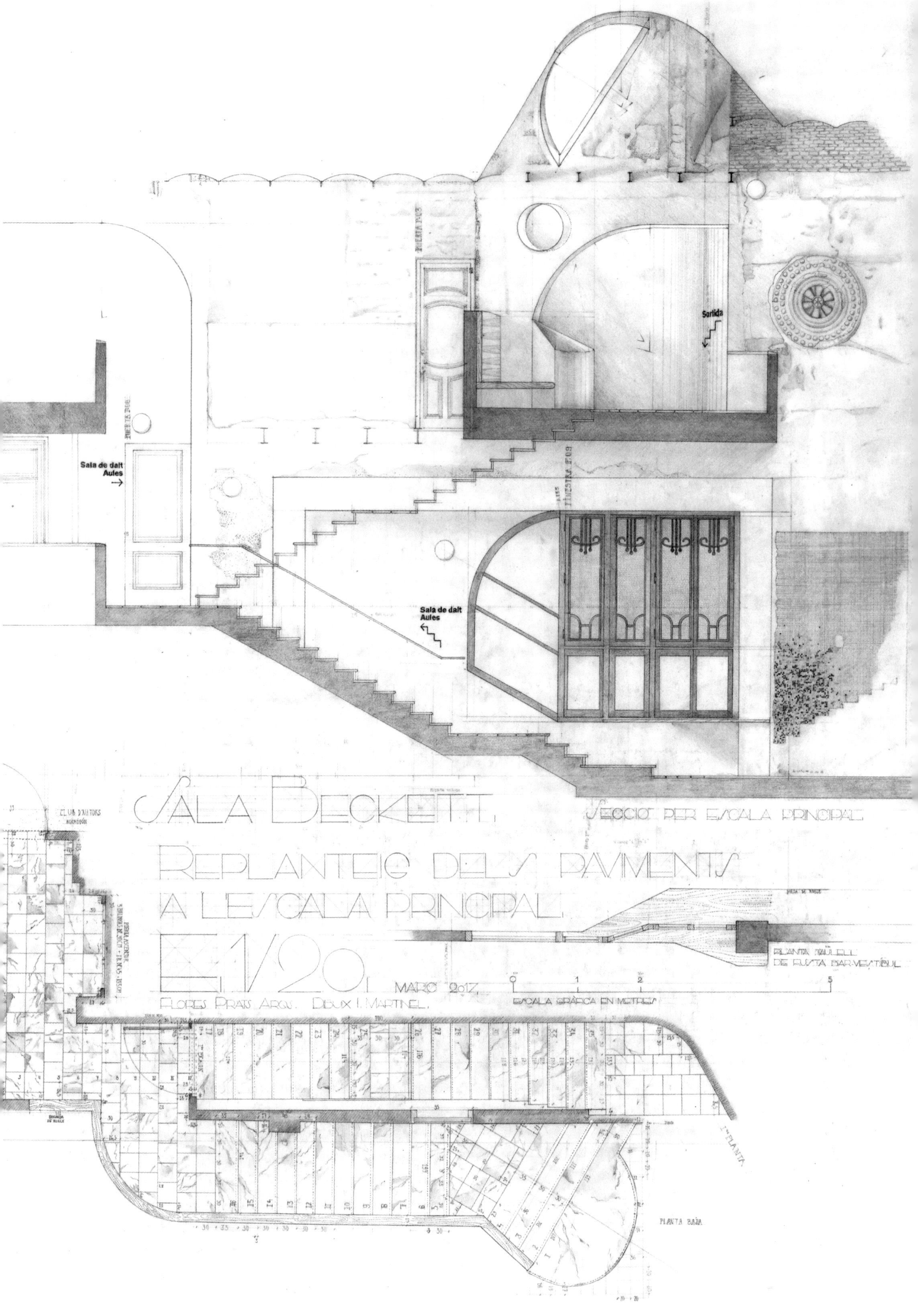

Sortida
Sala de dalt
Aules
Sala de dalt
Aules
SALA BECKETT
SECCIÓ PER ESCALA PRINCIPAL
REPLANTEIG DELS PAVIMENTS
A L'ESCALA PRINCIPAL
E.1/20
MARÇ 2017
FLORES PRATS ARQS. DIBUIX I. MARTINEL
ESCALA GRÀFICA EN METRES
PLANTA TAULELL
DE FUSTA BAR-VESTÍBUL
PLANTA BAJA
1ª PLANTA

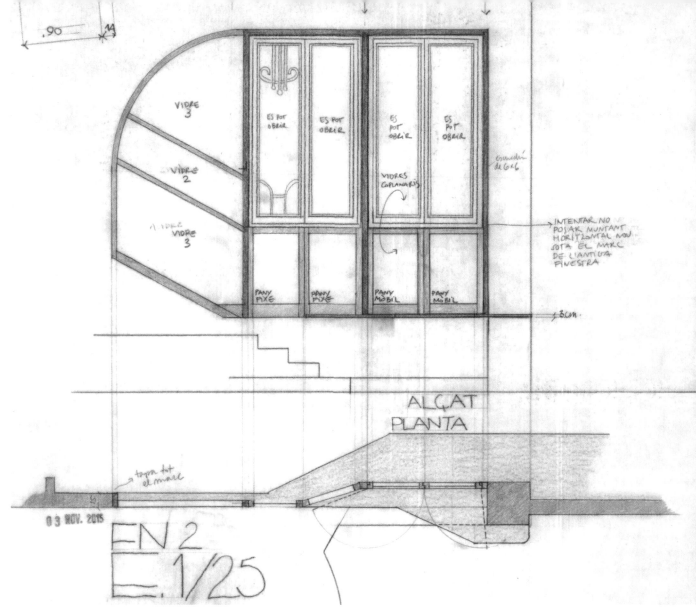

For the connection between bar and lobby we needed large doors and windows, so we chose doors more than four meters tall and windows more than two meters tall. Nevertheless, when installed in the new double-height lobby, they still lacked scale.

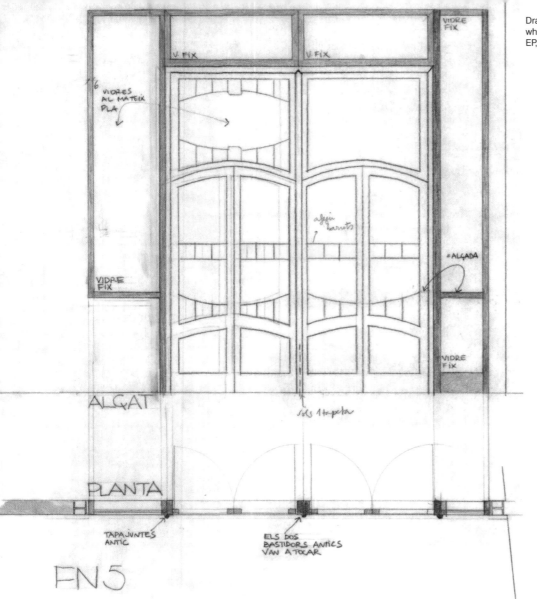

6 VIDRES AL MATEIX PLA

V. FIX

V. FIX

VIDRE FIX

algún barrots

=ALÇADA

VIDRE FIX

VIDRE FIX

ALÇAT

sols 1 tapeta

PLANTA

TAPAJUNTES ANTIC

ELS DOS BASTIDORS ANTICS VAN A TOCAR

FN 5

So we designed an extension that would accompany them and make them taller, without altering the original element.
The result was a new unit all painted the same color: a new generation of elements created out of the original ones.

Ninety percent of the doors and windows found in the preexisting building were salvaged. Most of them were modified in order to adapt them to their new locations, or to repair some part in poor condition. In the case of the upper-floor doors,

the difficulty was removing the 25 centimeters that the floor had risen, due to structural and acoustical reinforcement, without the original proportions of each element being lost.

The large windows on the façade were shortened by 25 centimeters so that the apertures on the façade would not have to be modified. In this case, the cut was made in the middle area, where there was less risk of losing the proportion of the whole.

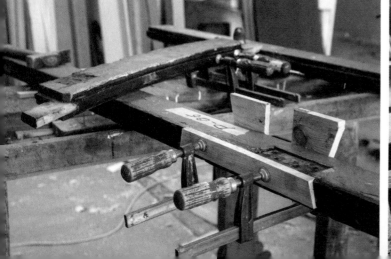

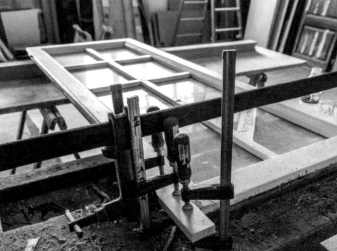

During the entire process, the carpenters restored the salvaged elements on site, avoiding the CO_2 emissions and other contaminants associated with elimination, new production, and transport.

Film *Feb 2016 - May 2017*
44 Doors and 35 Windows for the new Sala Beckett

We began to think about explaining this action of reusing elements with a stop motion movie, similar to those used on our Web page. We thought that a moving image would help to explain how these pieces moved through the building through the design process: the way they were in the air for a while— because we did not know where they were finally going to be relocated— and the long path that all of them had to take from the existing position to the new one, most of the time changing the floor and also their function.

We prepared the plans of the building and its elements at 1:50 scale to be able to move doors, windows or the wooden staircase easily with our hands. We started making all the elements in thin cardboard, to which we then pasted the colored drawings, leaving on them the code that each element had in the original inventory. Some of the elements, such as those that changed color during the construction, were manufactured twice, so that we could explain its initial and final state in the film. Then we hung all the plans on a studio wall, placing the same plan in parallel position twice to be able to move the elements horizontally, trying to be as clear as possible when explaining how these pieces changed position.

EA 03

We filmed the promenade of these elements by provisionally attaching the pieces to the plans with Blu-Tack, moving them very slowly, step by step, from one plan to another. So, the film is made with hundreds of photos of each small movement of these pieces in the plans, so that this movement seems continuous.

The film begins by showing the first floor of Sala Beckett, since it was the floor that contained the largest number of doors and windows to be relocated. While we were thinking about where to place these elements in the new building, the doors and windows were flying in our heads, trying to decide their final location. Therefore, the film shows this journey, a flight that allows them to land in a new location.

D 35 WINDOWS
SALA BECKETT
& PRATS

The film shows all the carpentry elements that remained in the building, but in different situations and levels. They become the characters of the film, all of them different: small, elegant, large, representative... Each one of them is

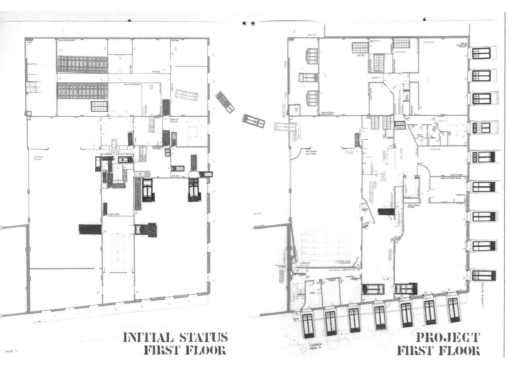

INITIAL STATUS FIRST FLOOR

PROJECT FIRST FLOOR

INITIAL STAT FIRST FLO

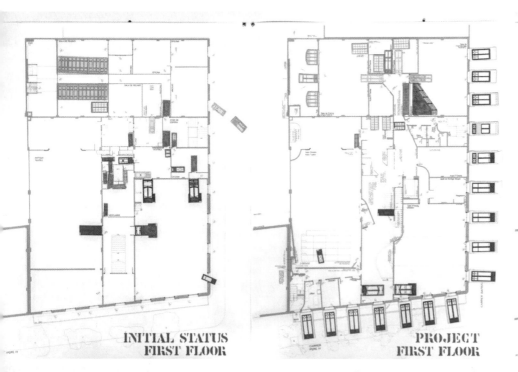

INITIAL STATUS FIRST FLOOR

PROJECT FIRST FLOOR

INITIAL STAT FIRST FLO

identified with a number and they are shown in the final credits as though actors of a movie. This film was made six years after having done the inventory, allowing us after so much time to retrace the path of all the doors and windows throughout the design process.

PROJECT
FIRST FLOOR

INITIAL STATUS
FIRST FLOOR

PROJECT
FIRST FLOOR

PROJECT
GROUND FLOOR

35
RECOVERED
WINDOWS

F03

F12

F15

P27

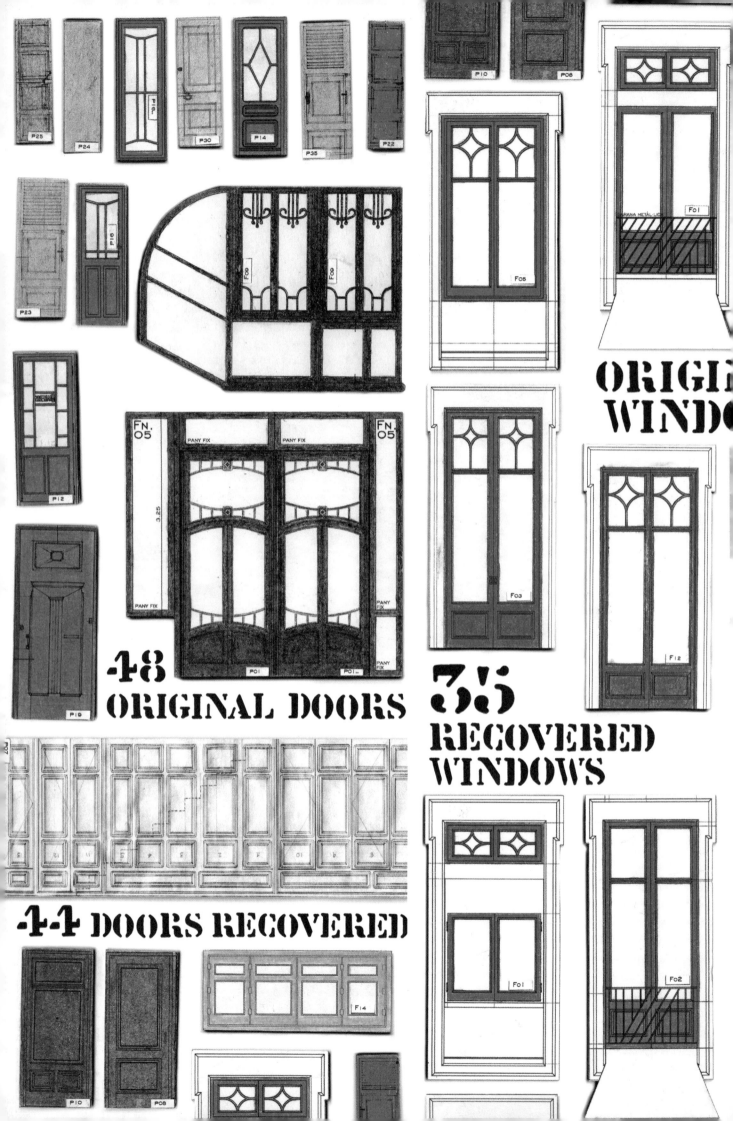

48 ORIGINAL DOORS

44 DOORS RECOVERED

35 RECOVERED WINDOWS

ORIGINAL WINDOWS

WINDOWS

FLORES & PRATS ARQS

SHOT AT THE STUDIOS
OF 12 TRAFALGAR STREET
FEBRUARY-MAY 2016

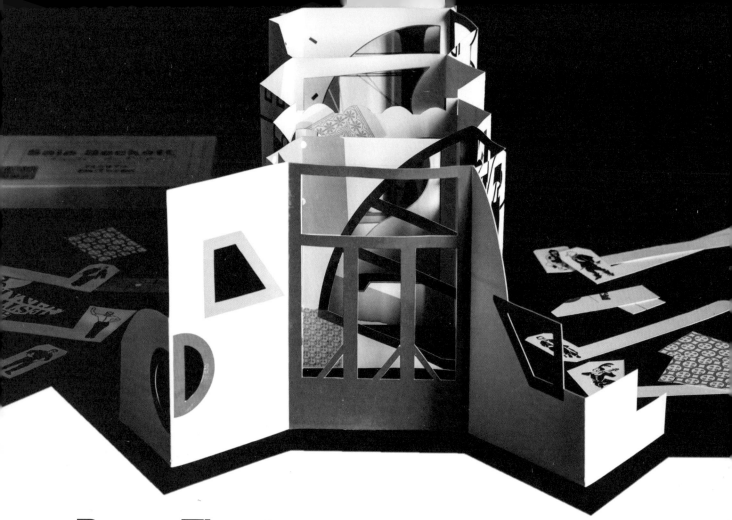

Paper Theater *Jan 2017 – April 2018*
Soraya Smithson

"In January (2017) I had a site visit, and I also attended a performance. And I was in the office and I had free access to the drawings and the models from early stages, and in a way I just then started playing with different elements, from what I've taken photographs of here and what I had seen, and then looking at their drawings and their models... kind of filtering through. One of the things that kept recurring in my mind was that Eva and Ricardo had done a very intense inventory of every aspect that remained in this building from the tiles, the doors, the windows, and they had made good drawings and worked out... and in a way rescued them. Because they saw this building as something that was an evolving history, that it started as one thing and that it has been through many alterations and occupations, and this was the current occupation, so you are layering history... They wanted to take the history that it had... and retain that but revive it for this new occupation. So, the doors and the tiles were part of that, how they were, how they reached the design and interpretation... it was a very evident and obvious piece for me to pick up on and want to show in an object I was making. In a way the celebration of this building."

First versions and tests.
Barcelona, January 2017.

"I am interested in the windows at the entrance of Sala Beckett because they are about how you move from one space to another. In the moment you go to the theater you are presented with this amazing little window onto an imaginary little time capsule, and they perform in front of you and then they disappear off the site through the doors and you are left and it's over... You open this window and you watch something and then you close the window, so there's always a bit of that. So, I think this building speaks of all of those things, and that's what I wanted to express by making the work."

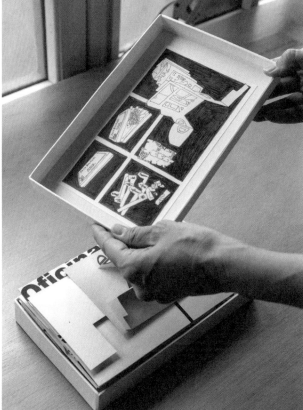

"There are other elements of art here, each one folds flat and will go in a box, so in a way you get a box and then it has other things inside, and it becomes a kind of something to play with and so it can occupy space and also be returned to be flat, small, almost like a book."

"Eva and Ricardo wanted me to do a bit of an intervention, because a lot of my work is about making objects that you can almost circulate around, and they take up space, and maybe ask you about how you interact with objects, and maybe making the objects almost into a subject, so they are real things and not just inanimate. And the crossover between the Victorian peepshows which were those layers of little dioramas that you look through had always intrigued me, partly because they are always of small size and in a way it feels ideal for a child because they get this little small view that only you are enclosed in this little world, and the Pollock theater, where you can manipulate it a little, change the stage sets and play again like dolls. A dolls theater that you can make up your own story but with these sort of set drops."

Fragments of the interview to Soraya Smithson for the film *Scale 1:5*.

E.1/50

SALA BECKET
ESTAT ACTU
PORTES I FINESTRES EXISTEN
FLORES & PRATS ARCHS DIBUXAT PER M ALLEVI I I MARTI
FEBRER 2016 I MARÇ 2

We frequently think about how to document the processes of projects in order to make a record of the actions carried out, and also to be able to explain them. In the case of the elements of carpentry that we found in the old Cooperative, we made two axonometric drawings: one of the existing states and another of the final state of the building. The two drawings show the building as a base. In the first one, all the elements identified at the beginning of the project are located, and in the second it shows where they ended up in the final project.

All the reused carpentry came from the first floor of the building, except for the red door on the ground floor on Batista Street. The existing doors and windows were sufficient in number to be distributed among the two floors of the building.

Most of the walls are drawn as transparent planes, like an x-ray, to reveal the various elements: doors, windows and tiles. Some of the elements can be tracked along the journey they have made to their new position.

The wooden staircase of the former cafe connected with a mezzanine where the members of the Cooperative were enrolled in sports or cultural activities. When the Café changed to become the Rehearsal Room, this mezzanine was no longer useful and therefore neither was the staircase. So, we thought that this mezzanine of 115 m2 could be useful as a dramaturgy classroom.

We dismantled the staircase and passed it through to the classroom's vestibule. We also removed the former brown access door to the mezzanine and passed it through to the opposite side, at the head of the relocated staircase. We painted the staircase and the door the same color as the rest of the classrooms, so that it did not stand out. Now this space is another classroom.

The new staircase at the first-floor patio takes the same geometry as the former one but with reduced steepness, in order to adapt to regulations. When we drew it again, we made one of the landings coincide with a window of the mezzanine; we turned this window into a door and now one can go out from that mezzanine to the patio through the staircase. The railing is made from the leftovers of railings from the former patio, which are now connected to make a longer one. The old sections that were reused had a steeper slope, so we added profiles below and above to get a set that meets the regulatory heights and gaps. In the end everything was painted in a single color to unify it.

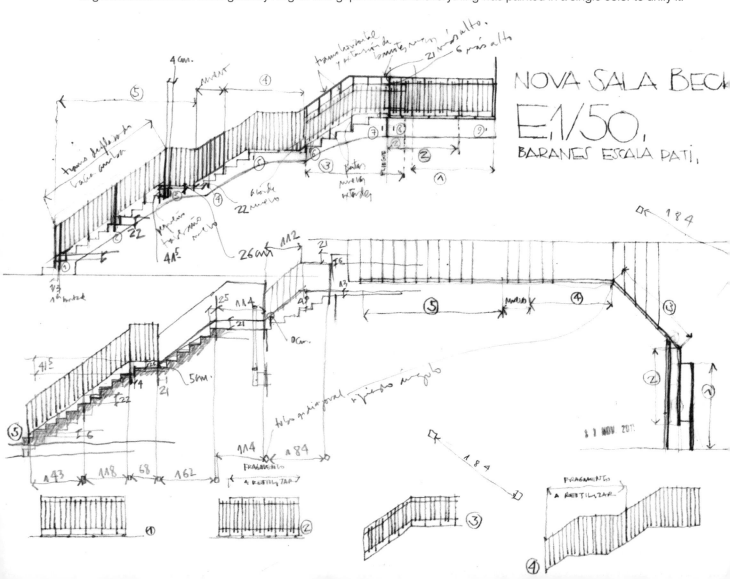

The patio on the first floor was expanded to twice its original size, bringing light to the centre of the plan and ensuring that it reaches the ground floor through the large openings. The railings of these openings are finished off with a piece of wood that turns behind the wall of the vestibule and enters the classrooms area, articulating the passage between the two zones. The yellow tile flooring also crosses this border between vestibule and classrooms, as does the patio window which folds and illuminates the long bench where the students memorize their lines. In the end, the passage from the vestibule to the classrooms is continuous because of this threshold loaded with activity, light and crossed views.

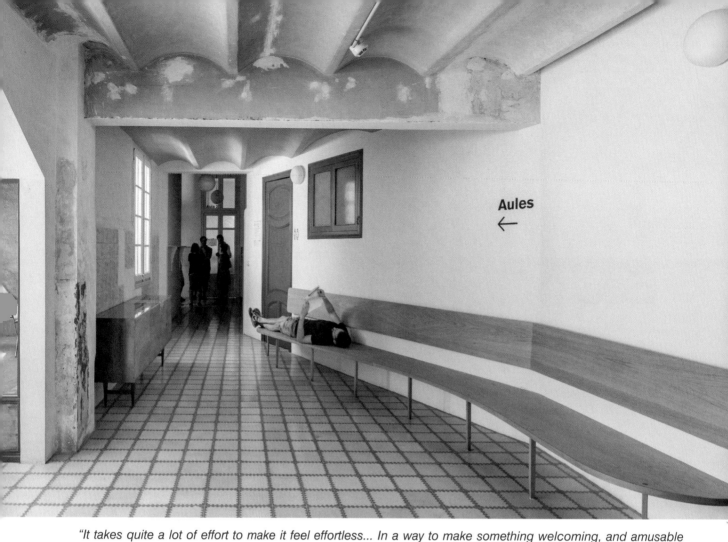

"It takes quite a lot of effort to make it feel effortless... In a way to make something welcoming, and amusable and inhabitable you have to do an awful lot of work, because otherwise it becomes kind of sterile and a barrier to feeling that you can come in here, and you can move the furniture around and you can occupy it...

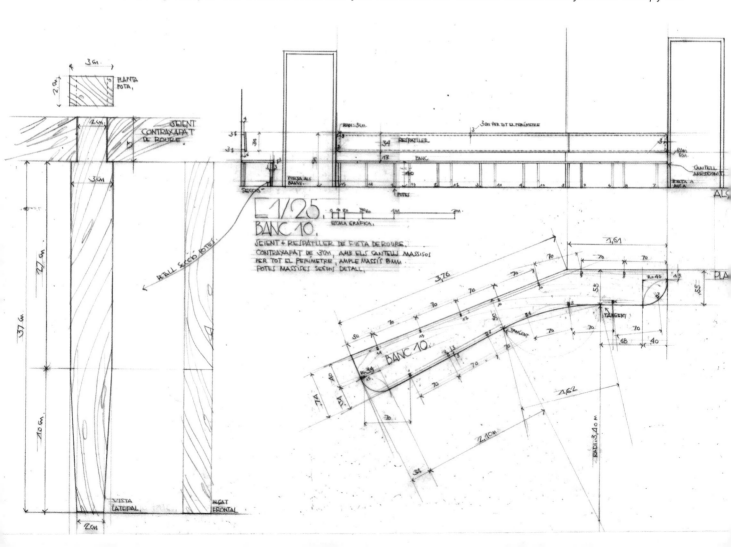

...and particularly in a theater space you want people to feel they can really occupy the space and move and articulate their bodies in relation to their space. So, I think they worked really hard to make it sort of loose, and playful and joyous as a space ultimately to occupy." Soraya Smithson. Interview for the film *Scale 1:5.*

"Part of Sala Beckett's charm is that there are elements that appear and that you do not know... 'is that architecture or is it...?' Of course, if you lean against a wall —say you are half resting—, at that moment you are using it as an element of rest, or if you lean on a railing, then that is furniture. Sometimes people refer to furniture as something that is movable, something that is independent, but this is perhaps a partial definition. I believe that playing with

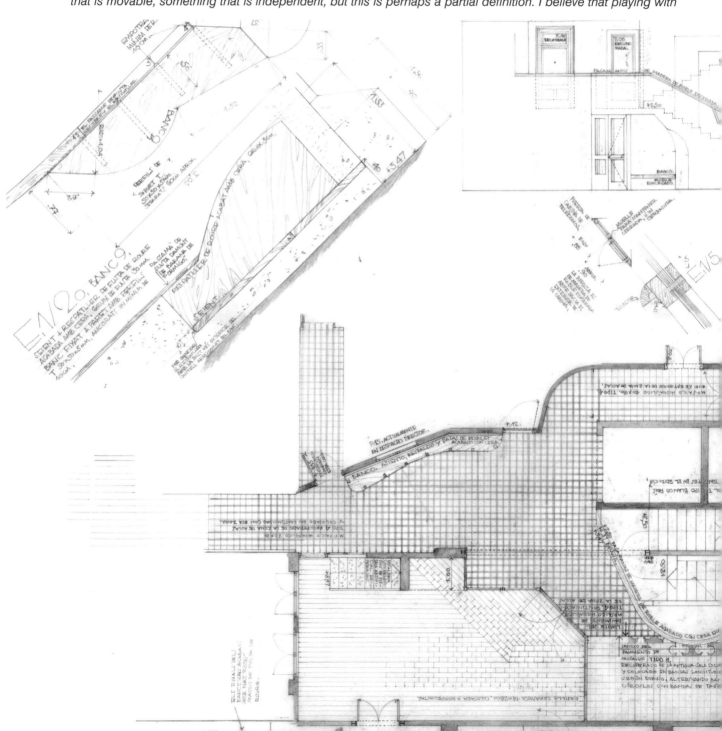

these areas that you do not know very well whether they do one role or another… this is life too, right? And perhaps in this sense you also recognize much of their interest in Jujol and Modernism, where you see these types of situations, suddenly a wall that is a bench and then another thing, that there is no clear distinction that 'this is this, and it serves for this.'" Curro Claret. Interview for the film *Scale 1:5.*

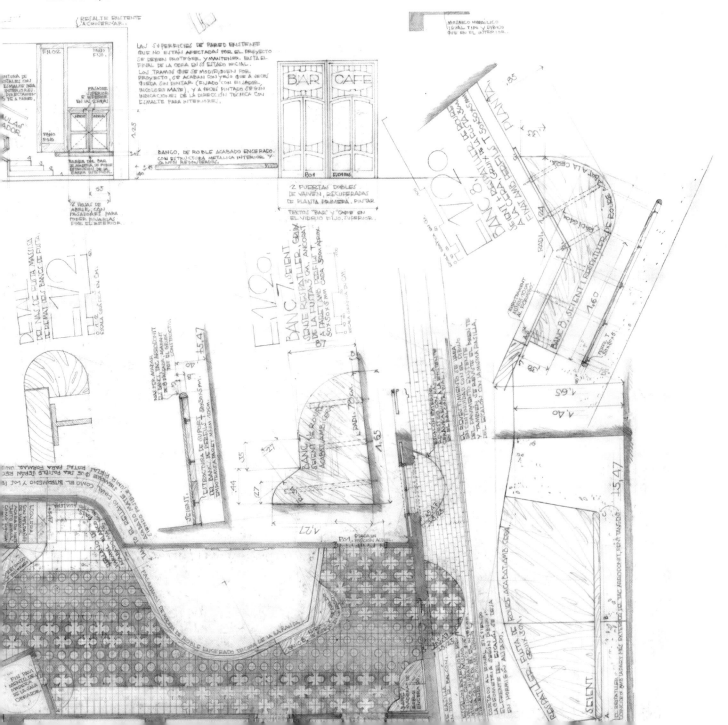

The red velvet sofa provides a very interior situation: it is cosy, soft, it holds you, it is waiting for you... The frame within which it was placed was originally open, letting the counter of the grocery store of the Cooperative pass beneath it. When we were drawing its enclosure, we bordered it in relief and with a depth that recall sits earlier life. The bench is placed inside this kind of niche: it is a small stage or camera that embraces you and creates an almost private place within the larger vestibule space around. When you sit down you leave the vestibule and it feels like standing behind scenery watching what goes on outside, in the vestibule, which itself has now becomes a theater full of people to watch.

"The theme of celebration is probably something that when people think of architecture or think of a space, does not appear so easily, but in the end, it is something vital. If we do not have the hope or the recognition that things have value and can get better, and that there is reason to recognize this and to celebrate or to enjoy this, then of course, there is almost no life, there is no next step. I would never have said it, but, I think it is very beautiful to understand that precisely what a theater should be —a space for questioning, for reflection, for talking about difficult things—, at the same time is a space to recognize the full value of life and the importance of enjoying and taking advantage of the moment. Then, to what extent do objects also accompany this moment, invite, and almost predispose, or hint, give clues... of course we all know that a stool is not just for sitting, right? A lot of things happen on a stool, it communicates a lot of things, preparing us to behave in a certain way, which is a role that it is fair to expect of it, and one that it must accomplish. Some people make it more evident and others not so much, and in this sense I'm sure that with Eva and Ricardo you recognize that there is a kind of life, of joy, of willing that people have a good time there, of being at ease, and to make this celebration appear." Curro Claret. Interview for the film *Scale 1:5.*

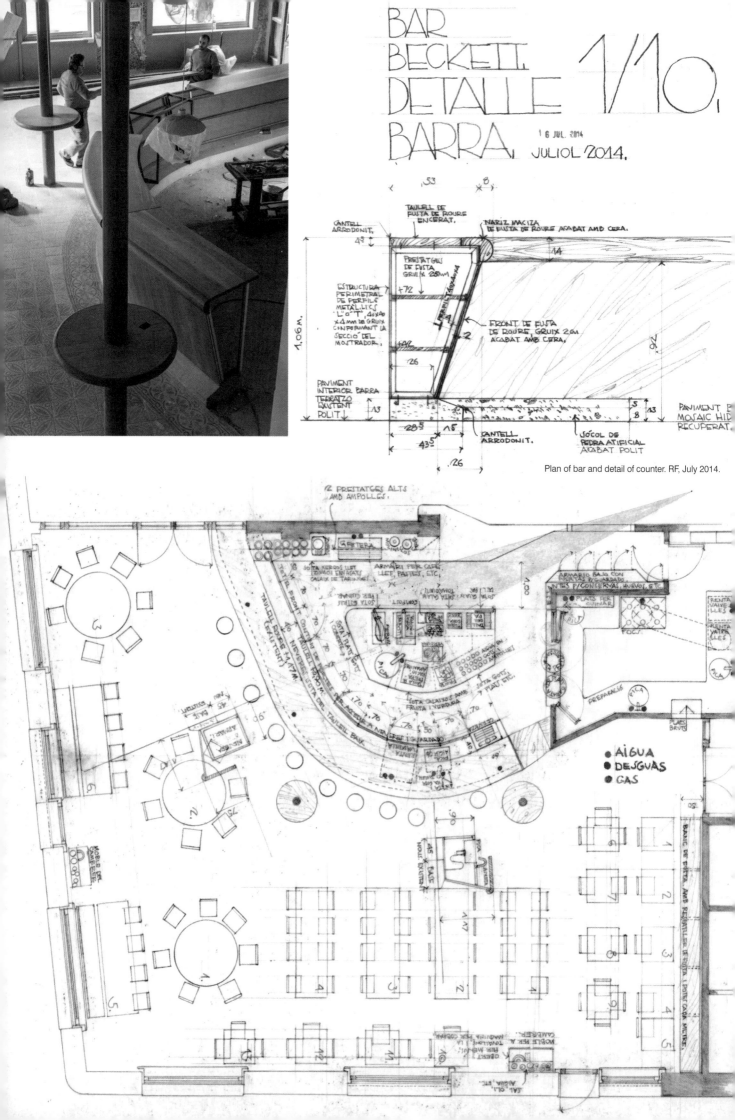

BAR BECKETT DETALLE 1/10.
BARRA. JULIOL 2014.

16 JUL 2014

Plan of bar and detail of counter. RF, July 2014.

"The bar is people; the bar is life. The bar is where things happen, where the masks fall if they are still in place, where total relaxation occurs. Eating and drinking is what we always need to achieve a level of calm, relaxed communication, one to one. A place without a bar is never a relaxed place. I went to University and spent more hours in the bar than anywhere else. It's the bar where you learn things, where you discover people, where you fall in love, where you fight, where ideas are born... A theater without a bar is a dead theater. And in fact, the bar was the last thing we opened in this building and we were all waiting for it with enthusiasm. Until the bar was opened, the Beckett was not working as it should. With a glass of wine and a piece of tortilla everything suddenly makes sense. Whenever someone asked me if the bar was important, I said the bar should serve to seduce. If the tortilla made in the bar is good, we will make people go into the theater. But it must be a first point of catching people who may not be interested in the theater or perhaps have not stopped to think that it might interest them. 'So, as a start, try the tortilla and then...'" Toni Casares. Interview for the film *Scale 1:5*.

"Giving this generous space to the activity of the bar is one of the great successes, because the bar is communicating with the neighborhood. It has independent entrances to the theater but everything is visible, therefore, the people from outside who come to this bar already know that it is a theater bar, seeing the face of Samuel Beckett hanging there in the bar, seeing that it is open directly to the Theater Downstairs, with the lockers by the door on the side... This connection makes the bar end up being the core as has been demonstrated: since it has been opened, they cannot meet demand and must expand the number of staff. This is a wonderful success, but also for us to have a meeting at the bar: because we are here and then suddenly will say 'Hey, let's continue the meeting over a coffee', and we go downstairs and we are inside the theater." Sergi Belbel. Interview for the film *Scale 1:5*.

Plan, cross section and elevation of wooden banister base of the main stairway, on the ground floor. EP, January 2015.

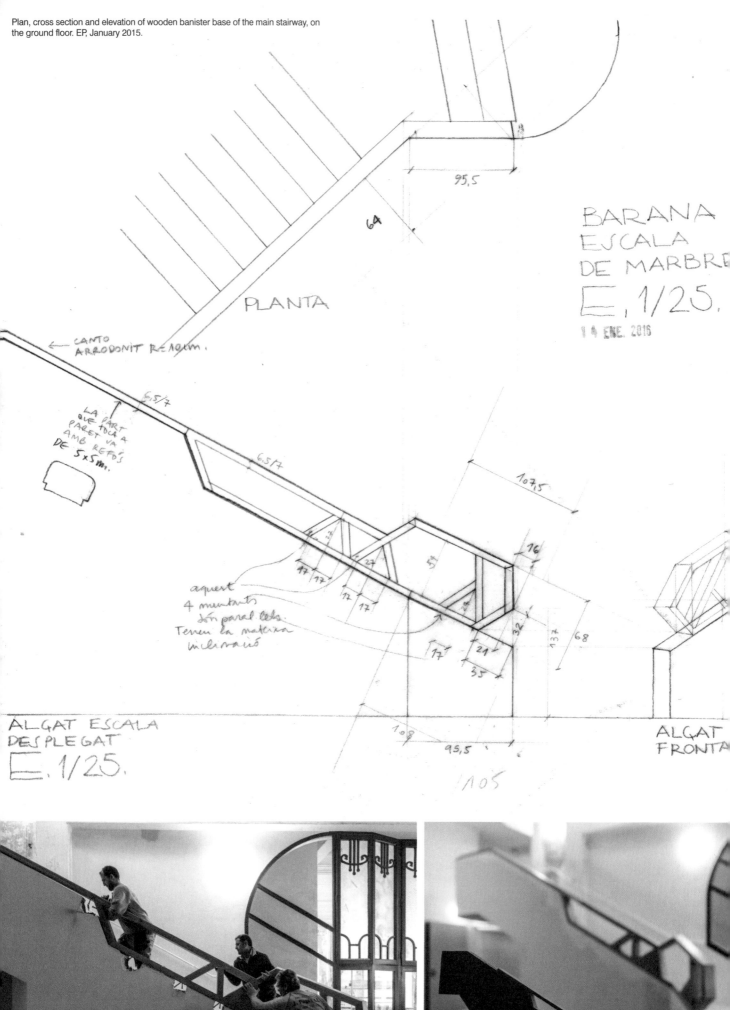

PLANTA

95,5

64

BARANA
ESCALA
DE MARBRE
E, 1/25.
1 4 ENE. 2015

← CANTO
ARRODONIT REAGIM.

6,5/7

LA PART
QUE TOCA A
PARET VA
AMB REFOS
DE 5x5m.

6,5/7

107,5

16

54

17 17

27

12 17

32

137

68

aquest
4 muntants
són paralels.
Tenen la mateixa
inclinació

17

21

35

ALGAT ESCALA
DESPLEGAT
E, 1/25.

108

95,5

1.05

ALGAT
FRONTA

"Knowing that the walls could be left in quite a state of ruin —with the difficulty that this brings, that normally when the wall is like this you do not approach because you think that you will have a piece of wall stuck to your clothes or that you will spoil something...—, we were interested in placing between the people and the walls a series of solid wood pieces, waxed oak that feels good to the touch, in places where you could sit or seek support: benches, railings, shelves, bar..." Eva Prats. Interview for the film *Scale 1:5*.

"One of the things that I find very positively intriguing in the Beckett is the game that they have made of taking things they had and using them in another way, so that in the end one does not know the reality... 'but was this exactly like this or not?' And I think this is very beautiful, the freedom to use something that existed before in the way that seems most appropriate to you, without the risk of: 'no, no, this was like that and we cannot touch it.'" How this use mixes and blurs what it was exactly before, it seems fantastic to me. When they had to do new things, they have seized this moment, selecting a material that they thought had the best conditions to take this role, and of course, everyone can see this. With all the new intervention they have done with wood it is evident that it has not come from the building, that it does not have a past, you can distinguish clearly what they have added, as in the case of these wooden elements, in comparison with others that came from before... If they had found some big wooden pieces maybe they would have made the furniture with that, I mean, I believe that it is the circumstances that have made them make it this way. There are also elements like the counter of bar that is all about contact and touch, but maybe what you find to fabricate it does not have these qualities... The same with a bench, where your hands make contact, you move them and find yourself playing with what it is..." Curro Claret. Interview for the film *Scale 1:5*.

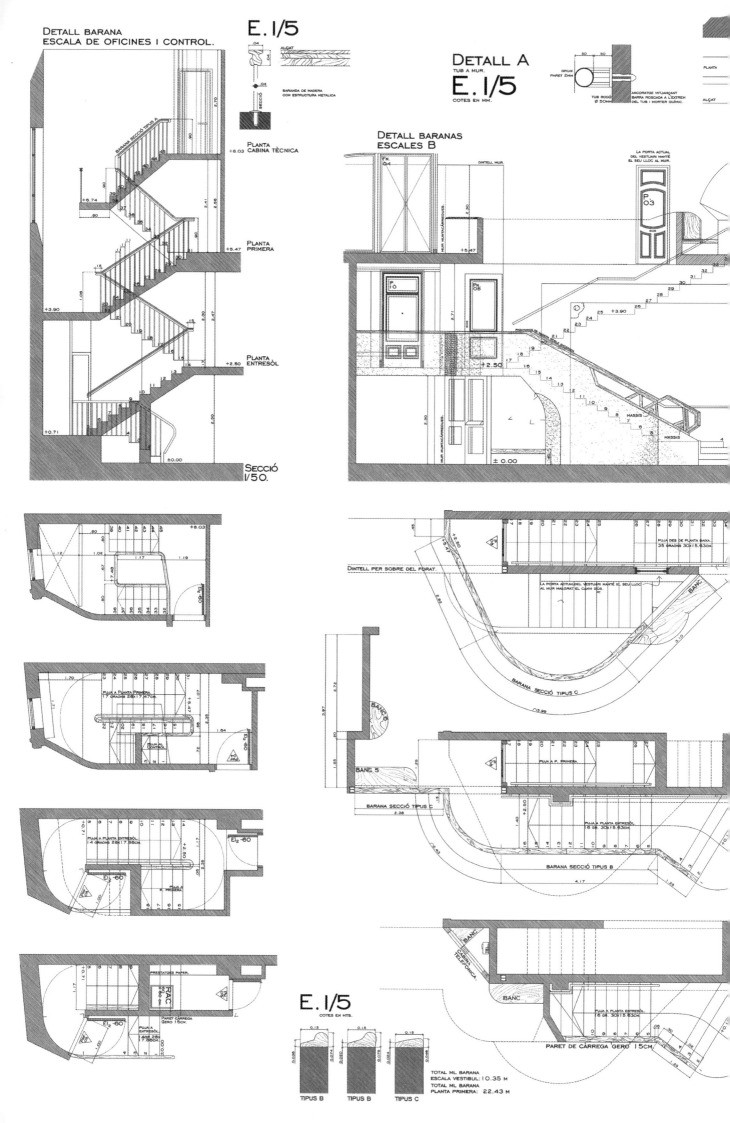

DETALL BARANA
ESCALA DE OFICINES I CONTROL.

E. 1/5

ALÇAT

BARANDA DE MADERA
COM ESTRUCTURA METALICA

SECCIÓ

PLANTA
+8.03 CABINA TÈCNICA

+6.74

+3.90

PLANTA
+5.47 PRIMERA

PLANTA
+2.50 ENTRESÒL

+0.71

±0.00

SECCIÓ
1/50.

DETALL A
TUB A MUR.
E. 1/5
COTES EN MM.

GRUIX
PARET 2MM

PLANTA

ALÇAT

TUB RODÓ
Ø 50MM

ANCORATGE MITJANÇANT
BARRA ROSCADA A L'EXTREM
DEL TUB I MORTER QUÍMIC.

DETALL BARANAS
ESCALES B

LA PORTA ACTUAL
DEL VESTUARI MANTÉ
EL SEU LLOC AL MUR.

P.03

DINTELL. MUR.

+5.47

+3.90

+2.50

±0.00

MASSÍS

MASSÍS

DINTELL PER SOBRE DEL FORAT.

+2.50

PUJA DES DE PLANTA BAIXA
35 GRAONS 30X15.63CM.

BANC

LA PORTA ACTUAL DEL VESTUARI MANTÉ EL SEU LLOC
AL MUR MALGRAT EL CANVI D'ÙS.

BARANA SECCIÓ TIPUS C

BANC 5

+8.03

FUJA A PLANTA PRIMERA
17 GRAONS 28X17.47CM.

FUJA AL
CONTROL

PUJA A PLANTA ENTRESÒL
14 GRAONS 28X17.36CM.

FUJA A
F. PRIMERA

BANC 5

BARANA SECCIÓ TIPUS C

PUJA A F. PRIMERA

+2.50

PUJA A PLANTA ENTRESÒL
18 GR. 30X15.63CM.

BARANA SECCIÓ TIPUS B

PRESTATGES PAPER.

RAC

PARET CÀRREGA
GERO 15CM.

PUJA A
ENTRESÒL
GR. 28X
17.36CM.

BANC

CABINA
TELEFONICA.

BANC

PUJA A PLANTA ENTRESÒL
18 GR. 30X15.63CM.

PARET DE CÀRREGA GERO 15CM.

E. 1/5
COTES EN MTS.

TIPUS B   TIPUS B   TIPUS C

TOTAL ML BARANA
ESCALA VESTIBUL: 10.35 M
TOTAL ML BARANA
PLANTA PRIMERA: 22.43 M

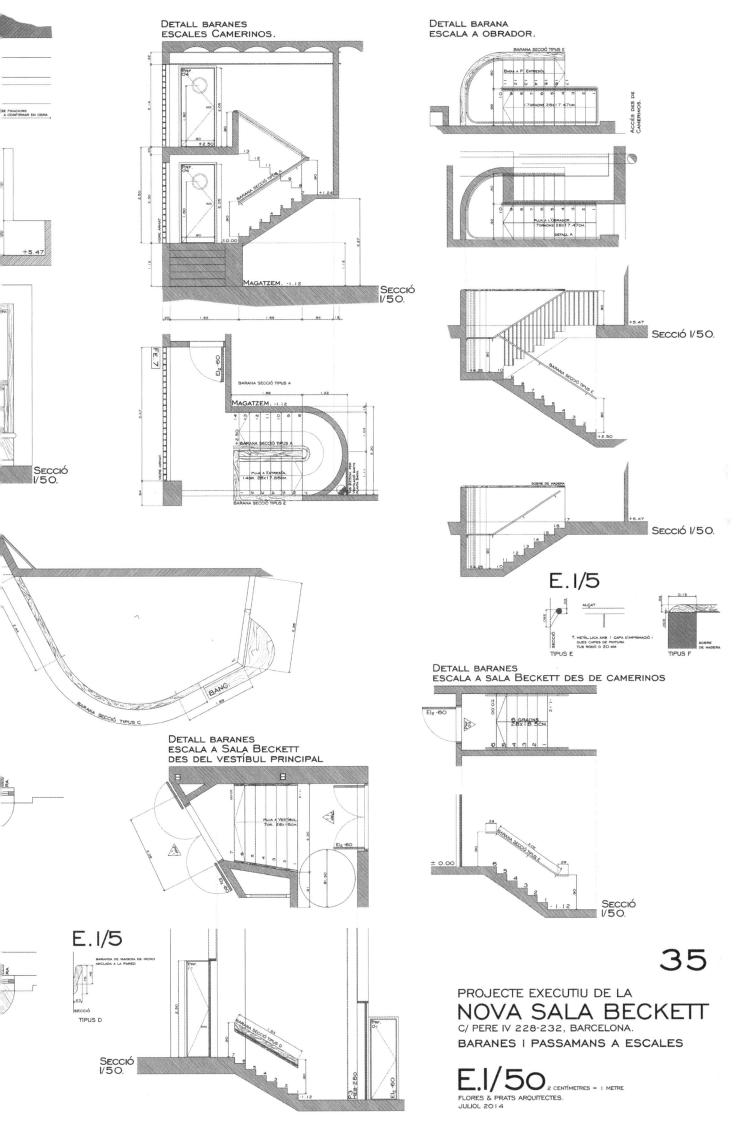

DETALL BARANES ESCALES CAMERINOS.

DETALL BARANA ESCALA A OBRADOR.

BARANA SECCIÓ TIPUS E

BARANA A P. ENTRESÒL

7 GRAONS 28×17.47CM

ACCÉS DES DE CAMERINOS.

PUJA A L'OBRADOR. 7 GRAONS 28×17.47CM

DETALL A

SECCIÓ 1/50.

BARANA SECCIÓ TIPUS E

+5.47

SECCIÓ 1/50.

SOBRE DE MADERA

+5.47

SECCIÓ 1/50.

MAGATZEM. -1.12

SECCIÓ 1/50.

FE. 7

BARANA SECCIÓ TIPUS A

MAGATZEM. -1.12

BARANA SECCIÓ TIPUS A

PUJA A ENTRESÒL. 14 GR. 28×17.86CM.

BARANA SECCIÓ TIPUS E

E. 1/5

ALÇAT

T. METÀL·LICA AMB 1 CAPA D'IMPRIMACIÓ I DUES CAPES DE PINTURA TUB RODÓ Ø 20 MM

SECCIÓ

TIPUS E

SOBRE DE MADERA

TIPUS F

DETALL BARANES ESCALA A SALA BECKETT DES DE CAMERINOS

El₂ -60

6 GRAONS. 28×18.5CM.

BARANA SECCIÓ TIPUS E

± 0.00

-1.12

SECCIÓ 1/50.

BARANA SECCIÓ TIPUS C

BANC

DETALL BARANES ESCALA A SALA BECKETT DES DEL VESTÍBUL PRINCIPAL

PUJA A VESTÍBUL 7 GR. 28×16CM.

El₂ -60

SECCIÓ 1/50.

E. 1/5

BARANDA DE MADERA DE IROKO ANCLADA A LA PARED

SECCIÓ

TIPUS D

BARANA SECCIÓ TIPUS D

SECCIÓ 1/50.

35

PROJECTE EXECUTIU DE LA
NOVA SALA BECKETT
C/ PERE IV 228-232, BARCELONA.
BARANES I PASSAMANS A ESCALES

E.1/50 2 CENTÍMETRES = 1 METRE
FLORES & PRATS ARQUITECTES.
JULIOL 2014

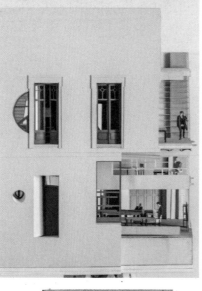

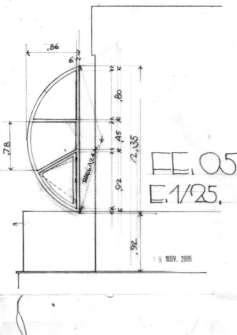

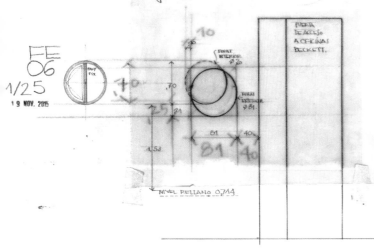

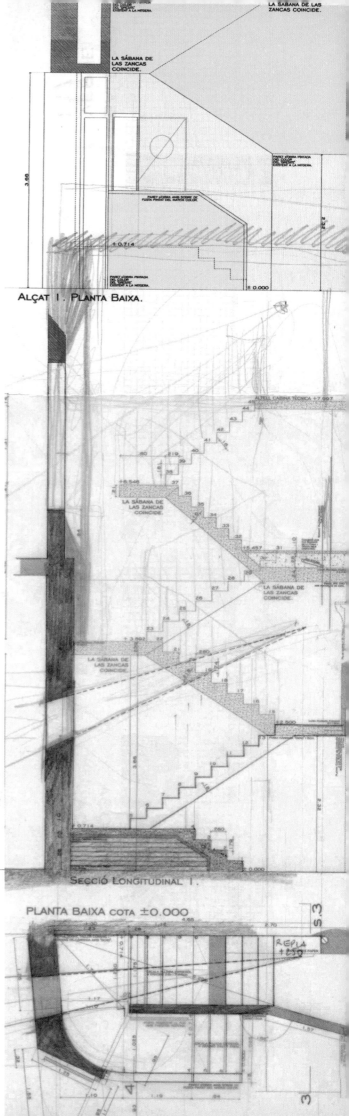

ALÇAT 1. PLANTA BAIXA.

FE. 05
E.1/25.

19 NOV. 2015

FE 06
1/25
19 NOV. 2015

SECCIÓ LONGITUDINAL 1.

PLANTA BAIXA cota ±0.000

The building needed a new fire protected staircase to adapt to the current regulations. It was decided that this would be placed at the corner of the facade of Pere IV abutting the neighboring building, connecting to the offices area. Two new apertures in the main façade help the staircase receive natural light and ventilation. Throughout the day this is the staircase which connects the ground floor, mezzanine and first floor offices, in addition to joining the two floors of dressing rooms and giving secret access for actors to the theater room on the first floor and the control cabin.

The entrance door to the offices is attached to this staircase, so it is a faster and more private access offered by the building to those who know how it works.

Section of the fire protected staircase and two wooden windows at Pere IV Street. EP + RF, Nov 2015.

At the time of starting to fabricate the signage for the facade there were some doubts about its size and location, so we decided to manufacture a few letters in thick cardboard at 1:1 scale in our studio, paint them black and, with the help of the builder, place them on top of the cornice to be able to see them from street level and decide on the design. Each letter is a box of metal sheet painted black, containing LED lighting inside. The front face of the letters is made of methacrylate, appearing black during the day and white at night when the lights shine from behind.

Defining the painting of metal shutters in ground floor windows. RF, Oct 2015

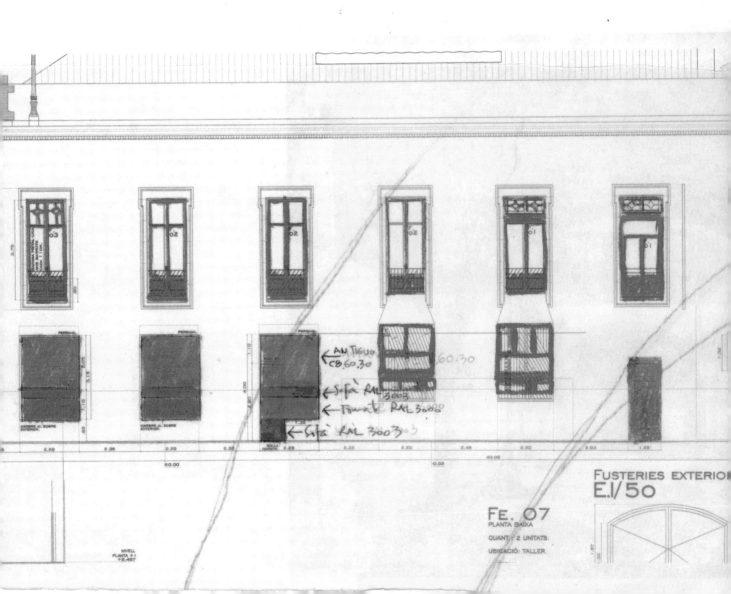

Detail of a door-window of the bar. RF, July 2015.

PLANTA A +3.30 M.

PLANTA A +2.30 M.

OB79

PROJECTE EXECUTIU DE LA
NOVA SALA BECKETT
C/ PERE IV 228-232, BARCELONA.

Finestra i Porta Tipus al Bar

E.1/10
FLORES & PRATS ARQUITECTES
5 AGOSTO 2015

PLANTA A +0.30 M.

SALA BECKETT AL POBLE NOU.
FUSTERIES DE FUSTA AL BAR DE PLANTA BAIXA.
DETALL FINESTRA-PORTA.
FLORES I PRATS ARQS. ESCALA 1/10.
JULIOL 2015.

SECCIÓ PER FINESTRA

ALÇAT EXTERIOR

PLANTA A +1.30 M.

Sala Beckett

What we found in the building, even in a much deteriorated state, stayed inside there. Probably because of this, the former members of the Cooperative who still live in the area and have re-entered the building, now a centre of dramaturgy, have recognized it as their own. Everything has been moved, but it also still seems that nothing has happened since they left the building about 30 years ago. The building now has a huge bar in its corner, with a row of large windows opening to the street. This makes it a very public place, so they usually meet there and those who are interested in the theater can see the most current shows that are on.

After the initial tests of labelling directly on the walls during the first occupation, we were able to collaborate with the designer Enric Jardí to decide sizes and positions of the lettering and signs that the building would need. We printed and tested them for a while to see if they were clear, if something was missing, or the positioning was wrong. When everything was checked, we painted them.

"It happens all the time that someone enters my office and makes a mistake thinking it was a rehearsal space, or I'm the one that makes the mistake when interrupting the rehearsal of a company, or someone from the bar looks for the toilets and does not know... I like that, because it makes the building alive, it makes people interact with the building. Both the building and the users themselves explain each other, and that is interesting for me." Toni Casares. Interview for the film *Scale 1:5*.

How were we supposed to paint there, next to a ruin that was already "perfectly painted"? We thought that the best way was to break the new walls into several colors, so that they fit the fragmented rhythm of the ruin where never just a single color is seen, and where the eye is used to receiving a large amount of information.

Instructions for the painters on which colors to apply in each part of the building.

We did not want a jump to occur when we looked from the old to the new walls, because the walk through the building was a coherent experience, without differentiating between what was already there and what was added.

Color definition on top of photos of the construction site. Lucía Gutiérrez, December 2015.

As we had done in the first occupation, we decided the colors by scenes, independently in each space, thinking from scene to scene in relation to those we found in each area: it could be the general color of the wall, or the one of a detail, of a door, the tiles on the wall or the floor tiles... we found clues in what was already there, in what had resisted the work or had moved and now helped us to decide how to repaint walls and ceilings. The photos of the construction site guided us in fixing those scenes inside the building, and so we tested the painting of new colors on top of them.

"...you notice in this building an interesting color arrangement that happens all around the building, and that is partly because of the history, because most of the doors had already been painted. Eva and Ricardo took that palette and kept the original windows and doors and the colors that they found in them, but then reiterated those colors on the walls and ceilings and you can read that in the building when you go around as I did, into the non-public areas

...you can see that there's a flow of green color, where the actors are coming up and down, the staircase between the dressing rooms and the public space is much redder... and then it moves into whites and pinks in the areas that are both public and private, or where the actors can join... So the colors are also making a sort of map."
Soraya Smithson. Interview for the film *Scale 1:5.*

Study of colors for the ground floor vestibule. RF, Dec 2015

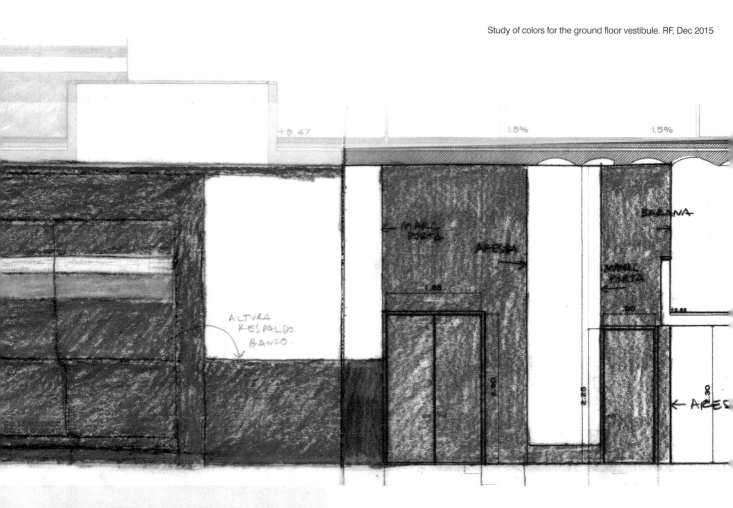

The Sala Beckett competition coincided with a study trip we had organized with the School of Architecture of Barcelona to take our students to draw four houses in the ancient city of Pompeii, near Naples. We spent hours inside observing them, drawing and taking measurements.

Toni Casares at the ruins of Pompeii, 2016.

Later, at the moment of having to decide how to paint the new walls of the theater, we remembered the rooms of those houses —the amount of information recorded there, the colors, their divisions in backgrounds and various borders, wearing away and with large broken fragments—, and how everything around you made you feel like a guest.

CARRER PERE IV

The decision about painting and colors was made when the construction was almost completed, because we could not know at the beginning how the building would resist all the actions on it, with excavators and structural reinforcements, during which at times we were afraid that the building would disappear.

CARRER PERE IV

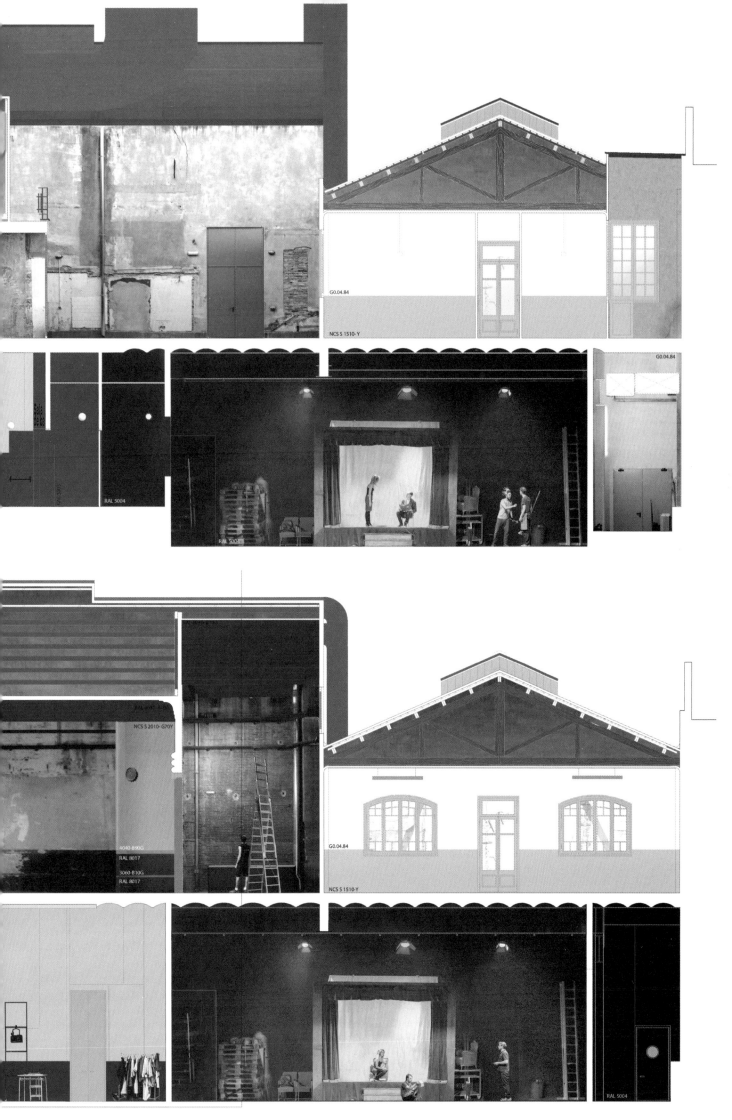

Only when the tiles, doors or windows began to return from storage and were placed in their new positions did the memory of the Cooperative reappear. When we reached that moment, we could start thinking about how to paint the new walls.

CARRER PERE IV

These sections collect all the information about colors that were designated within the different scenes. They record how the walls were at the end of the construction and, on each new color, there is a code to identify it when it is necessary to repaint.

Pop-Up *Oct 2016*

The idea of making a Pop-Up came with the interest of catching the backstage atmosphere of the central vestibule of the Sala Beckett, through an object. To make it, we used the longitudinal section through the vestibule as a base, a drawing that shows many of the spaces dedicated to the theatrical activities: the rehearsal room, the theater classrooms, the central courtyard and the Theater Downstairs. The light that enters in between the different cardboard planes of the Pop-Up expresses the qualities of the real space, where the natural light via skylights and patios that goes through holes and windows plays a key role in making the walls look lighter, weightless, empty from behind. At the same time, the new circulation that follows this path of natural light emphasizes the character that these walls adopt as curtains, people appearing and disappearing with the ease of a theater play.

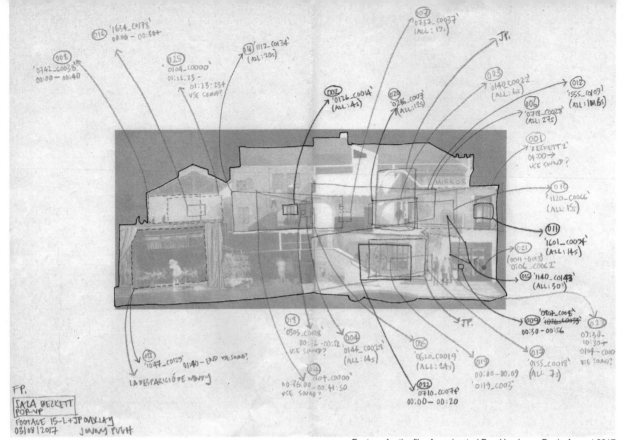

Footage for the film An animated Pop-Up. Jonny Pugh, August 2017

Film *Sept 2017*

An animated Pop-Up

A year after Sala Beckett opened its doors we thought it would be good to produce a short film that could explain the situation of simultaneous activities throughout the building, occurring throughout the day, every day. We wanted to show them all at once: a way of capturing the meaning of this building that is completely occupied and in action.

We planned to use the little Pop-Up as the container for these actions. So we used some recordings of activities that had taken place in the building since its inauguration to project them on the small paper walls, animating the different rooms that are seen in this object with the real events that had happened within.

When choosing the sound for the film, we remembered the final scene of the play that opened the new Sala Beckett in November 2016: *The Disappearance of Wendy*, by J.M. Benet i Jornet. In the last fragment of the play, a piano accompanies a narrator who explains a scene where a child receives a small toy theater as a birthday present from his parents. Within it the child begins to discover in its interior figures and characters that can move in and out of the scenery using fine cardboard sticks, being able to create new worlds from his imagination. The child is so trapped in this fantastic world that at the end the curtains of the theater fall, leaving him inside the stage forever.

Ghosts *Oct 2016*
The Café of Memory

INTRODUCCIÓ

Una vintena d'exalumnes dels dos cursos que vaig impartir a la Sala Beckett les temporades 2014/15 i 15/16 es varen animar, amb motiu de l'apertura de la nova seu a Poblenou, a realitzar-hi un laboratori de treball. Parlant amb en Toni Casares i l'Aina Tur, de seguida va sortir la idea de dedicar el laboratori a la memòria de l'edifici, a fer que tota l'experiència viscuda entre les parets de la Cooperativa Pau i Justícia no fos esborrada pel temps i tingués cabuda en les activitats de la primera temporada del teatre. Seguint la magistral remodelació que els arquitectes Flores i Prats han realitzat per convertir l'antiga seu de la Cooperativa en la flamant nova Sala Beckett, sense "pertorbar" les restes antigues de l'edifici i conservant-ne bona part dels seus detalls, fins i tots els més petits: rètols, andròmines, rajoles, fustes, penjadors, etc., el laboratori es volia plantejar com una reconciliació amb el passat de l'edifici, amb uns "fantasmes" que, en paraules del mateix director de la sala, en Toni Casares, "no havíem pas d'espantar", sinó amb els quals havíem de conviure i fer que, fins i tot, s'hi sentissin reconfortats.

Els vint intrèpids i meravellosos membres d'aquest "Laboratori de Peripècies", format per joves actrius i actors que també són "dramaturgs", és a dir, *escriptors de teatre* (a vegades aquesta parauleta porta a confusió) es varen trobar, els dies 1, 8 i 15 d'octubre de 2016, en el que abans era el bar de la Cooperativa Pau i Justícia (i ara una esplèndida sala d'assaig) amb persones que en varen formar part al llarg de la seva història. Es tractava de fer-ne entrevistes amb profunditat perquè cada entrevistat parlés de les seves experiències *personals* relacionades amb l'edifici i amb la resta de gent amb qui varen compartir vivències, aventures, feina, activitats, etcètera.

Les entrevistes tenien com a primer objectiu d'estimular els dramaturgs a escriure textos breus relacionats, *inspirats*, per les vivències que cada una de les persones els havia explicat en aquell *Café de la Memòria*.

Així doncs, el que llegireu ara són tots els textos que han escrit, amb més o menys llibertat creativa, els vint dramaturgs. Compte. No tots els textos transcriuen

4

amb fidelitat absoluta aquelles converses. Cada un dels membres del laboratori s'ha deixat dur pel seu instint, per un estímul creatiu divers i, a voltes, subjectiu. A vegades, s'han respectat els noms, d'altres, s'han canviat i se n'han inventat de nous. Hi trobareu narracions, petits poemes, cançons, obres breus de teatre (això que ara en diuen "microteatre"). Una mica de tot i variat. Això sí, tots els escrits han estat *inspirats* en tot moment per aquelles intenses trobades al Café, per tot el que una colla de gent esplèndida, vital, apassionada, entranyable i irrepetible els hi varen explicar.

És un autèntic motiu de joia que aquest jovent s'hagi emocionat tant i s'agafi aquest projecte amb l'energia, la força i l'apassionament amb què ho estan fent. El llegat de gent que va deixar la suor, el seu temps de treball i també de lleure i de passions en la Cooperativa, en l'escola, en aquestes parets, en aquest terra; gent que per a nosaltres fins fa quatre dies era anònima i que ara tenen cara i ulls i ens han prestat la seva veu i els seus sentiments... no es perdrà doncs del tot. Que dues i tres generacions més tard hagi aparegut una gent que reculli aquelles experiències, s'hi emocionin i les converteixin en art, a la seva manera, petita, senzilla, directa i desinteressada, per amor a la vida i al teatre, és francament emocionant i encoratjador.

Volem agrair a la Sala Beckett per afavorir aquest projecte i molt especialment a totes les persones, grandíssimes i meravelloses persones, que varen passar aquests tres dies pel *Café de la Memòria* i, per extensió, també a totes aquelles que, encara que no hi fossin, varen tenir alguna cosa a veure amb aquest edifici i amb el seu passat ple de vida que mai no hauria d'esborrar-se.

Sergi Belbel

5

"Twenty students from the two courses that I taught in the Sala Beckett for the seasons 2014/15 and 2015/16 were encouraged, on the occasion of the opening of the new building in Poblenou, to participate in a laboratory. When talking with Toni Casares and Aina Tur, the idea of dedicating a laboratory to the memory of the building arose immediately: the idea of giving the whole experience lived between the walls of the Cooperative Pau i Justícia a place in the activities of the first season of the theater, to avoid them being be erased by time. This idea followed the masterful remodelling that the architects Flores & Prats carried out to convert the old Cooperative into the brand new Sala Beckett, without 'disturbing' the old remains of the building and preserving a good part of its details, even the smallest ones: signage, tiles, junk, wood, hangers, etc. So, the laboratory wanted to reconcile with the building's past, with some 'ghosts' that, in the words of the director of the Sala Beckett, Toni Casares, 'we did not have to scare', but with who we had to live together, and even feel comfortable.

The twenty intrepid and wonderful members of this 'Laboratorio de Peripecias', formed by young actresses and actors who are also 'playwrights', that is, theater writers (sometimes this little word leads to confusion) they met, on the 1st, 8th and 15th October 2016, in the space which once was the bar of the Cooperative Pau i Justícia (and now a splendid rehearsal room), together with people who have been part of the building over its history. The aim was to carry out in-depth interviews so that each interviewee could talk about their personal experiences related to the building and the rest of the people with whom they shared experiences, adventures, work, activities, etc.

The aim of the interviews was to stimulate the dramatists to write short texts related, inspired, by the experiences that each of the people had explained to them in that Café of Memory."

Sergi Belbel. Fragment of the Introduction to the show *Ghosts. The Café of Memory*.

Axonometric of the common spaces of the Sala Beckett.
Constance Lieurade, Nov 2015.

SALA BECKETT.
TEATRE
A
TOT
L'EDIFICI

ESCALA
1/50.
FLORES & PRATS ARQS. NOVEMBRE 2015.
DIBUIXAT PER CONSTANCE LIEURADE.

Scenes from the performance of *Ghosts* in the Vestibule and the Ground Floor Dressing Room. Sept 2017

"In play Ghosts *the building functions as a stage. As soon as I saw what the architects were doing to this building, I proposed to do* Ghosts *with the 'Laboratorio de Peripecias', because it was clear that the stage had to be the entire Sala Beckett building."*

Scenes from the performance of *Ghosts* in the Bar and the Rehearsal Room. Sept 2017.

"Therefore, the journey that we do, —we make micro-pieces, micro-theater in fifteen spaces of the building where the public roams from one to another—, is also part of the experience, considering the whole architecture of the building as the theatrical space of our proposal." Sergi Belbel. Interview for the film *Scale 1:5*.

Axonometric of Public Circulation. Majo Cristiano + Jonny Pugh, June 2017

"It is a building that invites you to meet, to mix in a very balanced way, very quietly, very relaxed. It is inevitable that the spectators will meet the actors after the show, they will certainly meet each other, the students with the teachers, with the people from the offices... Here when one enters the building one sees the offices of production, the administration, next to the main entrance, facing the bar. All this makes mixing easy, in most of the spaces you enter one way and you can exit through another... this brings problems, many times, but also brings many advantages, in relation to unexpected encounters, and that's what it is all about." Toni Casares. Interview for the film *Scale 1:5.*

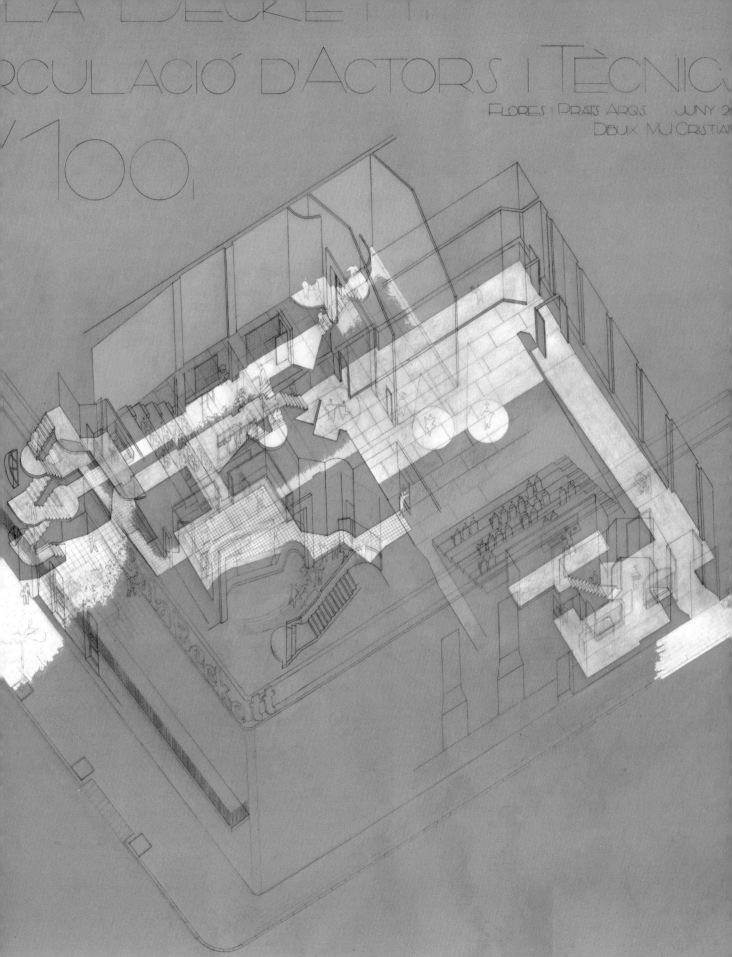

Axonometric of the Circulation of Technicians and Actors. Majo Cristiano + Jonny Pugh, June 2017

"When we were preparing Ghosts, the students said... that corridor there, where does it go? The great thing was to let one's own head trace the route from one place to another, it was great because we were planning that three groups of audience entered at the same time: one through the bar, the other through the vestibule and the other through the offices, and then the students asked: 'the group on the right should go from the bar to the patio above, but how should we go?' Ah, well look, we can go by the goods lift or we can go this way... or if we go down the stairs, we will go through the vestibule... going from one place to another was as if you were playing a game of 'choosing the shortest way' or 'choosing the most interesting way', there was always more than one possibility. This connectivity of everything with everything, which can cause certain mistakes, also has its grace because it is telling you that you are welcome everywhere." Sergi Belbel. Interview for the film *Scale 1:5*.

The Theater Downstairs, with the performance of *The Disappearance of Wendy*, Nov 2016.

"We are lucky to have been able to make two spaces that propose a different theatricality. And this is a very interesting discussion we had with the architects: to what extent the walls must be present or not during the fiction we propose. There is a kind of fiction that calls for absolute abstraction, completely forgetting about reality, a kind of theatrical convention that goes more towards naturalism, which asks the viewer to forget where he is, and therefore enters a magical world, new, that takes him and that abducts him: this is the type of theatricality of the Theater Downstairs...

The Theater Upstairs, with the performance of *Ghosts*, Sept 2017.

"...and another theatricality, which proposes a permanent dialogue between fiction and reality, and that asks you never to forget that you are part of the world, that you are part of a reality and that therefore the creator is interested that you see the walls of reality that encompass this fiction. This situation occurs in the Theater Upstairs. They are two valid theatricalities, both interesting, but both different. We are lucky that in the new Sala Beckett there are two spaces to practice these two theatricalities." Toni Casares. Interview for the film *Scale 1:5*.

"It's a domestic building, a place that not only me, who comes every day, but any person who enters feels very much at home, if not at his home, at someone else's home, in any case you feel at home, with everything that this implies, of a one to one relationship, of equal host and guest relationship, very affectionate, very respectful, nothing solemn, all this is explained by this building, just entering here relaxes people. It is a building that offers this relaxation, this comfort, and something that for me is essential for a place where artistic creation is made: an environment that invites you to make mistakes." T.C.

"I like that people make mistakes and enter a place thinking that it is one place but that it is another, and this extended to the creative projects... the creative projects are projects where testing and error must be possible. This way, nothing encourages you to do something through which you already can predict the result, how you have to articulate, instead it invites you to try, suggests ways, projects, things, but where nothing is too stipulated." T.C.

"This is one of the things that I think we have managed originating from the building. It is filled with extra spaces, spaces that do not serve for a single purpose, that depending on what you want to do, you can adapt them. This is also important. All these things I like." Toni Casares. Interview for the film *Scale 1:5.*

"There is something fundamental: Sala Beckett now has two aspects —in fact, it had them before arriving here— namely the production and exhibition of shows, and the training of professionals. But what is the grace of this architecture? Well, for one that the school and theater join to form one thing. Movement is as if a Moëbius band, but at the same time it is the spectacular exhibition of the theater spaces, like the Theater Upstairs or the one Downstairs, but also the corridors and the classrooms where the students will learn techniques of dramaturgy to be able to be authors, actors, dancers or whatever." S.B.

"What does a student do when they come here? They have to pass through the interior of the theaters, that is, at the same time the spectators who are going to see the functions and students who enter or leave classes are mixed. When the student leaves a class, they have to go through the vestibule, and if there is a queue to go in to see something from the Theater Upstairs, they interlock." S.B.

"What does this provoke? That when the student comes to learn they are aware that if they create something interesting in the class, the natural exhibition space of that creation will be the same theater where they are learning. Therefore, pedagogy and spectacle merge into one thing." Sergi Belbel. Interview for the film Scale 1:5.

ESCALA 1:5

una sèrie documental de 15-L. FILMS
dirigida per ALBERT BADIA i PATRICIA TAMAYO
amb el suport de FLORES & PRATS
i la col·laboració de SALA BECKETT

15-L. FILMS

Sala Beckett
Obrador Internacional
de Dramatúrgia

Film *Dec 2017*
Scale 1:5

Documentary series of 5 10-minute chapters on the process of creating Sala Beckett, with interviews with artists such as Curro Claret, Antoni Miralda, Soraya Smithson, Toni Casares and Sergi Belbel, and soundtrack by Maria Arnal and Marcel Bagés.

We knew we wanted to be close to the process of creating the new Sala Beckett. We visited what would become the new building with Eva and Ricardo, just before the construction started. We went there with them several times and decided to start recording the last moments of the construction and how the transfer of everything that came from the former Beckett would become settled in the new one. Thus, we accompanied this process until the new Sala Beckett opened in November 2016. Scale 1:5 is a documentary series that includes all these moments, with conversations with the architects themselves about their thoughts and with the interaction of special guests such as Curro Claret, Antoni Miralda, Soraya Smithson, Sergi Belbel and Toni Casares, who together with Flores & Prats star in each episode. Focusing on the materials and people that are part of this building, each chapter takes the name of a particular element: Roofs and Walls, Doors and Windows, Pavements, Stairs and Furniture. So, as with the building itself, the series invites experience both shared and fragmented, seen in parts or whole, but above all it is a claim to pay attention to details. This is how life becomes intense. Carlota Coloma and Adrià Lahuerta / 15-L. Films.

Albert Badia and Patrícia Tamayo filming in the studio Flores & Prats for the documentary Scale 1:5

Chapter 1.

Roofs and Walls,
with Toni Casares,
Director of Sala Beckett,
as guest.

"What is clear is that the building has helped us a lot in understanding what the hell it was we had in our heads when we said that Sala Beckett should grow, when we explained what the new Beckett should be. All this when explained only on paper, written, is very difficult. Once the building is finished, everyone understands it, and nobody doubts that this growth was necessary or that the city needed a space like this."

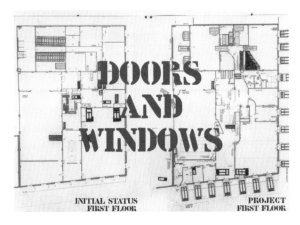

Chapter 2.

Doors and windows,
with the British Artist
Soraya Smithson
as guest.

"It takes quite a lot of effort to make it feel effortless, to make something welcoming, amusable and inhabitable you have to do an awful lot of work, because otherwise it becomes sterile and a barrier to feeling that you can come in here, and you can move the furniture around and you can occupy it. And particularly in a theater space you want people to feel they can really occupy the space and move and articulate their bodies in relation to their space."

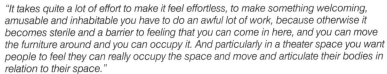

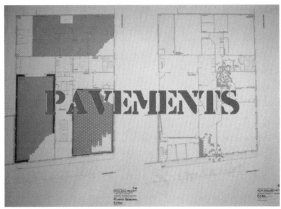

Chapter 3.

Pavements,
with the Artist
Antoni Miralda
as guest.

"This type of dialogue or proposal, is made of layers... it's a bit like what happened to us in 'El Internacional' [artistic project by Miralda New York 1984-86], behind that carpet, with a similar smell... we had been told that the place was half mafioso in the 70s, but of course, you raise the carpet and find another layer of linoleum and under the linoleum you find the terrazzo, etc. I mean, that the building itself is giving you clues to have a dialogue with these places."

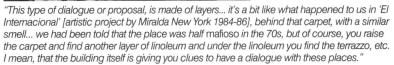

Chapter 4.

Stairs,
with the Playwright
Sergi Belbel
as guest.

"...they have managed to combine simultaneously a super new and super respectful aesthetic taste with something timeless -this thing of leaving the layers at sight, almost as if it were a geological cut, as when you make a cut in the earth and you see the Palaeolithic, the I don't know what... to keep the vestiges of time, an important value of memory, combined with the theatricality, that is, with the fact that it is a space designed to do and to teach theater."

Chapter 5.

Furniture,
with the Industrial
Designer
Curro Claret
as guest.

"One of the things that I find very positively intriguing in the Beckett is the game that they have made of taking things they had and using them in another way, so that in the end one does not know the reality... 'but was this exactly like this or not?' And I think this is very beautiful, the freedom to use something that existed before in the way that seems most appropriate to you, without the risk of: 'no, no, this was like that and we cannot touch it.'"

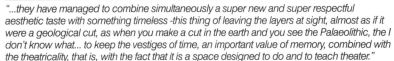

Cover of the newspaper ARA for the edition of Sunday 17th July, 2016. The issue is entirely dedicated to Catalan theater and interviews some of its best playwrights on the occasion of the opening of the new Sala Beckett. The following article by Manuel Guerrero, being the central critical piece of this special edition, recounts the rehabilitation process of the old Cooperative *Pau i Justícia* as a new centre of theater, through the steps followed by Sala Beckett from its previous venue in Gràcia towards this new house in Poblenou.

Beckett at the Cooperative
Manuel Guerrero Brullet

One of the great cultural news in Barcelona in 2016, during a time of general crisis, was undoubtedly the inauguration of the new Sala Beckett in Poblenou. A big event for the world of theater and dramaturgy but also for the world of architecture. Indeed, the extraordinary project of the new Sala Beckett by Ricardo Flores and Eva Prats has become an unavoidable reference of new Catalan architecture.

As all ambitious projects, it is the result of a long process that starts from the trajectory of the historic Sala Beckett founded in 1989 by the director and playwright José Sanchis Sinisterra. The Sala Beckett, which has been directed since 1997 by Toni Casares, was forced to leave its headquarters in Gràcia at Alegre de Dalt Street, because the londlords, Nuñez y Navarro real estate group, changed the rental conditions of the property in 2006. An agreement with the City Council of Barcelona made years later, opened the possibility of having new headquarters.

In 2011, in order to carry out the new project, the 'Sala Beckett / Obrador Internacional de Dramatúrgia Foundation' was created and an open architectural competition was called for the rehabilitation of the old building of the Cooperative *Pau i Justícia* in Poblenou. The design of the new headquarters was won by Ricardo Flores and Eva Prats. The first executive project was presented in March 2012 with a budget of 8.3 million Euros. Due to the economic crisis, it was decided to shrink the project and a new rehabilitation proposal was presented in January 2014 and subsequently approved, at a much lower cost of 2.5 million Euros.

In 2014, a collaboration agreement was signed between the Barcelona Institute of Culture and the Sala Beckett / Obrador Internacional de Dramatúrgia Foundation to carry out the refurbishment works of the Cooperative *Pau i Justícia* building as the new headquarters of the Sala Beckett. These works took place throughout 2015 and during the first six months of 2016. In the agreement, in addition of granting use of the building for a period of years, the City Council of Barcelona pledged to contribute two million Euros that, together with the one million Euros contributed by the Consortium for the Rehabilitation of Theaters, allowed these works to proceed on the old building of the Cooperative *Pau i Justícia*, located in Poblenou on the corner of Pere IV and Batista Streets. The new Sala Beckett, which is part of the network of Art Factories of the Barcelona City Council, has its specificity in the promotion of contemporary Catalan and international dramaturgy.

As with Beckett's writing, Toni Casares, the director of Sala Beckett, and the architects Flores & Prats had to reduce and condense the most ambitious original project to keep the essential: the rehabilitation of more that 2.900m2 that occupied the ground floor and the first floor of the old building of the Cooperative, built in 1924 and designed by the master builder Josep Masdeu.[1] This area tripled that of the former Sala Beckett in Gràcia, and would provide excellent working conditions, assuming all the necessary resources are found in the coming years.

[1] Images at pages 34 to 43.

An old Cooperative in ruin

In December 2014, before the beginning of the construction works, I was able to visit the old Cooperative building with Toni Casares, Ricardo Flores and Eva Prats. The two storey high building, very visible from Pere IV Street, stood out and stands out for its horizontal nature, with a cornice that goes round and connects the facade of Pere IV —with seven large windows on the first floor overlooking a long balcony— with the facade of Batista Street —which follows the same structure with nine windows, but without balconies. Old photographs show how the main facade used to be crowned by a pediment, probably Masonic, which has since disappeared.

We entered through the side door of Batista Street and climbed some stairs leading to the first floor where the school of the Cooperative used to be. It was humble and austere architecture, with the usual materials and popular decorative elements of constructions from the twenties and thirties of the last century. Ricardo Flores and Eva Prats showed me the cement tile mosaic floor on the first floor still in very good condition. They studied and classified them for months, recovered them during the rehabilitation of the building and placed them in the ground floor, where the bar and vestibule are now located. They also showed me the original wooden doors of the rooms they had drawn in detail. We visited the rest of the first floor where the theater and bar of the Cooperative used to be, still with visible remains of its ancient function, despite the effect of the years. The magnificent photos of Adrià Goula from 2011 allow us to see the state of the building at the time of starting the new architectural project.[2]

Flores & Prats, as real contemporary archaeologists, have inventoried all the remains of the decorative elements of the former Cooperative. It is as if they wanted to recover and dignify every detail of the worker and laborious spirit of this popular architecture of the Poblenou. They have made an exhaustive catalogue of all the flooring and tiles, and of all the doors and windows of the old building.[3] Without falling into historicism, the project wants to revive in the new theater all the different eras of the lives that once occupied the space. Ricardo showed me with fascination the wasted colors and the wounds caused by time on the walls that they finally preserved. We talked about Les Bouffes du Nord, the old theater rehabilitated by Peter Brook in Paris, which they have as an outstanding reference. The visit to Les Bouffes du Nord left them dazzled. There is no doubt that much of the preservation criteria of the old building and the old walls of Les Bouffes du Nord in Paris have been radicalized in the project of the new Sala Beckett of Flores & Prats. Throughout these years, the creative work and the collaboration between the architects and the director of the Sala Beckett to define the project and the construction of the new space has been exemplary. In that first visit, Toni Casares told me about the new functions of the space. The first floor will host the training and creative programme: in the former theater there will be the Theater Upstairs, a size of 23 x 11 meters, for 100 spectators, the former bar will be the Rehearsal room and the rest of spaces meeting rooms and production offices. We went down to the ground floor, where the grocery store of the Cooperative used to be. Unlike the first floor, everything here was destroyed. On the ground floor the project envisaged a vestibule, a bar, offices, dressing rooms and the large Theater Downstairs. The remnants of an old sauna were still visible. Where the hole in the pool could be seen, there is now the entrance of the new Theater Downstairs, a size of 19 x 14 meters and with a capacity for 250 spectators.[4]

A few months later, in February 2015, Ricardo and Eva invited me to their unique studio in Trafalgar Street. On the walls and tables there were numerous drawings, plans and models that allowed us to see the audacious evolution of the project and the careful work process that led them to study each detail. The studio resembled a craftsman's workshop, an architectural workshop to design a theater workshop. At that time they were also working intensely on another project, the Casal Balaguer in Palma de Mallorca. This was a project, developed together with studio Duch-Pizá, which was shown in the award-winning Spanish Pavilion of the Venice Biennale 2016. Flores & Prats, who met in the studio of Enric Miralles, are today two renowned architects.

Miquel Adrià, with his prestigious Mexican publisher Arquine, had just edited in 2014 in Spanish and in English a magnificent 449 pp. monographic volume dedicated to their work: *Thought by Hand. The Architecture of Flores & Prats*. We reviewed this book including texts by Juan José Lahuerta and Manuel de Solà-Morales among others. The book, which is an excellent introduction and study of their architecture and their particular artisan method of work, ends with the project of the new Sala Beckett.

The text "Ruins", signed by Flores & Prats reads: "The ruinous state in which we encountered the building was of interest, not because we wanted to restore it, but rather to take the ruin forward and make it participate, with its unfinished character of superimposed periods, in a new reality that would continue to be updated, with layers added upon its foundation."

[2] Images at pages 54 to 65.
[3] Íd. pages 66 to 83.
[4] Íd. pages 51 to 53.

The new Sala Beckett in Poble Nou

In June 2016 I visited the building once again. The construction works were practically finished. The historic Sala Beckett in Gràcia had closed and the whole team had just moved into the new building in Poblenou. Evidently, the building's facade had not changed much, the horizontality of the large balcony and the volumes of large windows had remained. However, just upon entering the new Sala Beckett the changes in the structure of the building were radical. Two large empty circles cut in the old ceiling that connect the vestibule with the first floor allowed surprising interior views, acting as skylights and allowing a spectacular entrance of light.

This was an architectural proposal that made me think of some of the dissections of buildings in some of the emblematic works of Anarchitecture from the New York artist and architect Gordon Matta-Clark (1945-1978). Like the "Conical intersect" (1975) in Paris, or the "Baroque Office" (1977) in Antwerp. "The result was a series of successive openings that insisted on Arabesque cuts that exposed the whole building to a tour of interior views," wrote Matta-Clark about this latest project.

A large, long and welcoming red velvet bench with curved shapes invites you to sit comfortably in the lobby before entering the Theater, and a lateral staircase that goes up to the first floor to the formation area are where the Theater Upstairs, the Rehearsal rooms and the classrooms are located, form the main elements found upon entering the building. Looking down to the floor, a large collage of cement tile mosaic floors, looking up at the walls, a pile of rosettes and elements of different eras offer a fascinating journey in time. The ruins of the Cooperative, the memory of Poblenou, the ruins of the 20th century survive in the 21st century in a new complex and integrating project. Enric Miralles's brilliant legacy and the winding memory of Josep Maria Jujol are reflected in the meticulous and detailed architecture of Flores & Prats.

On the first floor I met Ricardo and Eva, who had settled in a classroom during the last days of that month of June 2016 to draw some elements and to review the latest details of the finished work. An architecture designed in detail, a microarchitecture in which each space has a different form, a different finish, a logical or perhaps unexpected solution, a particular language that time has also created and built. Architecture is not imposed; it becomes a place to welcome, an open place for encounters and crossings, where dialogue, debate, movement, testing, creation and contemplation are possible.

The architectural space opens up to the visitor's experience, to that visitor who enters the building, who makes their way not to a monumental building, but to a building of common sizes and characteristics in the neighborhood where it is located. Yet, immediately, because of the space that opens up to their eyes and because of the different decorative and formal elements they find, as well as the abstract remains that they identify, they make a journey through time, to the styles and lived lives inside the building.

Jacques Derrida referred to architecture as an art of space. The architecture of Flores & Prats and, especially, the project of the new Sala Beckett, allow us to think of architecture also as an art of time. Like theater, architecture is also an art of space and time. Like the dramatic script, the architectural script of Flores & Prats deconstructs and builds space and time.

Three years later, in 2019, all those first impressions are already a consolidated reality. The Sala Beckett is already a true and ineludible cultural, theatrical and architectural reference in Barcelona. The spirit and the work of Samuel Beckett, and all the legacy of the workers' and cooperative movement, revive in the contemporary space of the old Cooperative of Poblenou thanks to the subtle architecture of Eva Prats and Ricardo Flores, the creative spirit of the Sala Beckett team, the public and all the people who participate in the training and theatrical activity of the project. The City of Barcelona Award for Architecture 2017 and the participation in the Venice Architecture Biennale 2018 has only confirmed the new Sala Beckett as a unique emblem of culture and of new Catalan architecture on an international stage. A place where, as Samuel Beckett wrote in Worstward Ho (1983), it is possible to: "Try again. Fail again. Fail better." To re-write, to do theater again, to get up again, to rebuild.

Sala
de dalt

Aules
90
→

Aules
→

S.Zaccaria
San Marco

VADO DETTO
LINEA 2

C   A   N   A   L   E

CANALE DELLA
GIUDECCA

PORTO FRANCO

CANALE DI S GIORGIO

ISOLA DI
SAN GIORGIO
MAGGIORE

CAPPELLA DEL
MATTINO
PADIGLIONE
VATICANO
S 1/1000

BIENNALE DI
DI VENEZIA 20

0   10   50   100   200
SCALA GRAFICA IN METRI

FLORES & PRATS ARCH: MAGGIO 2018   DISEG

Venice Architecture Biennale
May – Nov 2018

When the building had been in use for a few months we were invited to participate at the Venice Architecture Biennale 2018.
We decided to build there a replica of a fragment of the Sala Beckett inside Le Corderie building of the Arsenale.
This kept us mentally and physically in contact with the process material of this project,
giving us the opportunity to order and display the archives of this recent work
at the backstage of the scenography that we proposed for the event, presenting it to an international public.

ARSENALE

LE CORDERIE

LUCE LIQUIDA
MOSTRA FREE SPACE
SM1000

VIA GARIBALDI

GIARDIN DELLA BIENNALE

ISMARCO

CHITETTURA

VICTORIA BARRALE

Situation plan of *Liquid Light* at Le Corderie dell'Arsenale
and *Morning Chapel* at the Vatican Pavilion, Island of San Giorgio, Venice.
Ma. Victoria Barrale, Dec 2018.

Liquid light
Submission 1
Freespace, Venice Biennale 2018
Flores & Prats

A Social Club had been abandoned for about 30 years, rain, wind and pigeons where getting in, gradually destroying the building. The sun light was getting in as well, a ray of light right at the center of the old scenario; we read it not as a menace of destruction, but as an optimistic sign of a new possible future.

A theater group called Sala Beckett has been working in Barcelona for more than 20 years. Their main activity is to promote new drama stories, and to put them in stage for the first time. So what they found inside the old building was a great story to be preserved: a social club named "Peace and Justice" from 1924, a building raised by workers to have their own place for leisure: theater, Bar, dancing classes, celebrate weddings…

The rehabilitation of the old social club has turned it into the new Sala Beckett International Drama Centre. A ray of natural light is kept inside the building, changing the atmosphere of this central circulation space, all over the year.

Proposal for how we might exhibit a component of our work in response to the theme *Freespace*, after the invitation by Yvonne Farrell & Shelley McNamara, curators of the Venice Architecture Biennale 2018.

Our proposal for the next Venice Architecture Biennale, is to bring this ray of natural light inside the show.

We would like to build in plywood or plasterboard, in 1 to 1 scale, this fragment of Sala Beckett, using big photo reproductions on top of these walls to bring the athmosphere of the original spaces.

The piece can be entered inside, inhabited. As a passerby of the exhibition, the fragment can be crossed through, and by doing so it will offer the spatial experience of something which is far away.

The component is a replica of the Sala Beckett freespace in Barcelona, continuing to give surprise and emotion, but the light which makes the piece work is original, it is Venice's light.

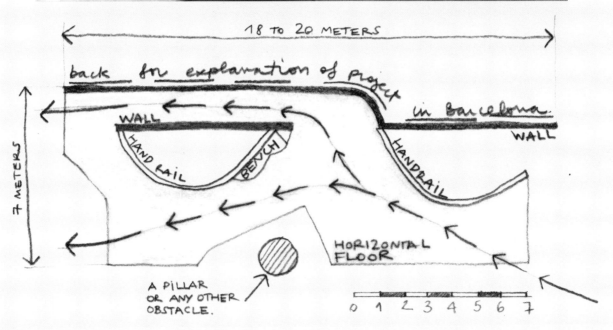

Liquid light

Submission 2
Freespace, Venice Biennale 2018
Flores & Prats

Our proposal for Freespace deals with natural light as water, with the idea of liquid light. We like to work with natural light and its capacity of concentrating intensity, passing through thick chambers, making its way to the inside, tirelessly descending, meter after meter, as found in ancient Egyptian burial chambers. The skylight proposed for Freespace will use and manipulate natural light, getting it from the windows of the Arsenale Pavilion in Venice to make it appear in the centre of the Sala Beckett in Barcelona.
A transposition of place, a translation of light.

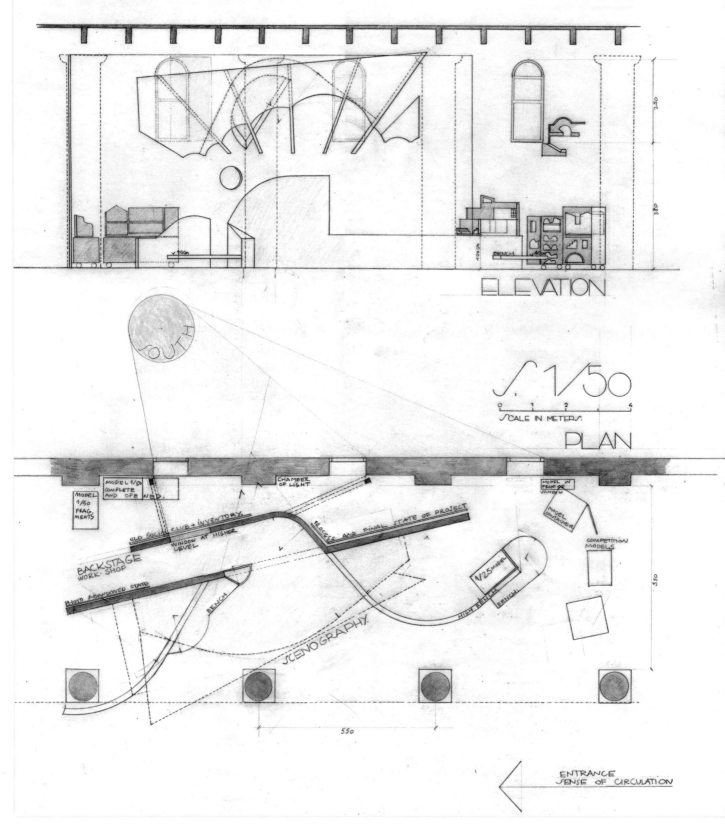

Submission 2, October 2017. Plan and Elevation of the installation Liquid Light. EP, Oct 2018.

Choreography.

This construction, which replicates the space and light of this new theatre in Barcelona, will make the effort of bringing in the light from these windows to the core of the promenade, provoking a change in the rhythm of natural light inside the Arsenale. It will keep the light in suspension, evidencing the capacity of natural light to create an atmosphere.

Visitors to the exhibition, promenading in the centre of the Arsenale, will find this 'sanctuary' lit up against the wall, pulling them toward it. This lighted space will provoke the surprise of finding an original work, inviting them to come inside, like inside a chapel, and find out where does the light come from. The fragment is therefore a space to be inhabited, illuminated by a light source that is out of sight. Seeing the light entering without seeing its source makes us feel as though we are inside somewhere far removed from the outside; we do not know how many layers or chambers the light has had to cross before reaching us.

Once the visitors cross the fragment of Sala Beckett and get into the backstage, they will find comprehensive information of the building and the process of making it, and will understand that the element they have just crossed is a skylight placed on a first floor in the centre of a far away building in Barcelona.

Position in relation to the Arsenale space.

The component proposed for Freespace is located slightly inclined in relation to the public's circulation, in order to present itself in an active position towards the promenade, as an apparition. For this reason we choose not to attach it to the back wall of the given space at the Arsenale, but instead to pull it towards the central corridor, leaving behind a back space which will allow us to expose the narrative of the project.

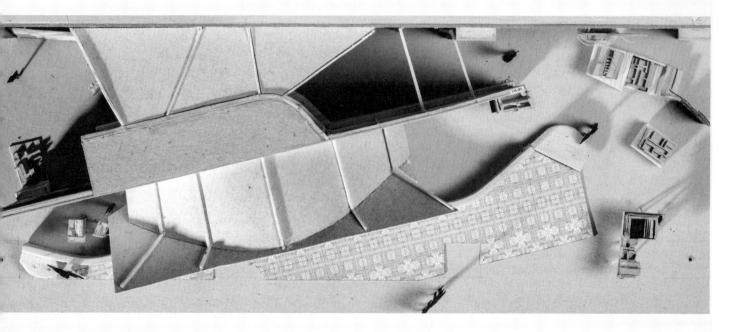

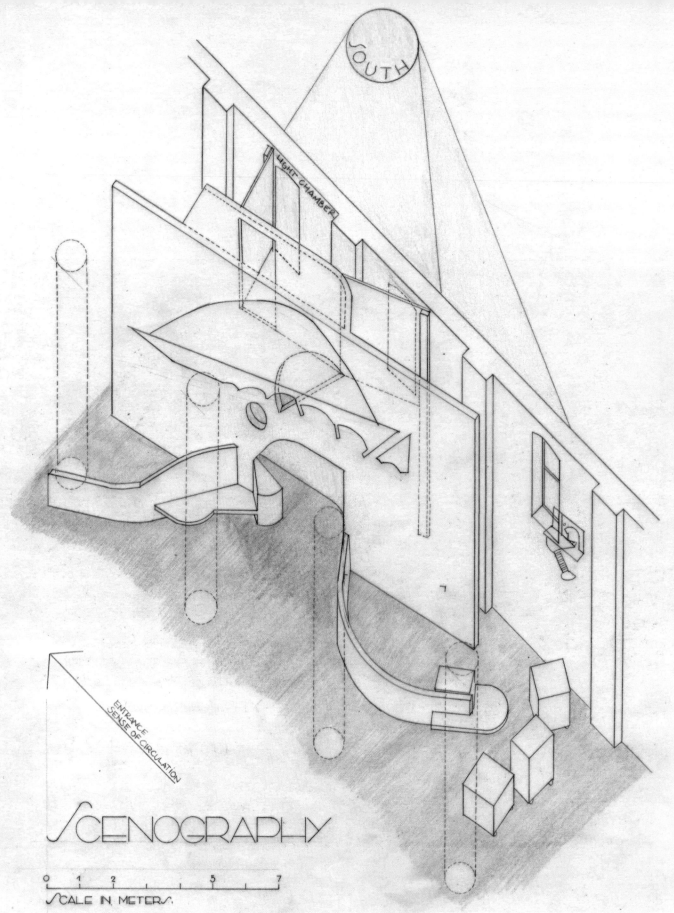

Axonometric drawing of the scenography for *Liquid Light*. EP, Oct 2018.

The exhibit will therefore have two parts.

1. One which reproduces the Sala Beckett skylight, facing the public main flow of the exhibition. In order to allow the light get to the dome and the arch, it would be optimum that the proposal is located in the south side of the Arsenale, as the original skylight which it refers to in Barcelona is also oriented south, and therefore we can be sure that the effect will be similar, here with Venice's light. The way we imagine that light will arrive in the same direction as in Barcelona is to take two of the three windows of our area in the Arsenale, and concentrate its light into one single opening in the back of the component. Given the strength of Venice's light, the piece will work well through the summer and autumn months of the exhibition.

Parallel to this natural lighting, we have considered that artificial light should be placed in the light 'chamber' behind the piece (in-between the piece and the Arsenale wall), hidden to the eye of the visitor, which will work with a sensor in order to start working as the natural light disappears —either towards the evening or on a cloudy day.

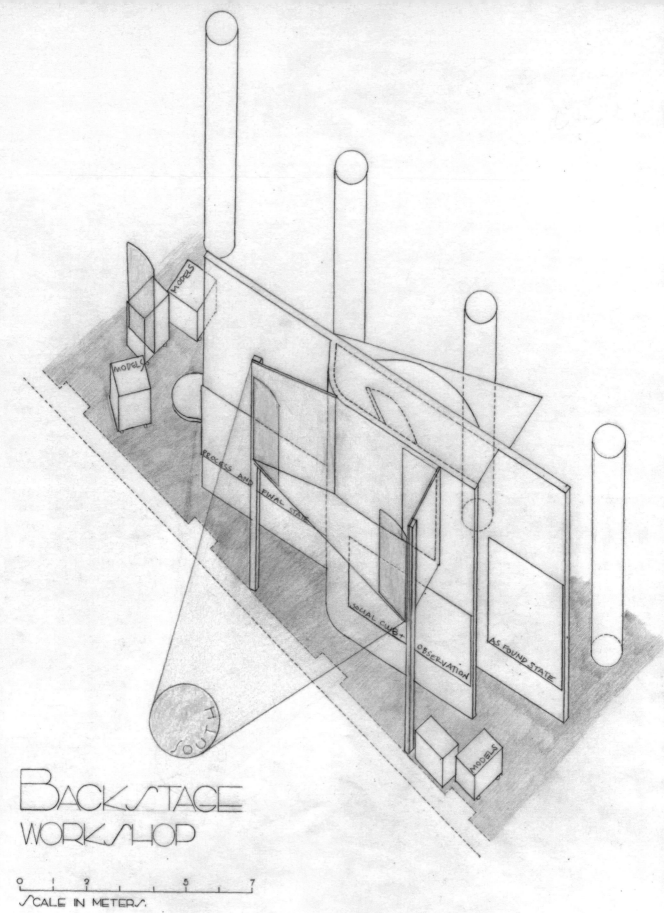

BACKSTAGE
WORKSHOP

SCALE IN METERS.

Axonometric drawing of the backstage for *Liquid Light*. EP, Oct 2018.

2. *A second part at the back of the component, a backstage occupying the remaining space towards the Arsenale wall, which will become a workshop containing an explanation of the spatial and material ideas of the project in Barcelona and of the fragment in Venice. This space will also allow us to explain how we fabricate things through process material such as models, drawings and photographs.*

The content of this backstage space will explain: a. Photographs of the as-found state of the building; b. Historical photographs of the Social Worker's Club; c. Observation drawings, Inventory of the as-found state; d. Models at different scales showing the design process; e. Design drawings (process and final proposal).

Constructed realities

Ellis Woodman

For the main exhibition of the 2018 Venice Architecture Biennale, Flores & Prats devised an ambitious installation called *Liquid Light*. It comprised a partial facsimile of Sala Beckett's upper foyer, produced by means of enlarging flat-on photographs of the original fabric to actual size. The distinctive composition of three curvaceous openings that heralds the arrival of the principal stair at the theater's upper level was recreated midway down the length of the exhibition's photographic tableau. Now, however, these cuts gave onto an unadorned "backstage" where models and drawings documenting the building's design development were displayed. The installation was sited in the Corderie at the Arsenale and Flores & Prats subtly adjusted Sala Beckett's original design in response to this new architectural setting. Three of the Corderie's monumental brick columns now found themselves absorbed within a reproduction of the theater's tiled floor, one column even being co-opted as the terminus of a low wall that paraphrased the course of one of Sala Beckett's curving balustrades. Aligning the three openings with two high windows in the Corderie's external wall provided a further means of anchoring the installation in its physical context. The shifting light of the actual Venice and the static light of the photographed Barcelona were summoned into mysterious coexistence.

The method of presentation drew attention to themes central to Sala Beckett's design, such as its preoccupation with transforming found material through creative framing and the critical role it assigns to daylight as a register of passing time. But perhaps the foremost impression conveyed was of the installation's ontological ambivalence. It could be characterized as a theatrical flat: a picture, lacking the substance, history, and phenomenal characteristics of the building that it represents. And yet the gestures towards situating this picture in the real world —the provision for inhabitation, the introduction of daylight, the incorporation of the existing columns— all served to ensure that it transcended a purely scenographic reading. However modest in scale, flimsy in construction, and short in lifespan, the installation ultimately demanded to be read as a work of architecture in its own right.

If the installation can be described as a picture that aspired to the status of architecture, Sala Beckett might be said to be the product of a contrary impulse. It is a work of architecture conceived in fundamentally pictorial terms. In justification of that claim I would like to consider three related attributes of the theater's design: the animation of its finishes; the articulation of its interior as a sequence of layers; and, finally, the improvisatory character of its component parts.

Particularly in Sala Beckett's public areas the walls and floors retain an artfully ragged condition that testifies to the near century of use and misuse that the Peace & Justice Workers' Cooperative building underwent before its conversion into a performance venue. In the foyer, to take one example, the stepping profile of an expanse of green and white mosaic carries the memory of a demolished staircase, as if providing its replacement, which climbs alongside, with a phantom twin. The archaeological record presented is not altogether reliable, the building's use as a gay sauna, prior to its abandonment and dilapidation, being one episode tactfully excised from the narrative. Significant material has also been shifted from its original location. Old windows and doors have been assigned to new openings and re-painted in colors that find precedent in the retained fabric but are now deployed to more dazzling effect. Rescued floor tiles have been reused in public areas, forming a ground articulated by carpet-like inlays of differing pattern and —after the meticulous cutting of many hundreds of tiles— an often sinuously profiled band around its edge. Redundant plaster ceiling roses have been upended and mounted on the foyer's wall.

In Flores & Prats' considerations of how to approach the wreckage of the old building, their late compatriot, Josep Maria Jujol (1879-1949), served as a valuable guide. During the early part of his career, Jujol assisted Antoní Gaudi on the design of Park Güell, taking responsibility for decorating the benches and the roof of the lower court using tiles, plates, bottles, cups, glasses and jugs —objects that were generally factory rejects or refuse. This Midas sensibility remained a hallmark of his subsequent career. As the architect and Jujol scholar, Josep Llinàs, has noted:

"Creating a mosaic out of waste ceramics and indeed waste recycling in general, is a constant of the Jujol work ethic, which builds consoles out of cardboard boxes, reworks farmyard equipment into a grille, employs fieldstones as mouldings and turns tin cans into lamp rosettes."[1]

One of Jujol's earliest independent projects, the Patronat Obrer Theater in Taragona (1908), suggests a particularly direct ancestral relationship to Sala Beckett. Working with a shoestring budget and the constraints

[1] Llinás, Josep & Sarra, Jordi: Josep Maria Jujol (Cologne, 2007)

of an existing structure, Jujol put to use whatever material came to hand. The ironwork structure changes profile from floor to floor —the columns on the upper levels being of the architect's design, those lower down being reclaimed from elsewhere. Windows in the dress and upper circles are also recycled; one is even a glazed door laid horizontally. Frequently resolving decisions through onsite consultation with his workforce, Jujol brings common purpose to a vast range of incidental design considerations through his insistence on their ornamental nature. Every aspect of the Patronat Obrer Theater is conceived as a form of visual play which, in the words of Josep Llinàs —who undertook the restoration of the building in the nineteen nineties— serves the honorable task of "removing work and solemnity from our horizons."[2] The design of Sala Beckett maintains a similarly ludic spirit. An economy of material means supports a profligacy of visual invention.

On the completion of his work to Jujol's building, Llinàs remarked that the experience had instilled in him the conviction that there was an urgent need for schools of architecture to "refloat the container of costume jewelry, froth, tomato sauce and fireworks that Le Corbusier consigned to the depths of the sea."[3] On the internal linings of Sala Beckett, Flores & Prats raise to the surface a handsome hoard of this long submerged treasure.

*　　*　　*

Extending for a distance four times greater than its width, the foyer maintains a street-like presence at the centre of Sala Beckett's plan. Midway down the length of its lower level a narrow space opens up to one side, highlighted in red and occupied by a long and shapely bank of upholstered seating. The pointedly theatrical effect is emphasised by the opening's treatment as a form of proscenium. Pushing the return flight of stairs to the outside of the foyer wall ensures that the threshold to the upper level takes on a similar character. The preoccupation with layering is also developed vertically by gestural openings cut into the roof and first floor slab. Cultivating long, tangential views and a Piranesian play of light and shadow, they draw the visitor into the building and then on to the more richly illuminated territory upstairs.

[2] Llinás, Josep: *Josep Llinás* , p. 12 (Seville, 1997)
[3] Ibid, p. 15

FIRST PROPOSAL FOR FREESPACE

PAPER THEATRE

CAFE OF MEMORY.
FORMER COOPERATIVE MEMBERS CELEBRATE
THE REOPENING OF THEIR BUILDING.

The abundant provision of internal glazing represents another contribution to the theater's layered spatial character. Mitigating the potentially oppressive effect of the deep plan, it opens views into territories beyond those prescribed for public access and ultimately of the city outside. Many of the reclaimed glazed doors and windows have a lattice-like character, and this quality is reinforced by the close spacing, and in some instances diagonal orientation, of the mullions in those that have been added. The application of brilliant color to their frames further ensures that they register as figures that occupy and apportion space rather than merely as voids.

Among the models displayed in the Venice installation, was one that communicated the effects that these devices engender particularly powerfully: a toy theater that Flores & Prats commissioned from the English artist Soraya Smithson in celebration of Sala Beckett's completion. Conceived as an abstracted representation of the building's foyer, this flat-packed assembly in printed paper concertinas open to reveal a miniature world, articulated by successive layers of paper of contrasting color and profile. This little construction deftly captures the sense that every part of Sala Beckett is a performance space: each opening framing an animated world beyond.

Soraya Smithson's toy theater also testifies to the place that Flores & Prats' thinking occupies within a network of close personal relationships. The architects' friendship with the artist dates back to late nineteen eighties, when

Soraya was employed as a model-maker in the office of Enric Miralles and Carme Pinós. Eva Prats was already collaborating with the practice, initially in her capacity as one of Miralles' students. On graduating in 1992 she took up a full-time role there as, a year later, did Ricardo Flores. Soraya's presence in the office had come about through the friendship that Miralles and Pinós had developed with her parents, the architects Alison and Peter Smithson, after the young Spaniards had attended the 1977 International Laboratory for Architecture and Urban Design in Urbino, where Peter had served as a visiting critic.

What is striking about this intergenerational network of Anglo-Catalan connections is that it is rooted in a shared set of artistic concerns among which a concern with the articulation of space in layers is one of the most prominent. As Alison and Peter Smithson wrote of the development of their own architecture:

"By the end of the nineteen sixties, the diagonal structural brace has been transformed from an expressed structure into a 'lattice' and had taken on entirely new meanings; to do with skin-depth, sense of protection; exploiting the sense of privacy and of fantasy that the lattice entrains."[4]

[4] Smithson, Alison & Peter: *Italian Thoughts* , p. 15. (Stockholm, 1993)

Flores & Prats are inheritors of those formal preoccupations and share the Smithsons' insistence on their psychological foundation. Encountering Sala Beckett in drawings or photographs, one is immediately struck by the singularity of its formal mannerisms but visiting the building is quite another experience. One's first impression is of the unique atmosphere of the place —of its conjunction of liveliness and intimacy, its freedom from institutional pretension, its tolerance of different kinds of use and different types of people. It is a building of collective use and public character but one rooted in its architects' empathy with the individual visitor.

*   *   *

The Smithsons' concern with the layer and the lattice found its most developed expression in the numerous interventions to the so-called Hexenhaus in Läuenforde, Germany, which they undertook between 1984 and 2001. The project represented a strikingly romantic turn in the architects' vocabulary, perhaps the sole precursor for which had been the determinedly non-orthogonal House of the Future (1956). While realised in painted plywood, that project's strikingly free form derived from the possibilities of plastic technology. By contrast, the interventions at the Hexenhaus are unambiguous works of carpentry —which in some instances repurpose existing joinery elements— lending them a quality of openness to subsequent transformation in response to changing needs. Their restless morphology supports this sense of irresolution: their oddly cranking profiles may be carefully tailored to animate certain lines of sight or to facilitate particular patterns of movement but they also imbue the project with a vital sense of adhocism.

A similar nervous energy courses through the design of Sala Beckett. Look, for example, at the way the window at the foot of the principal stair fidgets back and forth in plan or at the way the vermilion finish of the doors at the rear of the foyer bleeds onto an expanse of adjacent wall. Or look at Flores & Prats' most conspicuous addition to the outside of the building: the sign of large freestanding letters mounted at roof level that announces the theater's name. While the first nine letters of "Sala Beckett" are arranged along the building's main frontage, their positioning ensures that the two final t's are shunted onto a side elevation. A key effect is to enhance the theater's visibility on its principal approach from the city centre but the gesture also gives warning of an architecture composed of parts that are, if not exactly unstable, then unusually unencumbered by a sense of responsibility to a predefined and all-pervasive order.

This sense of an empirical imagination at play is nowhere more powerfully felt than in the composition of idiosyncratic elements at the top of the principal stair. Where the work of architecture typically comprises an assembly of repetitive parts, which develops consequentially from consideration of the horizontal and then the vertical plane, here no such systematic logic obtains. In many instances, the product of an act of extraction rather than assembly, each part is a singular presence albeit one that maintains a charged relationship to other elements of the composition. The largest opening's curved profile corresponds both to the fall of the bench's backrest and to the line of the wall at the top of the stairs; the circular opening rhymes with the form of the wall-mounted ceiling roses; the bands of shadow falling at the rear of the scene echo the exposed joists that project towards us in the foreground. The cumulative effect could be compared to that of a cubist collage, in which readings of solid and void, figure and ground, plan and elevation are lent a calculated ambiguity.

Certainly, the governing logic is pictorial or, to use a term with a more established place in architectural discourse, we might say that it is picturesque. That word has its origins in the development of the eighteenth century English landscape garden —a movement that abandoned the rigid geometries of the French tradition of garden design to privilege the individual's experience through an emphasis on qualities of variety, contrast and surprise. The picturesque landscape is a layered and episodic composition, which readily accommodates pre-existing features. It is an environment in which the visitor is constantly made aware of the presence of spaces beyond their own and which, at its edges, is contiguous with the wider world. Sala Beckett maintains a similarly delicate balance of naturalism and artifice. Much of the raw condition in which the building's fabric has been preserved embeds the project in the history and culture of its site, the sense of authenticity that it projects has been exceptionally hard won. Sala Beckett relates to the surrounding city as the landscape garden relates to nature, each representing its wider condition in intensely constructed form. Both are microcosmic worlds that afford the visitor a precious sense of situation. It is a gift that we are free to carry with us when we eventually step outside.

Credits

Sala Beckett International Drama Centre, Barcelona
First Prize in Restricted Competition.

Situation: 228 Pere IV Street, Poble Nou, Barcelona.
Promoter: Institut de Cultura de Barcelona + Fundació Sala Beckett.
Program: Rehabilitation of the former Workers Cooperative *Pau i Justícia* as the new headquarters of Sala Beckett / International Drama Centre, with two Theater spaces, a rehearsal room, reading and writing classrooms, drama acting classrooms, offices, working areas for technicians and bar/restaurant open to the neighborhood.

Competition: January 2011.
Collaborators: Eirene Presmanes, Jorge Casajús, Micol Bergamo, Michelle Capatori.
Area: 4.435m².

First Project: February 2011 - July 2012.
Area: 4.435m².
Budget: 8.000.000 euros.
Studio collaborators: Jorge Casajús, Micol Bergamo, Emanuele Lisci, Cecilia Obiol, Francesca Tassi-Carboni, Nicola Dale, Adrianna Mas, Giovanna de Caneva, Michael Stroh, Maria Elorriaga, Pau Sarquella, Rosella Notari, Laura Bendixen, Francesca Baldessari, Marta Smektala, Ioanna Torcanu, Carlotta Bonura, Florencia Sciutto, Georgina Surià, Elisabet Fàbrega.

THE THEATRE DOWNSTAIRS OF SALA BECKETT SCALE 1/25.

First Occupancy Project: December 2012 - January 2013.

Second Project: January - July 2014.
Area: 2.923m².
Budget: 2.500.000 euros.
Construction: April 2014 - March 2016.
Theater Engineer: Eng. Marc Comas.
Acoustic Adviser: Arau Acústica.
Structural Adviser: Arch. Manuel Arguijo.
Mechanical Engineer: AJ Ingeniería.
Quantity Surveyor: Xavier Badia.
Project Manager: D+M Tècnics / David Morros.
Studio collaborators: Jorge Casajús, Julián González, Valentina Tridello, Agustina Álvaro Grand, Monika Palosz, Shreya Dudhat, Jordi Papaseit, Judith Casas, Tomás Kenny, Filippo Abrami, Constance Lieurade, Iben Jorgensen, Lucía Gutiérrez, Gimena Álvarez Bertucci, Agustina Bersier, Mariela Allievi, Toni Cladera, Clàudia Calvet, Arnau Pascual, Alessandra de Mitri, Nina Andreatta, Inès Martinel, Majo Cristiano, Florencia Cotone.

Film *Scale 1:5*

Date of production: 2017.
Interviews: Eva Prats - Architect of Sala Beckett; Ricardo Flores - Architect of Sala Beckett; Toni Casares - Director of Sala Beckett; Soraya Smithson - Artist; Antoni Miralda - Artist; Sergi Belbel - Dramatist and professor of Sala Beckett; Curro Claret - Industrial Designer.
Script and Direction: Patricia Tamayo and Albert Badia.
Producers: Carlota Coloma and Adrià Lahuerta.
Production Assistant: Anna Asensio.
Editing: Jeffrey Frígula, Sergio Roldán, Patrícia Tamayo, Albert Badia.
Director of Photography: Albert Badia.
Camera operator during the construction: Carlota Bantulà.
Sound recording: Patrícia Tamayo.
Sound: Oriol Campi.
Music: Maria Arnal and Marcel Bagés, from the albums *Cançò de Marina Ginestà*, *Verbena* and *45 Cerebros y 1 Corazón*.
Produced by: 15-L. Films

Pop-Up

Date of production: November 2016.
Collaborators: Eva Blasco, Camila Morandi.

Film *An animated Pop-Up*

Date of production: 2017.
Animation of the Pop-Up: Jonny Pugh.
Music: Carles Pedragosa, for the play *The Disappearance of Wendy*, by Josep Ma. Benet i Jornet.

Paper Theater

Date of production: 2017.
Idea and design: Soraya Smithson.
Collaborator: Judith Casas.

Film *44 Doors and 35 Windows for the new Sala Beckett*

Date of production: February - May 2016.
Stopmotion: Agustina Bersier, Mariela Allievi.
Editing: Agustina Bersier, Judith Casas and 15-L. Films.
Photographs: Judith Casas, Miguel Angel Aguiló.
Music: Albinoni, Concerto for 2 Oboes in Fa Major, Op 9 Nº3, 3 Allegro. Advent Chamber Orchestra.

Liquid Light, Venice Architecture Biennale 2018

Situation: Le Corderie, Arsenale, Venice.
Project and Design of the installation: *Flores & Prats, 2017 - 2018.*
Studio collaborators: *Nina Andreatta, Jorge Casajús, Judith Casas, Eline Cooman, Makoto Hayashi, Inès Martinel, Rebeca López.*
Structural Adviser: *Juan Ignacio Eskubi.*
Lighting consultant: *Maria Güell / La Invissible.*
Design of the supports for the models: *Curro Claret.*
Coordination and construction of scenography: *Art% + Tempo.*
Collaborators in the installation of the backstage in Venice: *Jorge Casajús, Nina Andreatta.*
Special thanks: *Adrià Goula Photo for allowing us the use of his photographs for the exhibition, and at 15-L. Films for allowing the screening of the film Scale 1:5 in the installation during the six months of the Biennale.*
With the support of: *La Biennale di Venezia, Institut Ramon Llull, Ajuntament de Barcelona, Ministerio de Cultura de España, EGM Laboratoris Color and Cooperativa Jordi Capell.*

Photographs

Adrià Goula: Inner Cover, 2-3, 4, 6, 13, 15, 16-17, 25, 26, 29, 30-31 (model), 39, 44-45, 46-47, 49, 51, 53, 55, 56, 57, 59, 61, 63, 65, 81, 83, 88-89, 90-91, 92-93 (carpentries + facade), 94-95, 96, 97, 102, 117, 118, 119 (up), 120-121, 122-123, 124, 126-127, 130-131, 132-133, 134-135, 136-137, 138-139, 146-147(down), 148-149 (up 1 & 2 + down), 150-151 (up 1 & 3 + down), 152-153, 159, 160 (down right), 161 (down), 163, 167, 169, 174, 184-185, 189, 191, 192-193, 196-197, 198-199 (up), 200-201 (up), 208 (up), 212 (1), 213 (collage photos), 214-215, 216, 218-219, 220-221 (down), 223, 225, 228-229, 230-231, 234-235, 236-237, 243, 244-245, 246-247 (up right + down), 252-253, 258-259, 263 (up), 269, 271, 273, 274-275, 276-277, 280, 283, 285, 287, 288-289, 290-291, 292, 293 (left), 294-295 (right), 297, 298-299-300-301-302-303 (collage photos).

Judith Casas: 77 (up), 103, 104-105, 106-107, 144 (2 & 4), 147 (up), 149 (up 3), 151 (up 4), 158, 160 (up + down left), 161 (up), 164-165, 176-177, 178-179, 181, 186-187, 198-199 (down), 200-201 (down), 204-205 (1 & 2), 208 (down), 209, 212 (2), 217, 221 (up), 222, 224, 232 (up + down right), 233, 238-239, 240 (down), 262, 263 (down), 265 (down), 266, 293 (right), 294 (left), 298-299-300-301-302-303 (collage), 304-Inner Back cover.

Àlex García 30-31 (down).

Gabriela Zea Nadal 80

Miguel Ángel Aguiló 205 (3)

Flores & Prats: 72, 75, 77, 92-93 (up), 118 (down), 140, 144 (1 i 3), 156, 180, 232 (down left), 240 (up), 281.

Containers

The models must be very precise since they serve to verify proportions, and therefore it takes a long time to make them and it is difficult to get rid of them when the project is finished. So, they stay around us, on the shelves or hanging on the studio walls, as company.

But when we have time, we collect those of a specific project and build a container made to measure for them. On the one hand, it is a way to keep them safe from dust and damage, but also because by ordering them we can reflect on the project process again.

So, the first thing that must be done to design the container is to collect together from the shelves and walls all the models, fragments, templates, drawings, sketches, reference books, paper patterns... These documents of very different origins and formats that represent the project evolution are then placed on a large table, spacious enough to contain all at once, giving us the full spectrum of materials to store.

The next thing to do is to decide how to place the various models and fragments inside the container. This can be done chronologically, and for this it is key to have them dated at the time of their production, which now allows us to follow the evolution over the months or years that the whole process took. Another way to organize the models inside the container is by ordering the pieces by affinities or families, since some models and fragments are better seen together to explain more fully a subject or interest that has been tested, and not necessarily in chronological order.

When deciding how to hold together the pieces, one also has to decide on the shape or silhouette of the container. This can be defined by the dimension of the various pieces that will be kept inside and the manner in which they will be collated. Implicit in this decision is the way in which the container will finally look when it is opened, so that it helps us to remember the ideas that have led from one model to another, the jumps in the process of evolution of the project, the variations of a solution, and where the doubts and discussions about the project provoked different options.

Therefore, these are not just boxes but 'containers' that keep thoughts and all knowledge of the project within, things we must not forget. When it is opened and activated for an explanation or an exhibition, the sequence in which the different documents appear accompanies the narration, as a visual aid. Since these containers have wheels, they can move around the studio and make themselves disappear as soon as they get in our way...